KING TIGER

FRONTISPIECE: Reies Tijerina at the Poor Peoples' March, Washington, D.C., 1968. At the left: Hank Adams and Al Bridges, Indian leaders. At the right: Rev. Ralph Abernathy. Source: Patricia Bell Blawis, *Tijerina and the Land Grants* (New York: International Publishers, 1971), 164.

KING TIGER

The Religious Vision of Reies López Tijerina

Rudy V. Busto

UNIVERSITY OF NEW MEXICO PRESS | ALBUQUERQUE

©2005 by the University of New Mexico Press

All rights reserved. Published 2005

Printed in the United States of America

10   09   08   07   06   05   1   2   3   4   5   6   7

LIBRARY OF CONGRESS CATALOGING-IN-PUBLICATION DATA

Busto, Rudy V., 1957–

King Tiger : the religious vision of Reies López Tijerina / Rudy V. Busto.

p. cm.

Includes bibliographical references and index.

ISBN 0-8263-2789-3 (cloth : alk. paper)

1. Tijerina, Reies—Political and social views.   2. Tijerina, Reies—Religion.
3. Mexican Americans—Land tenure—New Mexico—History—
20th century. 4. Mexican Americans—New Mexico—Economic
conditions—20th century. 5. Land tenure—New Mexico—History—
20th century. 6. Civil rights workers—New Mexico—Biography.
7. Mexican Americans—New Mexico—Biography. 8. Civil rights
movements—New Mexico—History—20th century. I. Title.

F805.M5T5415 2005

978.9´0046873—dc22

2005022333

Design and composition: Melissa Tandysh

For my mother, Socorro Busto-Hiatt

And to the memory of my father,

Valeriano Ramos Busto

CONTENTS

ACKNOWLEDGMENTS

There are many people who helped this project come into being. Chief among them, of course, is Reies Tijerina. Reies's patience and long-suffering with a new generation of academics has been my boon. Although I do not expect him to agree with everything I have written here, my best hope is that he would find that I have tried to represent his life and work with respect and care. My fascination and awe with Tijerina verges on what scholars of religion call *tremendum et fascinans*.

The earliest support for this project came from my graduate advisor, Margarita Melville, who understood the power of religious conviction and its political consequences, and thus why writing about Tijerina was a good idea. My appreciation for her support and example of passionate scholarship only increases over time.

Others crucial to the shaping and organization of my ideas for this book beyond the dissertation include Susana Gallardo, Gastón Espinosa, Alberto Pulido, and Daniel Ramírez. Assistance from Stanford undergraduates Noah Rodríguez and Tanya Moreno in the form of library research is gratefully acknowledged. Friends and colleagues involved in the Hispanic Theological Initiative (HTI) have offered me moral support, as have Alice Bach, Davíd Carrasco, James Treat, Randi Walker, Gilbert and Renya Ramírez, Jennifer Michael, Priya Karim Haji, and Tony Stevens-Arroyo. Tangible support by way of specific information and assistance is gratefully acknowledged from Jay Maiorana, Mario Garcia, Andrés Guerrero, Peter Nabokov, Carlos Muñoz, Jr., Jorge Bustamante, Claude Clegg III, Amado Padilla, Evangeline Corona, drafting supervisor for the Pinal County Assessor's Office, Julie Hoff of the Arizona Capitol Library, Baptist historian, Bill Hunke, the staff at the Zimmerman Library (UNM), and numerous *nuevomexicanos* who smoothed my path at every turn in my research. Although I never knew him personally outside of a brief correspondence, an enormous debt is owed to the late Clark S. Knowlton, whose long view of Tijerina and the *Alianza* resulted in a valuable corpus of writing crucial to understanding Tijerina and his context.

Despite the assistance of all of these scholars upon whose work this book depends, I need only add that responsibility for the interpretation put forth, as well as any errors and omissions, is mine alone.

I am forever grateful to my family for all of their love and support, especially to my mother, Socorro Busto-Hiatt, for her unending prayers and instilling in her children the love of books and insisting on the power of Philippians 4:13. A large measure of love and gratitude is reserved for Tony Feudo and Maria Elizabeth Carlotta Feudo, who continually remind me of the priorities in this life, encourage me, and make it worth the effort. I acknowledge my cat, Puss Puss, the only sentient being who truly knows all that this project required.

The process of putting this book together has been lengthy, and so I owe a great debt of gratitude to David Holtby and Maya Allen-Gallegos of the University of New Mexico Press for their forbearance and oversight.

TERMS

The term "Mexican American" is used to refer to persons of Mexican descent living in the United States since the Treaty of Guadalupe Hidalgo in 1848. It is also used to refer to Mexican descent Americans prior to the 1960s adoption of the ethnopolitical term "Chicano." "Mexican" is used to denote nationality and as descriptive of cultures and traditions originating in Mexico (e.g., Mexican Catholicism). "Chicano" is used to describe the progressive, sometimes radical assertion of ethnic and political identity, particularly by young Mexican Americans beginning in the mid-1960s, and then as descriptive of the culture and scholarship arising out of the Chicano Movement (e.g., Chicano history). The term "Hispanic" is for the most part avoided, but used to describe the leveling of Spanish-speaking Americans by the federal government in the 1980s. Among Chicanos it is a derogatory term. On the other hand, "Latino" is the commonly accepted label encompassing the larger population of Spanish-speakers in the United States.

Regional Mexican Americans have their own labeling traditions, and so I use "Hispano" to indicate the people and cultures associated with the traditions specific to Spanish-speaking New Mexicans reaching back to the Spanish settlements in the sixteenth century. Similarly, I employ the local colloquialism, "vecino" (literally, neighbor) and "nuevomexicano" or "Nuevo Mexicano" to refer to land grant heirs in northern New

Mexico. "Spanish American" is an older regional ethnic term constructed around the history and continuation of the earliest Spanish arrival into what is now New Mexico and southern Colorado at the end of the sixteenth century. "Tejano" refers to Mexican Americans from Texas. "Anglo" is an awkward but common label used historically by Mexican Americans and Chicanos to refer to all European Americans. Clearly these are cultural and political labels more than they are racial ones.

The term "evangelical" is used as an umbrella term to denote a distinct theological worldview. Broadly speaking it includes traditions that subscribe to a literalist interpretation of the Bible, the intense experience of "born again" conversion, active missionary efforts, and the expectation that Jesus will physically return at a future date to gather up the saved. "Fundamentalism" refers to a harsher, ethically stringent and uncompromising form of evangelical belief and practice.

 # INTRODUCTION

"Right now we look like a cricket. What is a cricket? King of the Insects; a little, tiny animal. All the cricket can do is [say] 'cricket, cricket, cricket.' Just a noise, that's all. But you know, if that cricket gets in the ear of the lion and scratches inside, there is nothing the lion can do. There is nothing; there is no way the lion can use his claws and jaws to destroy the cricket. The more the lion scratches himself the deeper the cricket goes. . . ."

—Reies López Tijerina, 1971[1]

DURING HIS MOST ACTIVE YEARS IN THE ROUGH AND TUMBLE WORLD of New Mexican land grant politics, Reies Tijerina was fond of relating to his audiences the fable of the lion and the cricket. As the leader of a grass-roots Hispano land rights organization, the *Alianza Federál de Mercedes Reales* (The Federal Alliance of Land Grants), Tijerina's retelling of this pithy fable inspired members of his organization and potential supporters to put their faith in the persistence and strategy used by the small and weak in the face of impossible odds. As this book describes, so much of Tijerina's life and efforts—real, rumored, and mythologized—illustrate the ability of the "King of the Insects" to triumph in the face of overwhelming odds. This book is also about the forces that animate the cricket to lodge itself so firmly in the ears of many lions in the course of his life.

Tijerina, or "King Tiger" as the press dubbed him, is certainly much more than the cricket in his story. Even more than three decades after the June 5, 1967, infamous Tierra Amarilla County courthouse raid guaranteed him a legacy in New Mexican history and earned him a pedestal in the pantheon of Chicano history, Tijerina remains an important touchstone for New Mexicans—Anglo, Hispano, and Native American. All New Mexicans understand the painful and violent history surrounding the interdependent issues of land, water, language, economic development, sovereignty, political power, and rights to cultural formation in the southwestern United States. Tijerina's work in New Mexico has left an indelible imprint on Hispano culture there. Throughout the preparation of this book, requests I made to various libraries, archives, and newspaper offices in New Mexico were often helped along by *nuevomexicano* administrators and receptionists who at some point had been encouraged by the words and legacy of Tijerina that have played a role in shaping the consciousness of Spanish-speaking New Mexicans. When I requested information from an Albuquerque newspaper, the receptionist at the other end of the telephone whispered into her headset, "Oh, I would do anything for Reies," and went out of her way to assist me.

Not everyone, of course, who remembers Tijerina and the Alianza thinks fondly or kindly of the theatricality with which the organization and its supporters pursued its goals. Nevertheless, no one can deny that Reies López Tijerina has forever changed the way activists, scholars, and politicians go about the tricky business of dealing with land and Latino cultures in the Southwest. For Chicanos in particular, Tijerina's leadership of the Alianza remains one of the epic narratives in our history. Indeed, Chicano identity owes its existence in part to Tijerina's defense of New Mexican community land rights by appeal to history, legal means, and when pushed, armed resistance. His role in Chicano history has been told and retold in textbooks, films, and college courses on the Chicano/a experience. Despite this collective memory about him there is much about Tijerina that is unknown, and even more that is misunderstood and misinterpreted. And because he has always positioned himself in opposition to established power and frequently comes as an outsider to his causes, there is nothing about him that does not stir up controversy whenever his name surfaces in print and conversation.

It is into these unknown places, interpretations and controversies I venture. Thinking, reading, and writing about Reies Tijerina over the years has been a difficult process. For reasons hinted at above and explained in this book, the representation of Tijerina in Chicano history has been and remains frozen. This is the image of him that first comes to mind: speaking behind a microphone, one or both hands raised emphatically to make a point, wild-eyed and passionate in his dark preacher's coat, white shirt, and tie.[2] Every student of Chicano history knows this image and comes to embrace the same outrage that led Tijerina's followers to protest the theft of deeded Mexican American land to unscrupulous and greedy "Anglos" following the end of the Mexican American War. In fact, one could say that it is precisely this anger and sense of historical injustice that smolders still at the core of Chicano/a identity. Writing about Tijerina has meant having to navigate through sources full of anger, partisan agendas, and misinterpretations. I have also had to suspend judgment, and check my own biases and politics in my attempt to write an honest book about an extraordinary and complex man for whom I have enormous respect and who for more than a decade continued to live inside my head.

In the mid-1980s I was introduced to Tijerina's politics and activism in Ron Takaki's graduate ethnic studies seminar at Berkeley. At the time I was interested in cultural change and the religious responses by racial minorities to economic and political colonialism. Focusing on questions of cultural preservation and indigenous revitalization models of resistance, it seemed to me that Chicano assertions about their mythical place of origin and homeland, *Aztlán*, was similar in ways to the resistance by Native Americans to the westering sweep of the American republic. Comparing Native American legal and extralegal means of preserving land as the basis of economic, cultural, and spiritual power with Tijerina's own attempts at land grant reform piqued my interest. In the context of political and ethnic power movements in the 1960s and early 1970s, Tijerina's Olympian status in Chicano history as an uncompromising nationalist came about through his redrawing (retracing?) geopolitical boundaries in defiance of the maps produced by the history of land theft in New Mexico. Tijerina, according to secondary sources, wanted all of the lands Mexicans had lost north of the U.S.-Mexico border after 1848. To that end, the Alianza Federál de Mercedes Reales had taken possession of National Forest lands in 1966. In 1967, Tijerina and the Alianza had rained bullets down on the courthouse in the small northern New Mexican town of Tierra Amarilla. It was this image of Tijerina as the separatist Chicano nationalist willing to resort to violence if necessary that I encountered in what I read.

Several years later I was looking for a dissertation topic and stumbled across Tijerina's memoir, *Mi lucha por la tierra* (My Struggle for the Land).[3] In my search for scholarly reviews of his book I was surprised and puzzled that there were none. In fact, I was unable to locate—a decade after its publication—any mention of *Mi lucha por la tierra* in any bibliography on Chicano/Latino literature or autobiography. That non-Chicano scholars had ignored a book written in idiosyncratic Spanish by one of the architects of the Chicano Movement was no surprise. Rather, my astonishment was that not a single Chicano/Latino scholar had written a review, analyzed, or listed the memoir in reference compilations.

What accounted for the lack of interest by Chicano scholars in Tijerina's own account of Chicano history? What were the reasons for ignoring a substantial autobiography (released by one of Mexico's most esteemed publishers, no less) by one of the essential figures in the creation of a Chicano consciousness and political voice? These initial enigmas, as well as the desire to critically examine Tijerina's politics through the lens of religion, compelled me to undertake the project. These questions and the pursuit of answers to them eventually led me to Tijerina himself.

The dissertation highlighted the ways Chicano studies as an emergent academic discipline was burdened in subtle and not so subtle ways by an ideological cultural nationalism. There I argued that Chicano nationalist discourse contained, suppressed, and even erased dissident and religious voices from its collective ethnic memory.[4] Despite his status as a national Chicano leader, I argued that Tijerina was nevertheless the perfect victim of this Chicano nationalist silencing. His meteoric rise in the mid-1960s to the status of *movimiento* patriarch in the mythology of Chicano history made clear sense when viewed from a nationalist discourse in search of revolutionary models of praxis. On the other hand, the reasons for his sudden disappearance from Chicano activist discourse going into the 1970s were not forthcoming in any of the available Chicano histories. So complete was his absence in the post-Aztlán era consciousness that into the 1990s otherwise savvy Chicano studies students and scholars who asked about my work were shocked to learn that Tijerina was still very much alive and politically active.

Contributing to the issues about Tijerina's place in Chicano history is the fact that his Pentecostalism has never been discussed or put into context. In Chicano writing about Tijerina religion remains only a small part of his poorly understood biography. Tijerina entered politics applying the tools of reading and preaching he learned as a Pentecostal, but to read the secondary accounts one would never guess how profoundly an evangelical worldview pervaded his life. That is, in the construction of *Chicanismo*, the cultural ideology of the Chicano Movement, Roman Catholicism provided an assumed ritual and sacred canopy for the community. Evangelicals, and Pentecostals in particular, had no place in the movimiento's imagining and construction of authentic Chicano culture and politics. Fortunately for Chicano history Tijerina's brilliant life as a political activist appeared to move him beyond any concern for organized religion or even the sacred. As a mature political agent, according to this view, Tijerina was able to triumph over both the degrading poverty and deviant religion of his early years. The original intention of my project meant to reveal Tijerina's religious life as central to his political work and so critique the process of how Chicano history constructed and maintained itself in selective and predictable ways. However, when I began to read closely what Tijerina himself had written, the project shifted away from the critique of Chicano studies and toward addressing the silence around his Pentecostalism and later religious speculations. It is in his writing, and in particular his sermons and memoir, where Tijerina's relationship to the sacred provides clues to knowing who he is, what formed him, and what continues to compel him.

In the late 1980s, less than a handful of religion scholars were interested in the religious history and content of Chicano culture. There were even fewer Chicano/a scholars interested in religion, let alone evangelical and Pentecostal forms of Christianity. Compounding the difficulties in writing about a controversial figure in Chicano history is the absence of a theoretical literature that addresses in a productive or sophisticated way the relationships between Chicano group identity, politics, and religion. The sociological literature on religion and ethnicity, as expected, focuses almost exclusively on either the experience of European immigrants and their progress toward assimilation, or the "problem" of black religion in relationship to politics, civil religion, or mainline Protestantism.

It was not until the early 1990s that scholarship on Chicano religions (under the larger rubric of Latino religion) emerged as a definable subfield within American religion. Since then interest in the role of religion in Latino communities has deepened our understanding of the tensions and alliances between political/social movements and religious institutions, but less so the connections between dogmas and personalities. The theoretical literature as a whole, however, remains at an early stage of development. Thus despite the rapid advances in the historical and sociological data suggestive of how religion functions in Latino communities, studies of individuals as religious agents are only beginning to appear.[5] Given this lack of attention to the religious dimension in Chicano biography, an examination of Tijerina's rather singular life and writing requires a well-stocked toolbox. Devices are required to address historical and literary aspects, as are also tools calibrated for working the religious studies concerns for texts, sources, mapping the sacred, and taking seriously the visceral power of religion in the lives of individuals and whole communities. How then, might the privileging of religion, religious language, ritual, and cosmovision assist in our understanding of Reies Tijerina?

Out of that toolbox and a shameless poaching from other disciplines comes this book. It is my attempt to force a conversation between the disciplines of religious studies and ethnic studies. The combination of ethnic and religious studies will seem odd to some in ethnic studies who may have inherited strong suspicions about religion's place in the survival and self-determination of racially ethnic communities. However, it is clear that scholars working in comparative ethnic studies have only much to gain from a close look at the centrality of religion in the formation, survival, and maintenance of colonized minorities. Marxian perspectives, which determined to a large degree the questions and solutions throughout the "golden age" of ethnic studies in the 1970s and 1980s, have for the most part ignored the religious aspects of identity and political movements sometimes at the very center of ethnic communities.[6] Religion has been dismissed as sentimental cultural baggage, abstract, ahistorical, and part of an oppressive and hegemonic cultural system in the United States.

In the case of Chicano communities the historically poor treatment of ethnic Mexicans by the American Roman Catholic Church, and the paternalism of Protestant missionary efforts gives Chicano scholars more than a few good reasons to regard religion with suspicion. This explains, for example, the targeting of Roman Catholicism and its clergy as objects of derision by Chicano novelists and poets.

For its part, however, the study of American religion has only begun to tease out the real differences between the experiences of European ethnic immigrants and colonized racial minorities.[7] This study then, is an attempt to engage the field of American religion in a conversation with ethnic studies where appraising and quantifying the very real differences that exist between individuals and groups means taking seriously the centrality of race in the survival and struggle of minority communities. Ethnic studies also avoids the hand-wringing by scholars of American religion over matters of race and ethnicity and disrupts the irenic expectation that religion ought to be the agent of mutual understanding and acceptance. The best I might hope for in such a convening is a horizon of understanding between these concerns and a fruitful transgressing of disciplinary borders.

Despite my great concern for bridging academic and theoretical connections, the center of the book's focus is Tijerina's distinctive and utterly unconventional voice. Specifically, the book examines Tijerina's life through his collection of sermons, *¿Hallará Fe en la Tierra . . . ?* (the earliest collection of Mexican American Pentecostal sermons to my knowledge), key political tracts, speeches, interviews, and especially his overlooked memoir, *Mi lucha por la tierra.* The interpretive task here is to wade through a lot of secondary sources about Tijerina's life and work, balance them with primary sources, and steer a path through the meanings suggested in them. Some readers will be disappointed that this book is not a reiteration or assessment of Tijerina's political career. Almost all of the sources on Tijerina I consulted for this book focus exclusively on politics, and my biographical reconstruction (Chapter Two) is therefore necessarily organized around his political achievements and setbacks. Tijerina's leadership of the Alianza Federál de Mercedes Reales, and the events around the famous 1967 courthouse raid have been lavishly documented and vividly described by Peter Nabokov in *Tijerina and the Courthouse*

Raid, and to a lesser degree, Richard Gardner's *Grito!: Reies Tijerina and the New Mexico Land Grant War of 1967*. For sheer narrative punch, Nabokov's account is the best one. And even though hindsight should provide me the illusion of clear vision on those events at the height of Tijerina's political career, Nabokov's physical presence close to the action means *Tijerina and the Courthouse Raid* is as definitive a reading of the actual events outside of Tijerina's own version. The obvious limitation in Nabokov, Gardner, and other contemporary accounts is the view that the Tierra Amarilla County courthouse attack is the defining event in Tijerina's life.

This book moves in the opposite direction. By setting aside the courthouse raid as the centerpiece of Tijerina's life, not only do I place myself outside the need to explain the contexts behind the particularities of northern New Mexico's race relations and cultures, I also avoid obscuring the primacy of what I believe to be Tijerina's motivations and underlying religious vision. Key to this reassessment of Tijerina's life are his writing and words in sources that have never been examined alongside the public data of his life. Happily, turning to these primary sources provides me with a convenient way to circumvent taking up an overly defensive posture against what is already written about Tijerina. This reorientation is also crucial for grounding the analysis from his own writing. In the context of a polarized and unreliable secondary literature, it is best to let Tijerina map his own internal landscape. The task then, is not so much a determination for verifying or falsifying history as it is exploring the (re)constructions and (re)interpretations of events in an extraordinarily full life. While there is a great deal of historical narrative required to attain these goals, I am most interested in Tijerina's own selections and versions of his life, religion, and the past. More than a moderate amount of care has been taken to verify many of the facts presented in his biography and memoir. Greater emphasis, however, is given to Tijerina's story from his own perceptions and interpretations. To quote historian Mario Garcia, whose work involves retrieving Chicano biography, "History, as some suggest, is a selection of memories."[8]

The chapters are arranged to impose a chronological order and provide the necessary background for interpreting Tijerina's writing. Chapter One begins with a discussion of the received assessment of the public Tijerina. Here I examine four of Tijerina's biographies, noting their differences and how they deal with his religious life. The chapter then considers the interpretation of Tijerina in Chicano history, and observes how the writing of Chicano history required a specific, useful interpretation of Tijerina's life.

Chapter Two is a reconstruction of Tijerina's biography. Here my goal is to recalibrate the events of the late 1960s by taking in the longer trajectory of Tijerina's robust life. I have chosen to "sketch" Tijerina's biography rather than present an extended, conclusive biography. Because the focus of my analysis is religion, the emphasis on politics in the secondary sources prohibits—for the time being—the writing of a full, rounded Tijerina biography. Freed from the impossible task of telling yet another "objective" true story I am more concerned with presenting an overview, balancing Tijerina's activist years (1963–1970) with the early part of his life (1926–1962), and the postactivist years not available in his biographies or any single source (1971–present).

Chapter Three brackets the years 1940 to 1955, covering Tijerina's training as a Pentecostal evangelist in Texas, his itinerant ministry, and his growing disillusionment with organized Christianity. I examine Tijerina's book of sermons, *¿Hallará Fe en la Tierra . . . ?* and argue that the form and texture of his political work are rooted in his early theological writing.

Chapter Four tells the story of Tijerina's utopian community, Valle de Paz. Tijerina's attempt at creating a religious community in the Arizona wilderness is the only Mexican American experimental colony in American history. Essential to understanding this utopian venture, I argue, are the landscapes of Mexican American dreaming, visions, and the transformations of the desert itself.

Chapter Five considers why Tijerina's memoir, *Mi lucha por la tierra* remains a pariah text in Chicano letters. His political tract, "The Spanish Land Grant Question Examined," his letter from the New Mexico State Penitentiary, and relevant portions from the memoir provide the lenses through which his rise and fall in Chicano mythology are interpreted.

Chapter Six discusses Tijerina's horrific but illuminating incarceration in the Springfield, Missouri Federal Prison Hospital as recounted in his memoir. It is during this time that the origins of his dark view of the end times are founded. The chapter also examines Tijerina's startling revelations about the genealogy of Spanish-speaking peoples in the Americas.

The Epilogue revisits the major themes and arguments in the book and reassesses the relevance of Tijerina's life for understanding Chicano history and culture and the study of religion in the United States.

Finally, although it is obvious, it must be pointed out that this interpretation is only a beginning. Like the cricket in the lion's ear, this project continues to scratch and burrow. While completing the manuscript, the "King of Insects" continued to chirp. Tijerina is continually adding material to future assessments of his life. In October 1999, Tijerina appeared at the University of New Mexico to donate his personal archives to the Center for Southwest Research.9 His papers, which I saw in their original underground office, will be of inestimable value for those interested in the organizational and historical background to the 1960s New Mexico land grant movement. My desire to incorporate them in this study, however, was ill timed but definitively thwarted by their quarantine for the hanta virus suspected lurking in the papers. Similarly, I was unable to make use of recently declassified FBI files that include at least three folders concerning Tijerina. At some point the research must come to an end. I do so unwillingly, but am heartened by the knowledge that Reies Tijerina's continuing activism and reinvention of himself in the new millennium will attract others to the challenge of writing about a phenomenal life. I happily leave the cricket to its chirping.

1   CONTESTED TERRAIN

IN THE SPRING OF 1997 TWO HEADLINE NEWS EVENTS IN THE AMERICAN west resonated with the themes of this book. In early April the bizarre mass suicide tragedy of the Heaven's Gate "cult" was discovered. Its members left behind chilling videotaped farewells that revealed a melding of apocalyptic religious vision with science fiction and UFOlogy.[1] Scrambling to make sense of irrational religious action and devotion to a maniacal cult leader, the American media struggled with the fact that a group of educated and otherwise sensible people had somehow allowed the intoxication of cult religious belief to take control of and end their lives. The second event, which appeared as an odd footnote in the larger scheme of world news, occurred in rural southern Texas. A small group of armed "patriots" had drawn the borders of what they understood to be the legal Republic of Texas and were prepared to defend their tiny nation against the United States.[2] Although separate and unrelated, the Heaven's Gate "cult" and the irredentist Republic of Texas incident are both part of a continuing pattern of themes in the American west: religious innovation and the armed struggle over land rights.

The contested topographies of religion, community self-determination, and history suggested by the Heaven's Gate New Religion and the tiny Republic of Texas have all been traversed by Reies López Tijerina. Tijerina has led a group of religious zealots into the western desert, claims to have had a close encounter with extraterrestrial messengers, battled the federal government over land rights in the Southwest, successfully set up an independent Republic, and claims to have seen the future destruction of the world.

The year 1997 also marked the thirtieth anniversary of the Tierra Amarilla courthouse raid, an event in New Mexican history that forever changed the political and cultural landscape in the American Southwest. Reies López Tijerina, the leader of this spectacularly failed attempt by "Spanish-Americans" to arrest the New Mexico district attorney, became an immediate celebrity in the Chicano Movement. Hailed as the incarnation of Chicano outrage over the encroachment and theft of lands once belonging to Mexicans, Tijerina became the most visible symbol of Chicano nationalism. This book is about the extraordinary life of Reies Tijerina, as well as a number of landscapes—religion, race, history, memory, vision—all very much contested, and central to Tijerina's vision of himself and his relationship to the world.

Specifically, this book is about how religion can inform and provide a framework for one of Chicano history's legendary figures. Until just a few years ago the place of religion, the sacred, and sacred history in Chicano studies remained problematic in the interpretation and understanding of Chicano culture. Beyond perfunctory and usually suspicious treatments of Roman Catholicism in the canonical texts of Chicano studies, it was only well into the 1990s that larger questions about Chicanos and religion became interesting to more than a few scholars. Among Chicano scholars there resided a set of unspoken assumptions about religion (read Mexican Roman Catholicism) in Mexican American family culture and history. The theoretical and ideological trends of the 1960s Chicano Movimiento delayed religion as its own arena of scholarly interest for all of the 1970s and most of the 1980s.

Germinating out of a 1960s Marxist sociology the intellectual stalk of the Chicano Movimiento simply ignored (or was ignorant of) the power religion as practice, belief, and discourse wielded over ethnic Mexican communities in the United States. Presuming that most Mexican Americans were Roman Catholics suffering the paternalistic and racist policies of the American Roman Catholic hierarchy, the neat and simple movimiento analysis viewed Chicanos in asymmetrical power relationships with Anglos in the United States (as they were in labor and education). The feebleness of religion to confront this asymmetry required no further comment or analysis than the historical fact that Mexican American Catholics comprise over 90 percent of the Catholic population in some areas of the Southwest and yet it took more than 130 years (since the 1848 Treaty of Guadalupe-Hidalgo) for a Mexican American to be elevated to the position of bishop. At the same time the scholarly interest in and knowledge of Mexican descent mainline Protestants, Mormons, Evangelicals, and Pentecostals was practically nil. Since the mid-1980s, the trickle of scholarly output on Chicano religion has now pooled into a discernible body of writing. As a hybrid of interdisciplinary Chicano studies and the more conservative fields of theology and religious studies, the emergence of a critical Chicano religious studies has yet to overcome the agendas of its parent fields, and is still very much in its infancy.

While it is common knowledge that Tijerina pursued an intense Pentecostal evangelistic ministry prior to his New Mexican land grant activism in the 1960s, almost nothing has been written about this crucial and formative period in his life. For the most part, the secondary literature on Tijerina obscures his profound and sometimes blinding personal faith. My argument here is that it is the all-consuming fire of his religious faith that supports his political life and has always determined his view of himself in relationship to the world. Thus the net effect of ignoring Tijerina's complex relationship to the Christian tradition has been a greatly impoverished understanding of who he is and why his public life takes on seemingly bizarre twists and turns. My purpose here is not to advocate for Tijerina's positions so much as it is the exposition of his ideas and their origins in a particular theological mindset. Of course it would be difficult to defend many of his apocalyptic ideas and, beginning in the 1980s, murmurings of anti-Semitic thinking. But rather than suppress his recent theological formulations so that I might present a "cleaner" and more acceptable version of who he is (and fall into the same trap against which I am arguing), the reconstruction of his life and thought here must include this problematic material. It would have been quite easy to simply omit or finesse his controversial ideas about race in this study, but even these ideas, once framed by the religious foundations of his life and writing, permit us to at least comprehend his worldview.

That is, Tijerina's relationship to the sacred has always compelled him to action and to write polemically and prophetically on behalf of his vision of the world. How and why this is so is the task here. Whether he is arguing for international adjudication of Spanish and Mexican land grant treaty rights in the United States, or claiming for Spanish-speakers in the Americas the birthright given by God to Israel, the source of his sanctioning authority has remained constant into the new millennium: an ancient God of Justice who is exacting, jealous, and reveals himself both historically and through miraculous signs.

As tempting as the details of his life are, this study is not an attempt at psychohistory. Rather, I follow as a general model the work of historian Carlo Ginzburg and his reconstruction of the worldview of a heretical sixteenth-century miller, Menocchio.[3] In his exploration of Menocchio's worldview, Ginzburg shows how Menocchio bridged and combined the discourses of low/oral peasant culture and high/written culture into novel cosmological formulations. Ginzburg's study demonstrates how exceptional and autodidact individuals construct and imagine theories and systems of complex internal logic. His microhistorical approach to explaining, for example, how Menocchio read texts, is invaluable for showing the many ways ideas and texts are read, misread, assimilated, and manipulated. Menocchio, Ginzburg notes, read by "isolating words and phrases, sometimes distorting them, juxtaposing different passages, firing off rapid analogies." Menocchio's most notorious claim, at least as it is described through the mediation of the Inquisition's records, comes down to us as the stitching together of the Genesis account of creation with other books and traditions available to him: "I have said that, in my opinion, all was chaos, that is, earth, air, water, and fire were mixed together; and out of that bulk a mass formed—just as cheese is made out of milk—and worms appeared in it, and these were the angels. . . ."[4] Similar in ways to how Menocchio constructed his hybrid cosmology, Tijerina's weaving together of Christian scripture, legal text, race theory, science, and the memoir genre relies upon a tight, internally consistent and logical theology fashioned out of vernacular/local cultures and received official texts and traditions. If we are to understand extraordinary individuals like Menocchio and Tijerina, we must expose and explore the framework of sources and ideas that support idiosyncratic worlds. How such alternative worldviews overlap, challenge, and subvert dominant paradigms of knowledge and conventional thinking also demonstrates how orthodox discourses in society are imbricated with systems of power and domination. Menocchio, Ginzburg reminds us, paid dearly for promoting an eccentric theology. Eventually he was condemned as a heretic by the Inquisition, hauled twice before the Holy Office, and summarily put to death. Tijerina's political and historical "death" in the Chicano movimiento, comes as a result of his heterodox politics derived from religious experience. It is important to note here that in both cases judgment against Menocchio and Tijerina come largely in part through the distortions of their original ideas and words recorded and interpreted by others.

My interpretation of Tijerina's relationship to his reading and writing is also influenced by Steven Justice's work on the role that literacy played in medieval peasant rebellions.[5] Examining how peasants carefully manipulated official records and adopted manorial rhetoric and clerical tropes, Justice notes that the world of ideas and the powers inherent in the figures and institutions that control writing were not impervious to the noise of the masses. My adoption of medieval figures of literate resistance might appear far afield for some until it is pointed out that among many of my colleagues in Latino studies much of the texture and content of Latino religion, literature, vernacular culture, and medicine have managed to escape the regulation and rationalization of modernity. Mexican American Catholicism in particular, has often been faulted by church officials for its "pre-Tridentine" obsession with virgin and saint veneration, bloody crucifixes, and *mandas* fulfilled by crawling on one's knees from the far edge of the plaza to the altar of the Virgin of Guadalupe in Mexico City.[6]

We begin with an examination of how Tijerina has been represented and received through his biographers and Chicano historians.

Tijerina's Biographers

Tijerina's core religious worldview is not very well understood or appreciated. This missing dimension of his life is evident if one reads the secondary sources and especially the four biographies by Michael Jenkinson, Peter Nabokov, Richard Gardner, and Patricia Bell Blawis.[7] Tijerina's charismatic and strong-handed leadership appeared to be at its zenith at the time of the 1967 Tierra Amarilla Raid. These biographers, all writing while Tijerina was being tried for the courthouse raid, depicted him as a hero of mythic and Biblical proportions. Michael Jenkinson, for example, describes him in caricatured Old Testament images:

> He spoke of Moses leading his people out of bondage into the promised land. And let there be no mistake, his people—bitter, proud farmers who had scarcely enough land to turn a tractor around, let alone the money to buy one; pensioners in old Robert Hall suits—had waited, as had their fathers, for better than a century to be led to the Promised Land.[8]

This heroic portrayal of Tijerina occurs in all nonhostile treatments by Anglo writers at the time. Because the four Anglo biographies all appeared within four years of the 1967 Raid, their immediate goal is to provide the reader with an image of Tijerina at the height of his militant action and the Alianza's visibility and potential successes in the land grant effort.

These four biographies have influenced all subsequent treatments of Tijerina's life, providing the definitive data and interpretations of his political work. Survey and general secondary sources in Chicano history and politics, as well as mainstream academic sources, have relied almost exclusively on these four biographies, especially those by Peter Nabokov and Richard Gardner.[9] While the courthouse raid did catapult Tijerina and the Alianza into the 1960s consciousness, the presumption since then has been to view Tijerina's life as having been brought to a climax in the summer of 1967. Undoubtedly the courthouse raid changed Tijerina's life in dramatic and tragic ways, but the significance of the Rio Arriba County courthouse assault I feel has overshadowed later important developments in Tijerina's thinking. Rather, a longer view of his life must be presented, beginning with a reevaluation of his biographies and including a more substantive account of the full life in order to move beyond what has become the standard interpretation of Tijerina. Recasting Tijerina's biography (and so the reinterpretation) is not meant to diminish the importance of the Alianza's most celebrated event. The Raid, however, was not the only act of ethnic resistance in the Southwest at the time, and it is arguably not the most significant event in the life of Reies Tijerina.[10] Another way to view Tijerina is through the circumstances of his religious life and the way his theological sensibilities infuse his activism and thinking. This admittedly interpretive approach to biographical reconstruction opens up broader questions about his worldview and motivations. Because of the pervasive influence of his four Anglo biographers, it is useful to know how they understand religion in Tijerina's life.

Each of his biographers have noted that Tijerina was raised by a devout Roman Catholic mother, converted to Pentecostalism in his early teen years, and that he attended the Assemblies of God Bible Institute in Texas. The biographers also concur that Tijerina's life after his period of itinerant ministry (1946–1956) indicates a consuming passion for justice that replaces his religious life as he prepares to confront the United States government over the land grant issue.

Evidence of this shift from religious worldview to secular political activism is seen in Richard Gardner's *Grito!: Reies Tijerina and the New Mexico Land Grant War of 1967*. In his treatment, Gardner's narrative on the young Tijerina is organized through Biblical references as if to emphasize a youthful, if naive spiritual fire:

" . . . I found things, not outright things, but that I was a hypocrite, that I was not doing what I could do."

For that which I do, I allow not: for what I would, I do not; but what I hate, that I do.

"That urge had been building up in my soul for months, building up and building up, and every time I would stop to think or pray or read the Bible, I would feel the urge, that I was way back, way behind, that I had to overcome everything."

For I delight in the law of God after the inward man; but I see another law in my members, warring against the law of my mind.[11]

Gardner quotes Paul (Rom 7:15, 22) on the tensions between the demands of the religious life and pull of the "carnal" sinful life. Paul chose to submit to the religious life, while in Gardner's account, Tijerina's inevitable choice is to reject it. After Gardner moves beyond Tijerina's early adult involvement with religion, he makes no further references to the importance of scripture in Tijerina's life, nor does he reveal any lingering religious sensibility. At the end of his book Gardner interprets Tijerina's early religious life as grounded in his family life. He suggests that the "psychological roots of his dedication, along with the main source of its intensity, can be found in the details of his early life. Herlinda, the strong and pious mother who had died, left him with an uncompromising moral mandate."[12] An independent filmmaker and writer, Gardner presents a comprehensive and detailed narrative that is particularly valuable for its contextual background information on New Mexican politics and the filmmaker's eye for quirkiness and good storytelling. His book is engaging but his patronizing tone and caricatured depictions of Spanish-speaking New Mexicans is regrettable.[13]

Peter Nabokov's influential *Tijerina and the Courthouse Raid* still remains the definitive work on the circumstances and events leading up to and including the Tierra Amarilla incidents. A reporter for the *Santa Fe New Mexican* at the time, Nabokov's journalistic style and intrepid approach makes for a gripping account of a complicated set of nesting and overlapping stories leading up to the Raid.[14] And even though Tijerina later found Nabokov's chronicle "ridiculous,"[15] Nabokov's careful notes and collected documents are indispensable for understanding the Alianza's desperate position in the late 1960s.[16]

Nabokov is clear about the impact of Tijerina's early religious life, but never reaches beyond what is necessary for understanding who Tijerina was and what made him tick at the time of the courthouse raid. In *Tijerina and the Courthouse Raid*, Nabokov is sympathetic to the Alianza's cause and reveals a fondness for Tijerina. Yet, when it comes to figuring out who Tijerina is and what motivates him, Nabokov chooses to regard Reies as "an archetypal primitive rebel" leading "a classic peasant community insurrection, a rising against civil authority." Drawing from Eric Hobsbawm's classifications of peasant leadership in rebellion and Vittorio Lanternari's classic study, *Religions of the Oppressed*, Nabokov collapsed the revolutionary impulses of the social bandit with the blind faith of the messianic savior. He admits that he never really took the time to understand what compelled Tijerina except to refer to a vague "psychological process that was his mystery." Nabokov ends his book with a curious "hint" at this mystery, describing his last conversation with Tijerina late in 1969:

> It was during a cigarette break in the second raid trial. Tijerina lifted his head from a water fountain, slid his palm impatiently across his mouth, and waited for my question. I asked why, really, he had quit the Alianza. . . .
>
> "I tell you Pete. In that prison cell, forty days after the [NASA] moonshot, I had this dream, this experience, the most fantastic thing. I was laughing and crying when I awoke. I was afraid to reach out and touch the walls for fear my hand [would] go right through them. . . . You see, now the land grants are so much of my attention," he pinched his fingers in the Mexican gesture for *a little*, "but the Middle East is so much," he threw out his arms.

Tijerina continued with what could only have shocked the young reporter:

> "I saw in that dream that time and space are barriers to communication, and I was shown a new language, a universal language, the fourth-dimensional language. Then I looked in the Bible and read it all in a new way, and it all checked out. The Arab and Israeli peoples are both the sons of Abraham. So I am going to petition U Thant to send me alone as a civil emissary to the Middle East and bring these warring tribes together." Before he could elaborate he was tapped on the shoulder to return to the courtroom. We never had a chance to talk alone again.[17]

Unfortunately, Nabokov finished his book with Tijerina's comments uninterrogated. Tijerina's references to the American moon landing, and the relationship between Arabs and Jews, appear here as the ramblings of someone at the edge of delusion. Such odd remarks in Nabokov's book can only make sense, however, if we take seriously the critical role of dreaming in Tijerina's life. And to make sense of Tijerina's dreams, we have to understand the influence of his literalist Biblical hermeneutics. Nabokov takes none of these factors into account to explain the "mystery" spilling out here, even though he acknowledged Tijerina's rich dream life and the importance he placed on the Bible.

Michael Jenkinson's, *Tijerina: Land Grant Conflict in New Mexico* is the earliest of the four biographies. Published in 1968, just after Tijerina was acquitted of charges in the first of two trials on the courthouse raid, Jenkinson's account is limited historically by the unresolved reverberations of the Alianza's actions and by an overt sentimentality. His partial view of Tijerina and the Alianza translated into an unfortunate romanticization of Tijerina's life story. For Jenkinson, Tijerina's religious experience and training as a young man met their practical ends in Tierra Amarilla:

> But the Promised land offered by Tijerina was not an economic panacea, the things talked about by governors, eager sociologists, young, intense Marxists, and representatives of the Office of Economic Opportunity. He proposed to return all those things that had been snatched from his people by an errant spin of history, that had made their cultural heritage seem somehow shabby. He spoke as Moses to the sun-creased people who had watched their offspring wheel off in backfiring Chevies toward cities that would hurt and change them, plastic saints magnetized to dashboards.
>
> Reies López Tijerina indicated he would restore their dignity as a people.[18]

Jenkinson's short book is written for a popular audience and is the least analytical of the four biographies. It was nevertheless useful to both Peter Nabokov and Richard Gardner. Jenkinson does not credit his sources, but Nabokov reports that they shared research materials.

The fourth book-length biography is Patricia Bell Blawis' *Tijerina and the Land Grants: Mexican-Americans in Struggle for Their Heritage*. Blawis makes no reference to any of the other three works, but it is unlikely she was able to write her book without knowledge of the other three already published biographies. A member of the Communist Party, Blawis frequented Alianza meetings and was predisposed to interpret the land grant movement as class struggle. Her book takes a forthright, politically left viewpoint, and to her credit she locates Tijerina's organization against the larger background of American racism.[19] While her Marxian view predictably dismisses religion's role in Tijerina's political activism, Blawis acknowledges that his religious training provided a firm foundation for his rhetorical skills and his style of public presentation:

> Some have said that the biblical framework of his speech is a gimmick, others that he is a religious fanatic. Neither is true. Like his dark suit, Tijerina's religious terminology stems from the days of his itinerant evangelism. He spices his rhetoric with biblical references, as did the silver-tongued orators of our grandfathers' day and for the same reason.
>
> Although Tijerina is basically a religious man, he does not attend church nor urge others to seek salvation in prayer. When Reies describes events in biblical terms, it is because these are allusions most familiar to his listeners. It is a cultural, literary expression rather than a religious one. Most of the Alianza members are at least nominally Catholic. Reies' former Protestant denomination embodies a militant anti-Catholicism. So, there is no question of what some have called a "religious rebellion." Tijerina's is a rebellion against impossible conditions of life.[20]

Blawis's ideological bias notwithstanding, it is ironic that among the four biographies, hers is the most accurate description of Tijerina's core religious personality. Tijerina's own estimation of these four works, I should note, is one of disappointment. In his memoir, he reports that Peter Nabokov was "commissioned by the University of New Mexico to write a history of Reies López Tijerina and the Alianza," and that the resultant book was therefore in its very conception flawed. "I did not like that a stranger would interpret my life and struggle," he points out, "because it would be done from a puppet's mentality in the service of his *patrones*. But I couldn't do anything about it." Tijerina also reports that when he was given a copy of Nabokov's book in 1969, "a shiver went up his spine" because he realized it would be used against him.[21] Questioned directly about his preference for any of the available interpretations of his life, Tijerina told Carlos Muñoz, Jr., that none of them were capable of capturing the motivations and essence of who he is, or what he was doing in the late 1960s. "No, none of them do me justice," he emphatically insists, "because they have all wanted to present me in a limited way, and from a journalistic point of view. They have left out the spirit of the cause. They've left out my dreams, my objectives; what inspired me."[22]

If for no other reason than Tijerina's own dissatisfaction with the existing studies of his life and work, a retelling of his life story is in order and benefits from the critical distance elapsed since the work of his four Anglo biographers. Tijerina's criticism that the existing biographical presentations are superficial and "journalistic" indicates a need for investigating the sources and motivations that have been present throughout his life and continue to inform his thoughts and actions. Despite their limitations, the Nabokov and Gardner accounts would be the definitive works on Tijerina were it not for his memoir, *Mi lucha por la tierra*. It might appear useful and interesting to compare their biographical accounts against the memoir, though there is no clear advantage for doing so. There is little, if any, contradictory information on the basic facts or events during the period, 1963–1970, Tijerina's most politically active years. The sheer bulk of media reports and eyewitness accounts, as well as general consensus among his biographers, means that there is already a credible and accurate dating of events in Tijerina's life during this period. The memoir's narrative, beginning in 1956, is also fairly consistent on these matters. But biography and history are of course never simply a matter of chronology, and every act of selection and translation of experience into text is interpretive. My aim here is to translate and so interpret Tijerina's life somewhere between the existing biographies and Tijerina's own work. Other texts, those of Chicano historians, represent yet another view of Tijerina.

Chicano History and the Four Horsemen Tradition

Tijerina's research and activities around Spanish land grants in the Southwest are the basis for his status as a Chicano Movement patriarch. Although the Alianza's assault in Tierra Amarilla remains the event most often associated with him, Tijerina is largely responsible for reinvigorating land grant issues throughout the Southwest and initiating ongoing debates over the legality and enforcement of the Treaty of Guadalupe

Hidalgo.[23] His research in colonial documents reaching back through five hundred years of Spanish, Mexican, and U.S. colonial administration, and his dogged pursuit and reinterpretation of precedent legal texts uncovered the Iberian legal roots of Chicano history. His collection of Spanish colonial documents created a documentary foundation for cultural nationalist myths about Chicano claims to the American Southwest as Aztlán, the ancestral homeland of all Mexican descent peoples.

Tijerina's role in New Mexican land reform cannot be overestimated. The florescence of land grant scholarship after the rise and fall of the Alianza is a quantifiable indication of his ability to force into the open complex land ownership issues simmering beneath the cultural conflicts in the Southwest that periodically erupt in violence. With more bite than previous attempts by its predecessors, the Alianza inspired political interest groups and legal factions in New Mexico (and eventually Texas) to gather land grant documents and interpret for themselves the convoluted history of land rights, tenancy, and use. For example, in response to Tijerina's advocacy, the New Mexico State Government sponsored the *Land Title Study* in its attempt to take an objective position on the issues while trying to co-opt and discredit the research efforts of land grant organizations like the Alianza.[24]

Tijerina's Pentecostal Bible Institute training, his career as an evangelist, and the 1950s Valle de Paz communal experiment were all forgotten by the time the Alianza Federál de Mercedes Reales began to have an impact in New Mexico. When in the early 1970s Chicano historians began to construct narratives of resistance and Mexican American agency, Tijerina was reborn as the incarnation of borderlands *bandido* heroes. The movement and its supporting historiography propped him up as the paradigmatic Chicano nationalist icon.[25] For example, Jesus Treviño's film *Yo Soy Chicano* used cinematic techniques to suggest the connection between Tijerina and the nineteenth-century Mexican social bandits that reflected the "collective omniscient spirit" of Chicano communities.[26] Even as recently as the 1996 documentary produced by a consortium of Chicano filmmakers on the Mexican American Civil Rights movement, Tijerina's relationship to Chicano politics and identity remained circumscribed by promoting a flat, static image of him framed by a nostalgic indigenist connection to the Southwestern landscape.[27]

In one of the earliest attempts at synthesizing Chicano history in the late 1960s and early 1970s, Matt Meier and Feliciano Rivera's *The Chicanos: A History of Mexican Americans* dubbed the male leadership "the Four Horsemen" of the Chicano Movement. In this clever apocalyptic formula, each one of the four leaders—César Chávez, Rodolfo "Corky" Gonzáles, José Angel Gutiérrez, and Reies Tijerina—represented a particular style of political leadership, symbolizing the collective resistance of distinct regional Mexican American communities.

By the middle of the 1960s, César Chávez and his California farmworker's movement had catalyzed an emergent Mexican American consciousness. Attracting national attention with his successful campaign for the labor rights of a predominantly Mexican, Mexican American, and Filipino American agricultural labor force, his Alinsky style of community organizing in the California fields became the struggle of righteous racialized labor. Set against the backdrop of Black Civil Rights agitation, Chávez's well timed efforts were aided by the support of nationally recognized luminaries including then U.S. Attorney General, Robert Kennedy, Catholic Worker activist, Dorothy Day, and other labor leaders.

Rodolfo "Corky" Gonzáles, an ex-boxer and ex-director of a War on Poverty program, initiated the "Crusade for Justice" organization in 1965 in the urban *barrios* of Denver. Promoting strong cultural and traditional Mexican American family values as a strategy for community empowerment, Gonzáles would be best remembered for his 1967 epic poem, "Yo Soy Joaquín/I Am Joaquín," that dramatically narrates the historical rise of a proud indigenous Chicano people. Gonzales's poem voiced a cultural nationalist mythology many young Chicanos were beginning to embrace. "Corky" is also credited with organizing a series of Chicano Youth Liberation Conferences beginning in 1969, which focused and crystallized the movimiento's energy and produced the nationalist manifesto, *El Plan Espiritual de Aztlán*.

The third "horseman," José Angel Gutiérrez, was the youngest of the four men, and the only leader with a college education. Gutiérrez's contribution to the Chicano Movement was to initiate the Texas La Raza Unida Party (LRUP) in 1970. Conceived as an alternative political party for Mexican Americans, LRUP was successful at breaking through the electoral stranglehold whites had historically maintained over the largely

Mexican population in South Texas. LRUP's victories in electing Chicanos to local school boards and city councils encouraged the spread of LRUP chapters across the Southwest. Although LRUP eventually fell prey to internal division and overly ambitious goals, the Raza Unida Party had disproven the longstanding image of Mexican Americans as politically weak and tied to the Democratic party.[28] Gutiérrez's organizing and cultural nationalism proved popular with a new generation of Mexican Americans who resonated with his commitment to both local community activism and higher education.

Poised alongside these three leaders, and representing another style of political mobilization, Reies Tijerina completed the Horsemen posse. If Chávez, with his pacifist Gandhian approach to political struggle occupied one end of the Chicano leadership continuum, then Tijerina with his fiery rhetoric and gun toting outlaw image occupied the opposite pole. By the time Meier and Rivera introduced the four horsemen formula, the Tierra Amarilla courthouse raid had become a defining event in Chicano history. Each horseman had earned his place by virtue of a significant achievement: Chávez and the 1965 Delano Grape strike; Gutiérrez and the election of Mexican Americans to the Crystal City, Texas, city council; Corky Gonzáles and *El Plan Espiritual de Aztlán*. Tijerina's achievement at Tierra Amarilla would forever define his place in Chicano history.

The Four Horsemen ideal—masculine, powerful, and apocalyptic—organized and united four distinct and only tenuously related political movements. Moreover, it dovetailed with traditional Mexican concepts of *caudillismo* or autocratic male leadership. Each of the four movements (there were others) represented by the horsemen spoke to particular issues and to specific Mexican descent populations. It was only when they were viewed in relationship to one another through a nationalist frame that the power of the horsemen ideal (and so the power of the Chicano Movement) could be fully articulated. As a labor movement, César Chávez and the United Farm Workers came to be identified as the strategy of traditional, rural Mexican Catholic *campesino* moral piety set against the Goliath of corporate agriculture, big boss Anglo growers, and the rival Teamster's Union. Gonzáles's work typified a youthful, idealist, and urban Chicano voice; while Gutiérrez's electoral politics resonated with the older, impoverished, historically present Mexican American population along the U.S.-Mexico border. Tijerina's Alianza Federál de Mercedes Reales represented the land grant struggle of the isolated northern New Mexican *Hispano*. Neither Tijerina nor Chávez saw themselves as cultural nationalists. However, articulated from within the rhetoric of the movement and in relation to Gutiérrez and Gonzáles, both of them became associated with the nationalist Aztlán ideal.

Tijerina certainly understood his leadership role in the context of the larger movement as useful for his work in New Mexico. However, his status as one of the movement's horsemen needs to be clarified and examined against the ideological underpinnings of Chicano cultural nationalism and the revisionist tendencies of the earliest Chicano historiography. Complicating this inquiry is the role and influence of Tijerina's Anglo biographers, all outsiders to the northern New Mexican communities and offering sympathetic portraits of him. In addition, Tijerina's harshest critics were New Mexicans themselves, both Anglo and Hispano, particularly politicians and professionals such as state historian Dr. Myra Ellen Jenkins, *Albuquerque Journal* editor Bob Brown, and anthropologist Nancie L. González. Among the Hispanos themselves, there remains no consensus as to the legitimacy or popularity of Tijerina and the Alianza.

From the view of Chicano activists and scholars (the latter themselves almost always activists) Tijerina and the Alianza were adopted wholesale as representative of the New Mexican Hispano struggle. Part of the explanation for why Chicano scholars and activists presumed Tijerina to be the voice of New Mexican *Chicanismo* was the political desire to bridge the historical and cultural differences between northern New Mexico Hispanos and other Mexican descent communities in the United States. Bringing together disparate populations of Mexican Americans was a prerequisite for the purposes of building a pan-Chicano culture and political movement. Tijerina's outsider status in New Mexican Hispano communities and the realities of local New Mexican land grant factionalism were all ignored by Chicano Movement ideology. The New Mexican land grant issue, by virtue of its ancient and legal claims to the land played a crucial role in the nationalist cause. Recognized legal precedent to Hispano ownership of New Mexican lands gave substance to the dream of the Chicano homeland of Aztlán. Without Tijerina's research and arguments flowing from legal documents on the land issue, Aztlán remained empty rhetoric.

This is not to suggest that Tijerina's place in Chicano history is only a product of Chicano Movement ideologues. Rather, what must also be taken into account is the extent to which Tijerina's ability to act was circumscribed by movement ideology and contained by the teleological hope of the Chicano Movement as it passed into the 1970s. The enduring legacy of revisionist Chicano history, with its idealization of the family, naive trust in proletarian values, and its romanticized vision of a pre-Columbian indigenous communalism, has been responsible for limiting Tijerina's image to one that conformed to the ideals and goals of the movimiento.[29]

Tijerina's life and work was thus forged by Chicano scholars. Meier and Rivera's *The Chicanos* and especially Rodolfo Acuña's epic *Occupied America* reveal how and why Tijerina's presence was essential to the mythological structure of the Chicano Movement. But these texts are also in large measure the reason why he vanished from the movement narrative later in the 1970s. Although Meier and Rivera released the Four Horsemen into the collective Chicano historical memory, Acuña's *Occupied America* remains the most influential Chicano history text illustrating the intersection of historical narrative with a revisionist political agenda. Now in its fourth edition, *Occupied America* presents a sweeping survey of Chicano history beginning with the systematic and violent takeover of northern Mexico by the United States in the nineteenth century. *Occupied America* continues to be the standard college textbook in Chicano studies and has been noted for its landmark importance in both scope and historiographical significance. A review of *Occupied America* here illustrates the pervasiveness and longevity of its nationalist discourse.[30]

Critics of Rodolfo Acuña's work have noted that he is all too aware of the changes he has made over four editions of his book. In the second edition of *Occupied America* (1981) Acuña confessed that the original release (1972) was too contentious and guided by a Marxist, internal colonial model of history. In his first revision of the text he "attempted to purge polemics" from the analysis that interpreted Mexican Americans as an internal colony of the United States through the nineteenth century. Sixteen years after the first edition, the third edition of *Occupied America* (1988) returned to a moderately polemical view. Animated by what he saw as the decline in Chicano activism, Acuña admitted that the book's purpose was "to dispel the myths that are manufactured by scholars who take refuge in patriotism" (viii). In fact, *Occupied America*'s turn away from the moral outrage and influence of Franz Fanon's political philosophy in the original edition toward a measured and less politically charged second edition, to an exaggerated concern for class analysis in the third edition, and finally to a more contextual approach in the fourth, represent changes in Acuña's scholarship, as well as the changing fortunes of Chicano communities since the 1960s. Reading Acuña's revisions through the changes in the American political climate does in fact coincide with the changing tone of the narratives.

The first two editions of *Occupied America* frame the Chicano historical experience through two centuries of racial oppression and labor subordination. In the case of the nineteenth century, Acuña depicts Mexican Americans as the colonized victims of an expansionist, capitalist United States following a bloody military conquest. This colonial legacy thus sets the stage for Chicano challenges to dominant American society in the late twentieth century.[31] In the third edition, however, Acuña leaves behind his heavy handed anticolonialist critique and instead frames the twentieth-century Chicano experience within a class analysis. Alex Saragoza notes that Acuña's first edition of *Occupied America* "derived much of its information from extant literature" and was guilty of a "facile acceptance of internal colonialism as an interpretive framework." Although Acuña "pruned" the colonial framework in the second edition, Saragoza pointed out that "the emphasis on the victimization of the Chicano continued."[32] But by 1988, in the third edition, *Occupied America* located the contemporary danger to Chicano communities in the "intensification of methods of social control" as well as the "defection" of a Chicano middle class. Lapsing into the language of the first edition, Acuña promoted a widening of a "progressive counter-hegemonic ideology within the community, and [a call] to plan the class struggle that is inevitable."[33]

In the fourth edition of *Occupied America* Acuña once again shifted his emphasis.[34] The flood of new historical research, a larger and diverse Latino population, and the emphasis on women and gender in the 1990s required him to broaden his approach. Ever the curmudgeonly patriarch of Chicano scholarship, Acuña aimed his criticism at an increasing number of corrosive forces threatening Chicano communities in the intervening twelve years since the third edition.

The importance of Acuña's text in the substantiation and interpretation of Chicano history is acknowledged by all Chicano scholars, whether or not they are in accord with his views. As the prime example of Chicano revisionist history, the "them versus us" drama in the narrative has informed three generations of students in Chicano studies.[35] For our purposes, *Occupied America*'s central role in creating Chicano history and defining the arena of Chicano historiography provides us the opportunity to trace the origins of the Four Horsemen paradigm in Chicano mythology. More to the point, it reveals how Tijerina's status changed between the height of the Chicano Movement (as promoted in the first, 1972 edition of *Occupied America*) and the postmortem analysis of the movement's failure (the fourth, 2000 edition). The changing portrait of Chicano leadership in Acuña's text supports the idea that Chicano history is held to particular ideological standards that protect and sanction revisionist and cultural nationalist historical narratives. Again, Saragoza correctly observes that "given the political context in which Chicano scholarship originated, the search for common historical threads paralleled the search for a means to organize Chicanos into a viable and coherent political force. Activists in this sense 'used' history as an ideological base for concerted action."[36] Thus, Acuña's texts not only sanction the portrayal of Tijerina in Chicano history, but more than any other historical treatment of the movement, *Occupied America* is responsible for the disappearance of Tijerina as an historical subject/actor after his release from prison in 1971.

Besides Saragoza, other scholars have commented on the nationalist character of Acuña's treatment of movement leaders. Carlos Muñoz, Jr., reminds us that although Acuña assumes that César Chávez was part of the Chicano nationalist strategy, Chávez preferred to see himself as working primarily on behalf of unionized farm labor.[37] I would add that Acuña's portrayal of Tijerina as a cultural nationalist is a similar misinterpretation. Certainly Tijerina's rhetoric often bordered on nationalist concerns and members of the Alianza often made the leap from local land grant efforts to Chicano nationalism, particularly after 1969. However, even a casual reading of the documentary sources indicates that Tijerina did not advocate or embrace outright secession or the larger hope for a return to Aztlán. In general he carefully avoided using the ideological vocabulary of the larger movement.

In the first edition of *Occupied America*, Acuña took inspiration from and constructed his text around the potentially revolutionary ideals and meanings that Tijerina held for the Chicano Movement. Quoting Tijerina extensively throughout the text as proof of the radical nature of Chicano activism, Acuña adopted Tijerina's phrase about Mexican Americans having only "Freedom in a Cage" for the title of one of his chapters. Celebrating Tijerina's direct action politics, Acuña linked the New Mexico land grant movement to a larger Third World struggle against western imperialism. "Only through a broader understanding of history," Acuña declared, "will we appreciate the protests of men like Tijerina."[38]

A decade later Acuña produced a "purged" second edition. Revised after the revolutionary zeal of the Chicano Movement had waned, Acuña reduced his treatment of Tijerina to less than half of what had been written in the first edition. Gone was Tijerina's voice in the rest of the text. When Acuña set about to revise *Occupied America* the first time, Tijerina had already changed the direction of his politics. After two years spent in federal prison Tijerina was pursuing interests well beyond the concerns of most Chicano activists. Acuña's vagueness about what had happened to Tijerina after his release from prison in 1971 indicates that he still considered Tijerina useful in his narrative, but evidently found him problematic when he was revising his book. In the second edition, Acuña no longer writes about Tijerina as part of a larger historical process linked to liberation struggles in the rest of the world. The most disappointing omission in the revision, however, is that Acuña completely ignored Tijerina's recently released memoir, *Mi lucha por la tierra*, relying almost entirely on Nabokov's and Gardner's biographies.

In the 1988 revision, Acuña further abridged what he had said about Tijerina in the second edition, relegating him to an era that was short lived, naive, and crowded with a diverse set of leaders:

The 1960s produced heroes at every level of protest, from Joan Baez, to Che Guevara, to Stokely Carmichael, to Herbert Marcuse. With the growth of nationalism, it was natural for Mexican

Americans to identify leaders who best expressed their frustrations. During the 1960s, therefore, Chicanos, for a brief time, had heroes that were legitimated by them and not by the state.[39]

Not coincidentally, into the 1980s José Angel Gutiérrez and Corky Gonzáles, like Tijerina, had also dropped out of the collective Chicano consciousness. César Chávez and the UFW, on the other hand, continued to pursue justice in the California agriculture arena and Acuña returned later in the text to describe farmworker efforts to mobilize and survive under Republican policies. On the final pages of the third edition, we read that three of the original four horsemen (excluding Chávez) are reduced to the phrase, "were still active; the scope of their activity was nevertheless restricted."[40] Thrown into Acuña's class analysis of Chicanos in the twentieth century, the failure of three of the Chicano Movement horsemen is attributed to "changes in the mind-set of society and of Chicanos themselves." From the vantage point of the late 1980s, Acuña could afford to be nostalgic about the 1960s "Day of the Heroes." Casting about for villains, he blamed upwardly mobile Chicanos ("Hispanics"), lamenting that they had "joined the former baby-boom radicals in the mainstream of North American society. Unlike the 'heroes' they did not aspire to lead the masses or to remake society." No longer useful to the challenges or concerns facing Chicanos in the late 1980s, Acuña trapped Tijerina in the 1960s heyday of Chicano activism. Summarizing Tijerina's life after 1971, in both the second and third editions of *Occupied America*, Acuña simply observes: "Tijerina was released [from prison] in the summer of 1971."[41]

This final sentence in the third edition of *Occupied America* appears in slightly altered form in the fourth (2000) edition: "He was released in the summer of 1971." But unlike the previous editions, Acuña continues his discussion of the land grant struggle. In line with the fourth edition's recognition of women and gender, he adds two paragraphs profiling the work of María Varela, a veteran of the civil rights movement who helped start *La Cooperative Agricola*.[42] For all intents and purposes, and despite a continued struggle in Tierra Amarilla, Acuña still managed to kill off Tijerina in his text even as Tijerina continued to work in the region well into the 1990s.

Other representations of Tijerina in Chicano scholarship have adopted the pattern set by Acuña. In Juan Gómez Quiñones's *Chicano Politics: Reality and Promise, 1940–1990*, he describes Tijerina and the Alianza as "seminal influences" in the movement and supportive of a nationalist agenda. Gómez Quiñones correctly indicates that Tijerina's role and influence in the Alianza declined after 1971 when the organization disintegrated. Noting that into the 1970s Tijerina was no longer able to provide effective "organizational leadership," Gómez Quiñones sums up Tijerina's post-movement activities in a list that includes writing his autobiography, "denounc[ing] an alleged international conspiracy, and involv[ing] himself in lawsuits; he changed the spelling of his name and stressed that he too was heir to a land grant."[43]

Gómez Quiñones concludes his review of the Alianza by noting its passing and the reinvigoration of the land grant question through the efforts of traditional electoral politics. His analysis of the Alianza and Tijerina's relationship to the land grant movement is not without merit and offers insight into the importance that male leadership like Tijerina's played in the development and character of Chicano politics. In general, Gómez Quiñones's summary of Tijerina's post-Alianza work is accurate. However, like Acuña's revision of *Occupied America*, *Chicano Politics* relies, predictably, on Nabokov, Gardner, and pre-1971 sources. He does make limited use of the memoir, *Mi lucha por la tierra*, but completely misunderstands its motivation and summarily dismisses it as "rambling."[44] There is no mention made of Tijerina's land grant work in Texas or the San Joaquín "city-state" where Tijerina was living at the time, both activities falling squarely within the framework of Gómez Quiñones's concern and arguably constituting significant political action. Thus Gómez Quiñones's analysis of Tijerina, while better than most, ultimately failed to consider changes in the direction of Tijerina's thinking. Like Acuña's erasure of Tijerina after 1971, Gómez Quiñones is unable to imagine Tijerina outside the nationalist framework and the four horsemen formula. Despite Alex Saragoza's claim that Chicano related historical writing had overcome a uniform revisionist perspective by the late 1970s, a review of Tijerina's treatment in this literature proves that a detectable ideological current connected to an earlier movement era still operates in Chicano historiography.[45]

More recently a lingering nationalism is still visible in the framing and historical portrayal of Tijerina in the text by Francisco Rosales accompanying the documentary *CHICANO! The History of the Mexican American Civil Rights Movement*.[46] Leaving aside the numerous historical and factual errors about Tijerina in this account, Rosales elevates him as "the undisputed leader of the movimiento" during the late 1960s; "a mantle acquired not through design but through demonstration of sheer daring." Yet in his recent life, Tijerina is portrayed as a pitiable survivor, "the subject of a personality cult."[47] As with previous treatments, Rosales emphasizes political activism and encapsulates Tijerina's religious life in a single short paragraph.[48] It would seem that even with the benefit of historical hindsight, the nationalist narrative continues to define one of Chicano history's most central actors and ignore his religious impulse.

The changes in Acuña's *Occupied America*, and subsequent texts in Chicano history and politics, are indicative of how Chicano scholarship has evolved since the early 1970s. The four horsemen paradigm that formed the central narrative about the movement period forged a seamless, heroic Chicano mythology promoting a sense of unity across Chicano communities and reinforced traditional forms of patriarchal leadership. Beginning in 1971, Tijerina turned to a broad, coalitional political platform of "brotherhood awareness" and later began to read the place of Mexican Americans within an apocalyptic reinscription of Spanish Americans as the lost tribes of Israel. Clearly these ideas made him a liability to Chicano activism and advocacy scholarship. Unable to reconcile this postprison Tijerina with the heroic bandit image of the late 1960s, Chicano history froze the earlier image and banished any substantive mention of Tijerina's work after 1971.[49]

Tijerina himself consciously facilitated his entry into Chicano history and politics early in the 1960s with his conversion back to Roman Catholicism, aware that his Pentecostalism would hamper his acceptance into New Mexican Hispano culture. Tijerina has never been innocent in his own use of Chicano discourse and politics. So it is that his problematic Pentecostal past is rarely if ever acknowledged or discussed by Chicano scholars. And even though Nabokov's and Gardner's biographies (treatments that Chicano scholars have been heavily dependent upon for their work) hinted at the centrality of religion in Tijerina's life, the essentially religious quality of his work goes unnoticed by Chicano history. As recently as the 2000 edition of *Occupied America*, Chicano scholars continue to ignore, diminish, and dismiss Tijerina's non-Catholic life. Capturing this aversion to religion, Acuña's 1988 summary of Tijerina's most formative period fills one sentence: "Tijerina became a preacher."[50]

Fortunately we have Tijerina's memoir, *Mi lucha por la tierra*, which serves as a check and potential corrective to his biographers, critics, and interpreters. It is no surprise, however, that Tijerina's own memory of his past has also been dismissed and ignored by Chicano scholars. In Chapter Five I discuss how *Mi lucha por la tierra*'s reception constitutes yet another example of the influence that the master narrative of Chicano history wields in the fabrication and maintenance of a Chicano mythos. But until we get there, the next chapter is my attempt to reconstruct an alternate view of Tijerina's life and work.

2   REVEALING KING TIGER

1926–1956: Finding God

REIES LÓPEZ TIJERINA WAS BORN ON 21 SEPTEMBER 1926, NEAR FALLS City, Texas, one of five sons and two daughters to Mexican American sharecropping parents. Born during a period of intense social and economic changes along the Mexican-Texas border, the Tijerinas experienced first hand the ambivalence of their position as Mexican American laborers in the south Texas agricultural miracle. In the 1920s Mexicans and Mexican Americans constituted the dominant agricultural and ranching workforce in Texas. Mexican cotton labor was most common in central, west, and south Texas, and tenant farmers like the Tijerinas had gradually replaced black labor in this western, historically peripheral southern state. Perceived by growers as less ambitious than whites or blacks, Mexican laborers became the preferred workforce among agricultural interests. As an overall generally poorly educated population, Mexicans also appeared to be less likely to protest their exploitation, while their propensity for large families translated into increased labor productivity.

What we know about Antonio and Erlinda Tijerina's struggling family life corroborates the many accounts of Mexicans inside a labor-repressive agricultural system. It was a dangerous and racist order that would school the young Reies in his first lessons in racial injustice.[1] The poor treatment of Mexican labor in the commercialized and impersonal economy set in

Tijerina's mind a lasting bitterness brought on by a racial caste system, low wages, and harsh living conditions. The tyranny of white landed farmers and the impotence of local law enforcement were offset by Tijerina's larger than life mother who provided most of the economic and spiritual sustenance for the family. Erlinda Tijerina gave birth ten times, Reies being the fifth child of the seven surviving. Cleaning pastures, clearing fields, weeding, tending, and picking cotton, the Tijerinas lived in a one room house and at least thrice endured the humiliation of being cheated out of payment for an entire season's work. The endless round of agricultural tasks meant that Erlinda Tijerina was forced to work through her pregnancies to full term. Tijerina recalls that on the day he was born his parents were working in the cotton fields. "It was around, between four and five o'clock in the afternoon . . . and the [labor] pains arrived, and it was there that I was born on a cotton sack, half-full."

A formidable woman, Erlinda Tijerina could carry full sacks of cotton. During the Depression years she supplemented what meager foodstuffs the family had by hunting jackrabbits with a bow and arrow. The mythological stature of Tijerina's mother in his memory is indicated by his comment that during the harshest of times, "she would catch snakes with her bare hands!"[2] During these harsh years Tijerina and his brothers helped their father "gather bones, bags, scrap iron to sell" and more than once survived on ground squirrels they dug out of the ground. Antonio Tijerina at one time had been forcefully dragged off of his land in Laredo by whites and is remembered by Reies with regret for not having stood his ground against them on various occasions. Crippled in one of these physical attacks, Antonio depended heavily upon Erlinda, who at times had to carry him to and from the fields.[3]

Tijerina's religious education began with his mother whom he describes as a devout Catholic who "prayed before meals, and in the evening . . . read the Bible a lot." His father, however, "became a Protestant out of fear in Texas . . . of the [Texas] Rangers [who] don't like Blacks and don't like Catholics." Baptized into the Roman Catholic Church Reies was extremely close to his mother and took from her a profound sense of piety. Antonio Tijerina's Protestantism did cause some friction, but Erlinda seems to have remained Catholic to ease relations with her extended family.

At a very young age, Reies's life begins to show an extraordinary tendency for vivid and startling dreams. When only four or five years of age, he remembers an episode brought about by his frustration over having only half a cup of tea made from pecan tree bark for a meal.

And I didn't touch it and I went to sleep and that was it! I died! [laughing] I didn't get up until the next day! The next thing I know is what I saw when I was awake, and what they tell me [laughing].

Yes! That they made, you know, the coffin. They were making the coffin and they were crying and, you know, they go through the procedures when somebody dies. And I remember that I was cold when I got up. . . . And very hungry! . . . I ran to the kitchen and saw a piece of tortilla . . . and I grabbed it and ran outside eating it. And that's where people, my family [saw me and] got completely shocked. Shocked! And then, the next day, and throughout the years, my uncles used to talk about me . . . "There goes the dead boy," you know, "there goes the resurrected boy."

During this "death" he dreamt that

somebody was holding my hand . . . in my belief, in the dream, as a child, this could have been, because my mother was talking to me about Christ, I don't know! But in my mind, he was, you know, what I knew as Jesus. And I was . . . I feel, I was feeling through his hand and my hand. He never talked. He didn't say nothing, I felt something through his hand, you know, I was sure as long as he had me by his hand . . . I didn't have to worry for nothing. And the place— beautiful! Like Spring. Green; birds flying and green grass all over. It was beautiful scenery. And we were traveling in a little narrow road and I was pulling, with my other hand, I was pulling a little red wagon. See I never had . . . now that I could believe that I dreamed that because I always wanted a toy, and I didn't have no toys! That can be interpreted that way, but I remember that little red wagon![4]

In another recurring childhood dream, Reies would watch a driverless car moving toward their small house: "It would drive on up without a driver, and I would shake. I would shake from fright because I was afraid he [the owner] would think we had stolen it and come and shoot one of us. I would wake up trembling."

Tijerina's active dream life, while perhaps not unusual among children, set a lifetime openness to dreams, visions, divining signs in nature, and a search for meanings attached to these extraordinary experiences. One of Tijerina's strongest memories of his mother is that she would ask him to recall his death dream, "what you saw in heaven," whenever he awoke startled from the driverless car dream.

After the death of his mother when he was still very young, Reies recalls that it was her "conscience that stayed with me. That was all I had in my heart, what she left me." Leaving behind the sadness in Texas, the Tijerinas spent the next five years as migrant farmworkers following jobs northward and returning during the winter months. At the age of eleven Tijerina's father sent him to San Antonio to begin elementary school. As a migrant laborer constantly on the move, however, Tijerina was forced to abandon school after the third grade when it became impossible to complete a regular school year. In sum Tijerina's education was rudimentary at best; about six months total. The Tijerinas were so poor that Reies reportedly went barefoot until the age of thirteen. Life following the seasonal harvesting of crops across the states was difficult beyond having to locate work and lodging. "We'd sleep on the highway when we were going to different places to work." And even when employment was secured and wages paid out, "the men would guard the road against Klansmen that were trying to take that money."[5]

As early as age fourteen or fifteen Tijerina's impatience with the injustices of migrant labor found him confronting Anglo ranchers over working conditions. He was driven by an "inner force to defend my rights, to tell them they weren't paying us enough or doing right by us."[6] Unhappy with the mistreatment and labor caste system in Texas, Tijerina and his brothers headed north for the next few years, taking jobs in Indiana, Ohio, and even working in Michigan automobile factories.[7]

At about age fifteen, while laboring in the Michigan beet fields, Tijerina came into contact with a [Southern?] Baptist missionary. Samuel Galindo was evangelizing among the migrant Mexican laborers. "He came . . . where we were chopping beets and it was at that time . . . that he gave me a Bible as a gift when he saw that I was an enthusiast and that I liked listening to him." Already familiar with the Bible from his mother's instruction, the young Tijerina took to Galindo's preaching. He was soon converted and baptized in a local river in obedience to Baptist doctrine.

In his retelling of these early events, Tijerina's consuming passion for living out the lessons of the Old Testament patriarchs and prophets as models are preeminent:

> And I read in the Bible that mercy and truth met, and justice and peace hugged. So then it was the religious life for the satisfaction of the yearning of my heart for justice. And my idols [began] with Moses on. This is what I got from religious life. I gathered up the strengths and liberties of justice out of the lives of those Biblical men of old.[8]

In fact, the Bible became more central to Tijerina's religious formation than any denominational affiliation. In interviews he is precise about the importance of the text over and against the particularities of human institutions. He has been careful since the 1960s to portray his faith during his early adulthood as nondenominational. "Nothing, not Baptist, not Methodist, no denomination. I knew they would tie me down. It was just the Bible that I believed in." Recalling his full immersion baptism, he is deliberate to say that he was "baptized as a Protestant." Although in the Baptist tradition this ritual usually coincides with a commitment to a particular congregation, Tijerina's willful vagueness on this otherwise life-changing event draws narrow attention to the primacy of the Bible and not to sectarian dogma. The point is a minor one in the larger biography but indicates a consistent and careful memory that Tijerina has maintained over the course of a long public career. Taking time to familiarize himself with evangelical Christianity and mainline Protestant groups, he eventually joined the Assemblies of God, the largest Pentecostal denomination at the time.

In 1944 he entered the Instituto Biblico Latino Americano in Saspamco, Texas. Referred to facetiously as "Canaan Land" by its students, the Instituto lay just outside of San Antonio. Established in 1926 to train Mexican missionaries, preachers, and ministers, the Instituto Biblico was part of the Assemblies of God Latin American District.[9] Tijerina's three-year education at the Bible Institute fed his young, hungry mind with invaluable exegetical and homiletic skills that would serve him well throughout his life. Bible-centered and emphasizing the pragmatic applications of Pentecostal theology, the Instituto education opened up windows of possibility for Tijerina that he would not have otherwise had as a Mexican American Baptist, Presbyterian, or Methodist. "It was very good my early training because the center of it was the Bible . . . it was the bouncing board; or the means that inspired me to read and study the life of Buddha, the life of Mohammed the Prophet, the life of Christ, the life of Moses . . . it was a starting point and a driving force, the Bible."[10]

During his time there Reies developed a friendship with a female student, Vicky Rivera. He was reprimanded several times for violating strict regulations against students found unchaperoned with members of the opposite sex.[11] Eventually this friendship resulted in his expulsion from the Instituto, thus ending his formal theological training just prior to his graduation. It is unlikely, though, that this forbidden friendship was the sole reason for Tijerina's termination at the Bible Institute. Rather, charges of his increasingly unorthodox theology by the Institute's Superintendent, Kenzy Savage, were the actual reasons behind his expulsion, his association with Vicky Rivera merely the catalyzing transgression.

Prohibited once again from completing his education, Tijerina managed, nevertheless, to receive credentials from the Assemblies of God to preach as one of their own. Although the facts and dates are vague, Tijerina was given charge of several small Mexican congregations in Texas and spent some time visiting Assemblies churches throughout the Southwest. Tijerina's ministry as a sanctioned Pentecostal preacher on both sides of the Mexico-U.S. border lasted from his "graduation" in 1946 until the Assemblies of God stripped him of his ministerial credentials in 1950. Losing his denomination's endorsement over questions of orthodoxy, he set off to continue an independent itinerant ministry throughout the next six years.

Up to this point, Tijerina's family life had remained fragmented. Because of his father's chronic illness, Anselmo, the eldest son still at home, had stepped in as head of the family. Tijerina's older brother Margarito, always an independent child, had left home at age seventeen, moving first to El Paso, and then on to Michigan. Ramón, who later followed Reies into the political arena, followed him first to the Bible Institute. There is no mention of what happened to his sisters. In 1946 Reies and Ramón married a pair of sisters who had also been students at the Bible Institute. The youngest brother, Cristóbal, was only nine months old when Erlinda Tijerina had died and was being raised by a Native American friend of the family. Through the 1940s Cristóbal continued to live apart from his brothers.

After leaving the Bible Institute, now accompanied by his wife, Maria, Tijerina might have settled into a struggling but predictable life of a Pentecostal minister. Most graduates of Pentecostal Bible institutes went out into the world without financial support from their denominations and relied upon a combination of day jobs and a congregation's irregular financial support. Driven by faith and the sacred commission of the gospel, if they survived the first most difficult years of their ministry, Bible Institute graduates were faced with meager incomes, modest lives, and humble congregations.[12] Burned by his expulsion from the Bible Institute but eager to live out the challenges set out for him by the gospel, Tijerina, only twenty-one at the time, took his new wife and set out to reform Christianity. He began by retracing the round of churches he had pastored or visited when he was sanctioned by the Assemblies authorities.

The year 1947 found the young couple, now with their first child, David, pursuing a full-time traveling ministry. Most of the time they walked, living from hand to mouth and relying on the generosity of congregations and whomever they met on the road. Tijerina's suspicion of material wealth sometimes meant refusing the payment offered him in churches where he preached. Forced to make the most of their poverty, Maria did not appreciate her husband's voluntary asceticism and was unhappy with his acts of material negation. By 1953 the Tijerina family had spent six long years on the edge of poverty. And with three children in tow (Reies, Jr. ["David"], Rose, and Daniel) Maria could hardly afford her husband's theological excesses. "When I read that Socrates' wife was always angry because he wouldn't take money, I would rejoice," he told Peter Nabokov,

> because my wife was always angry because I gave everything of my own away one time to Mexican nationals who [were hoeing beets].

I gave them my gas and my car, taking them to town and wherever they wanted to go. Three times I felt the need to dispose of all my possessions and give [them] away free to people to feel at ease with my heart's desire. Once I gave away my new watch [and] four suits. Those deeds raised opposition from my wife, because she said I was taking bread from my children.[13]

Tijerina's itinerant ministry between 1947 and 1955 took him through the Southwest, the Midwest as far north as Saginaw, Michigan, east to Puerto Rican congregations in New York City, and several times into Mexico.[14] More than once he would give away all of his possessions, indicating a growing dissatisfaction with his abilities as a minister to effectively live out the gospel commandments concerning material poverty.[15] "Because I kept on having a struggle with my conscience, my soul," he recalled,

I was not satisfied, I was always finding that the Bible rebuked me. I found things, not outright things, but that I was a hypocrite, that I was not doing what I could do. . . . That urge had been building up in my soul for months, building up and building up, and every time I would stop and think or pray or read the Bible, I would feel that urge, that I was way back, way behind, that I had to overcome everything.[16]

Feeling that he was as yet inadequate to serve God, Tijerina announced to Maria sometime in the early 1950s that he was going off on his own "to seek the light, a better opening." Finding a cave on a hilltop near El Monte, California, he lined it with cotton from an old car seat, covered it over with brush, and burrowed into it "like a snake" and waited. He resolved that he "wouldn't leave that place until God would show me my duty."

I don't know how long I was there, but it was days, and I had great illuminations. I found that there were not so many religions as they had taught me in Bible School, there was just the two strong powers of good and evil. I saw that those of different religions were all the same, they all wanted new automobiles, they were full of pride and coveted the same things, and so I learned that there was no difference between Protestant and Catholic after all. Being subject to certain pressures, they would all act the same. And so, I went back to my wife with a new interpretation for the Bible, just literally, the way it was, and I started out preaching again.[17]

According to Kenzy Savage, the superintendent of the Bible Institute, even as a student Tijerina was zealous in his attempt to enact what he was reading in the Bible and learning in the classroom. Savage described him at the time as "fanatical, more peculiar in his thoughts, I guess—he was not orthodox. When he went to school he was a very sincere student. I don't know, when he left school, he began to get these rather far-out ideas about how people ought to conduct themselves."[18] Apparently Tijerina's heterodox ideas were not too unorthodox, as Savage accompanied him on evangelistic work around Santa Fe on at least one occasion in the late 1940s.

Tijerina's ideas about how Christians "ought to conduct themselves" translated into direct confrontation with the Assemblies hierarchy. The Assemblies of God flock that he pastored in Eden, Texas, was the location of his final break with organized Christianity. There Tijerina's preaching from his Old Testament prophet heroes against materialism and weak faith proved too much for the Assemblies' superintendent who summarily relieved Tijerina from his pastorate and locked him out of the church building. "They closed the doors and all the members, fifty families were kicked out with me," Tijerina recalled.

They [Assemblies of God] wanted to kick me out, suspended me. And all the members came to the front [of the church], you know. They said, "No! No, Reies is not speaking against nobody. He's rebuking. He's exhorting the people. He's advocating reform . . . but he's not talking about a new religion or a new institution or organization. Nothing of the kind." So they closed the doors and we continued having services [in another location], me and the fifty families.

That same year, in Chama, New Mexico, he refused to accept the "love offering" taken up during the service for the guest preacher unless the members of the congregation agreed to "follow Christ" and give the money to the poor.[19] On another occasion he flattened the collection plate with a hammer during his sermon to illustrate his point before a stunned congregation.[20] And again, when a member of a small church had heard enough of Tijerina's unorthodox theology and began to walk out, Tijerina grabbed a collection plate and flung it at him, the plate barely missing the man and crashing against the exit door.[21]

Tijerina's biographers take note of his radical theological transformation going into the first half of the 1950s. In interviews with Tijerina in the late 1960s, a period when Tijerina downplayed the influence of Christianity in his political life, brief overviews of his religious training and life as an evangelist contribute to a vagueness about the details of his ministry. Descriptions of Tijerina's ministerial life in the decade following 1946, unfortunately, gloss over his turmoil in trying to reconcile the inclusive theology of Pentecostalism with a growing awareness of pervasive racial oppression in the lives of his Spanish-speaking congregants. Both Gardner and Nabokov highlight conversations between Tijerina and mysterious unnamed Anglo men that trigger his shift from religion to politics.[22] These anecdotes, crucial in the biographies for explaining the change in Tijerina's career do not, however, help much toward understanding this critical period of his life that was anything but worldly or politically driven. Gardner's depiction of Tijerina's radical break with religion is illustrated in the following anecdote:

> On one of my first trips to Mexico, I went to Jalisco to ask a very famous holy man what I should do with my life. When I got there, he was still in bed, and his retainers said it was forbidden to wake him up. I told them that I had come 400 miles to seek this man's counsel, and I said, "What kind of a holy man is this that won't talk to a pilgrim seeking help. Saint Paul wouldn't do that, Jesus wouldn't turn away someone in need." And I left and went to Mexico City and gave my car away to the poor.[23]

Jenkinson's account of Tijerina's itinerancy and life of poverty is a more accurate description of these years than Gardner's or Nabokov's young revolutionary in the making. He quotes Tijerina's summation of these long, tedious years as a time spent

> teaching, talking to the people . . . farmworkers, in the towns going from one church to another where I was invited. I would sleep under bridges, or in the open. Drunkards and poor people would give me a dollar to keep me going—some would invite me to their homes to eat. It was a training period. My beliefs were greater than my experience.[24]

Despite all of the wandering, Tijerina managed to write and finance the publication of a collection of sermons under the title, ¿Hallará Fe en la Tierra . . . ? (Will Faith be Found on the Earth?). This slim volume captures the dark and brooding theology of the serious young preacher. In formal, baroque Spanish, Tijerina's sermons warn his readers of the dire consequences of lax faith and predicts God's use of the atom bomb as the instrument of divine justice. Chapter Three will examine this collection of Tijerina's sermons.

By 1955 Tijerina had made a complete break with institutional Christianity, gathering around him a band of loyal followers. Hard years of searching for authentic Christianity and the subsequent disappointments in his efforts took their toll on his trust in the Christian message he had been taught by the Assemblies of God. A growing disenchantment forced him to withdraw from the sinfulness and corruption of the world around him. The anger preserved in his sermons, and his conclusion that all institutions—religious and secular—were flawed sparked a crisis in his faith that could only find resolution by taking on the challenges put to him by the gospel. "I had fought with the 'church' (with all religion) for ten long years, trying to get them to take the side of the poor in their struggle against the rich, but had failed," he writes in the opening pages of his memoir. "They threw me out, and I was convinced that my struggle was useless. I began to look for an alternative."

That alternative struggle took the form of a utopian community organized with a group of followers that he named Valle de Paz (Valley of Peace). Tijerina's profound desire to set into motion the principles of the New Testament church ended his peregrinations. He answered for himself and his followers in the affirmative the question from Luke 18:8 he had used for the title of his book of sermons, "Will faith be found on the earth?" Tijerina decided to rebuke the world by creating the perfect Christian community. "Days of vanity, these approach us, and the just clamor for a new order [*correcion*]" he had preached a year earlier. Now he took it upon himself to "correct" the error of the churches by building that new order in Valle de Paz.[25] He aimed his rhetorical corrections to those true believers who had "fallen into the hands of tyrants" and were deceived by false teachers. They had all "invalidated the commandments of God eternal," he thundered: "Oh! If the people only knew the evil that awaits, and the end of their days!"

The Valle de Paz experiment, which I discuss in Chapter Four, is a forgotten episode in the history of communal religious settlements in the United States. It is also the only Mexican American attempt at religiously based communalism in American history. Tijerina's sectarian withdrawal into the Arizona desert put him at the crossroads between fulfilling a desperate search for heaven on earth. But earthly matters would eventually take center stage after an extraordinary dream/vision he had in 1956. In this "superdream" he was charged with leadership responsibilities by three angels. The terrifying event became a turning point in the direction of Tijerina's life. Forced to flee the Valle de Paz settlement within a year, Tijerina also abandoned his search for the elusive promises of the spiritual life and looked for his ideal community in the realm of politics.

1957–1963: The Fugitive Years

Tijerina refers to the period between the year of his decision to flee the Valley of Peace (1957) and the year he earnestly began to pursue land rights issues (1963) as his fugitive years. Charged with possession of stolen property in Arizona and, later, attempting to break his brother Margarito out of the Pinal County jail, Tijerina, his family, and a handful of followers caravanned east into New Mexico early in 1957.[26] Remaining on the property were a few Heralds of Peace left to care for the abandoned utopia. But for all intents and purposes, the community had failed.

He moved constantly to avoid arrest and extradition to Arizona. Frequently separated from his family, Tijerina took odd jobs, hid within the anonymity of migrant farm labor, and took refuge in the homes of friends he had made during his itinerant ministry. Living such a haphazard existence only seemed to heighten his restless sense of purpose and mission. He had plenty of time to think about the commission he had been given in his superdream. Late in the 1950s Tijerina had become interested in the history of Spanish land grants in New Mexico and began to learn from anyone who would speak to him. In his superdream he had come across a forest and a cemetery full of frozen horses that he interpreted as symbols of the New Mexican land grants awaiting reanimation.

In May 1958 Tijerina was given the opportunity to speak at a meeting of the Abiquiú Corporation. A grassroots New Mexican organization, the Abiquiú Corporation had for decades pursued legal channels in the defense of Spanish-speaking Tierra Amarilla land grant heirs and claimants. Originally established in the 1930s as the Tierra Amarilla Land Grant Corporation, the organization offered an "establishment" alternative to the violence and covert resistance by *Nuevo Mexicanos* against an equally violent and covert theft of land by Anglos. The Abiquiú Corporation defended Spanish and Mexican land grant heirs through litigation and friendly contacts with politicians.[27] At his first meeting Tijerina was introduced firsthand to the suspicion and violence dividing the land grant efforts. He had just begun to speak to the membership, some one hundred people, when a voice in the audience ordered him to stop. An agitated member suspicious of Tijerina's motives demanded that nonmembers be expelled from the meeting. Pausing to explain that the president of the organization had given him permission to speak, Tijerina resumed but moments later was clubbed in the head by the sergeant at arms. Tijerina's brother, Anselmo, and a companion, Rodolfo Mares, jumped to his defense and wrestled the assailant to the ground. "That day I discovered that it was not only a fear of the Anglo that would hinder me," Tijerina would later write, "but also the jealousy and envy among the heirs who were purely impoverished and honorable, and [some of them] the little puppet friends of the Anglos who had stolen the land."[28]

There is no record of what he intended to say to the Tierra Amarilla claimants. His knowledge of the byzantine New Mexican land grant history could only have been rudimentary and anecdotal at that time. He had learned about the local New Mexican situation from community elders there during a trip in 1956 and had taken a trip to Mexico later that year to "look for everything we would need for this struggle." He did not, however, have the sophisticated and detailed knowledge that would come steadily through the 1960s.[29] "Those first years were like prospecting. I traveled all over, I went to meetings, I talked to everyone I could," he said of the years after abandoning his Arizona utopia.[30] Most certainly his status as an outsider to the closely knit northern New Mexican villages would have made most of the Abiquiú Corporation more than a little suspicious of his interests and motivations.

Between September 1958 and September 1959 Tijerina was in Mexico. He spent that year immersing himself in the history and politics behind the signing of the Treaty of Guadalupe Hidalgo. Learning the details of the agreement ending the war between the United States and Mexico in 1848 was crucial spadework for him. This was at least his third trip into Mexico, setting a lifetime pattern of lengthy periodic visits across the border that continues to this day. "In 1950 I had come [as a preacher] with my family," he said of his initial fact-finding journey to Mexico. "Now I had another mission." While there he attempted to interest Mexicans in the plight of Mexican Americans, but he was only able to catch the attention of journalists who were more than happy to cast the United States in an unfavorable light. The articulation of what would become the goals of the Alianza organization were evident as Tijerina had hoped to deliver to the president of Mexico a petition describing the plight of Mexican Americans. According to a Mexican source from that time, Tijerina brought

President López Mateos a petition signed by hundreds of thousands of Mex-Americans, soliciting the intervention of the Mexican government before Washington, demanding the enforcement of the respective clauses of the Treaty of Guadalupe Hidalgo and the observance of the Universal Declaration of Human Rights, signed by Mexico in the General Assembly of the United Nations, celebrated on 10 December 1948, in Paris, which [the United States] is violating to the detriment of the Mexican residents in the southwestern United States.[31]

The basic message of the 1958 petition demanding protections for Mexicans and Mexican Americans in the United States as specified in the Treaty of Guadalupe Hidalgo later became a cornerstone of the Alianza. Even after Tijerina's activist years were over, the refusal of the United States to seriously consider an examination of the Treaty remains a constant point of contention for Chicano activists.[32]

Tijerina's family was able to join him for part of his Mexican trip, but after six months Maria and the children returned to the Texas cotton fields to earn money. Limited by his lack of resources and frustrated by Mexico's disinterest, Tijerina slipped back into the United States under an assumed name at Laredo and rejoined his family.[33] He and his brother, Cristóbal, would make another short trip to Mexico in the spring of the following year and may have had contact with radical political factions gathered around the memory and widow of Mexican revolutionary, Pancho Villa.[34] Back in the United States Tijerina accelerated his research into the history of land grants in the Southwest and began to campaign for collective action among the Spanish American land grant heirs. Because he was still a fugitive from the law (he told Nabokov that by 1960 he had escaped from the law seventeen times), his access to public libraries and archives was limited, and so he relied upon materials he carried back from Mexico and the information gathered from his supporters.[35]

Prior to the incorporation of the Alianza Federál de Mercedes Reales in 1963, Tijerina's status in the New Mexican landscape was marginal. He had two obstacles to overcome: religion and outsider status. During his trip to New Mexico in 1956 he had been introduced to Cristino Lovato, an elder member of the semisecretive Catholic Penitente brotherhood. It was Lovato's friendship and connections that paved Tijerina's way into the New Mexican land grant terrain. And although Tijerina had learned to condemn Roman Catholicism as false religion, he was easily won over by the Penitentes because they had kept alive the oral history of land theft in New Mexico and appear to have shared it all with him. Endorsed by the Penitentes, Tijerina was better able to overcome a well-deserved suspicion Catholic New Mexicans had of Protestants who ridiculed New Mexican Catholic practices and were often associated with Anglo land thieves.[36] For more than a century Hispanos had been visited by evangelical missionaries fueled by the belief that New Mexican Spanish Americans were caught in the web of "pagan" practices and the errors of Mexican Catholicism. The Penitente brotherhood, with its staged crucifixions of its members during Easter and secret bloodletting rituals, had been singled out as the most alarming evidence of New Mexican Catholic barbarism. Pentecostal evangelists in particular were held in great contempt by northern New Mexicans because of the odd nature of their charismatic worship, condemnation of Catholic culture, and rumors of evangelist indiscretions with local women.[37] Tijerina's close connection to the Penitentes suggests that he had quickly and successfully (and for good reasons) dropped his Pentecostal/fundamentalist identity after arriving in New Mexico.

Tijerina's increasing popularity and endorsement by New Mexican Hispano leaders was also in some measure influenced by a local folk tradition prophesying the arrival of a leader from the east who would turn back the Anglo enemy. New Mexican scholar Nancie González writes that, "Incidents have been told of old men who, after hearing Tijerina speak at public gatherings, have gone to him on their knees to kiss his feet, proclaiming him the messiah of the legend." According to another source Tijerina was considered by some "the prophet of Montezuma who will miraculously return in the imminent future to punish the Anglos for their appropriation of Hispano lands."[38] His rising credibility was also tied to his vast knowledge of sacred scripture and his newly acquired information on property rights, as well as New Mexican Territorial history in Spanish and Mexican colonial documents.

These years preparatory to the incorporation of the Alianza Federál de Mercedes began to bear fruit. In December 1959, Tijerina sent a letter of complaint to U.S. President Eisenhower informing him of the Hispano plight. He asked the president for "justice because the situation of our people, victims of unjust politicians and judges had reached a crisis."[39] Two months later he received a response from the White House he describes as "a few lines, cold and dull." Angered by the casual dismissal of his letter Tijerina moved closer to direct action. Five months later, on the Fourth of July, 1960, a group of *vecinos* organized against a government radar station located near the Tierra Amarilla land grant town of Vado. The installation had been placed there despite complaints by the land grant heirs that it was an illegal affront to their rights of *ejido* (common land use). Timing candles to ignite strategically placed kerosene torches, the installation was set ablaze. Afterward a party to celebrate the successful act of resistance was held back in Tierra Amarilla. Tijerina recounts this incident in his memoir in great detail, but takes no responsibility for having planned or participated in it. He refers to the perpetrators in the third person. He does, however, say that he had to hide from local police after the event and that Anglo ranchers in the area assumed he was responsible.[40]

By 1960 Tijerina and his family were settled in Albuquerque, though his fugitive status required him to remain underground. He continued to work at anonymous jobs, but otherwise the family was dependent upon Maria's domestic employment.[41] When he was not working Tijerina continued to widen the network of land grant heirs and supporters. Continuing his research into the labyrinth of Hispanic land grants, he pursued both documentary evidence and oral histories from land grant heirs. He later told Nabokov that none of the families with whom he had spoken at the time knew much about the Treaty of Guadalupe Hidalgo or owned a copy. Later in 1961 he would discover the archives in the University of New Mexico library and begin to pore over colonial and territorial documents there. In the summer of 1960 he traveled to Texas to visit his brothers Cristóbal and Ramón and spent the summer picking cotton with his family. With their earnings the Tijerina family rented a small three-room adobe house in Albuquerque for thirty dollars a month. It was then that he learned that a rancher in Arizona had offered to buy the Valle de Paz property for thirty-five dollars an acre. Realizing the increasing value of the land he had abandoned, he returned to Pinal County disguised as a woman to pay the back taxes on the property.[42] By the end of the year, with Maria working and the children adjusting to life in Albuquerque, Tijerina was able to secure a custodial job in a local Presbyterian church.

The following year Tijerina traveled to Chicago to visit his brother, Margarito, who had just been released from an Indiana prison and was living with their sister Josefina. Two years earlier Tijerina had come across a magazine article featuring Nation of Islam leader, Elijah Muhammad.[43] When he arrived in Chicago he requested a visit with the Black Muslim leader. Inspired by Muhammad's organization and leadership position among black people, Tijerina was eager to meet and speak with him. The Messenger of Allah appears to have received Tijerina with open arms, granting him a week of private afternoon conversations and putting him up in one of the Nation's guest apartments complete with delivered food and car service. Tijerina writes that in those private meetings, Muhammad "revealed to me what I wanted to know," presumably about the nature of Anglo society, as well as other "secrets."[44]

It is tempting to speculate about the content of these conversations and what, if any, influence the leader of the Nation of Islam had on Tijerina. On many things they held similar views, although in the early 1960s the aging Muhammad had constructed and realized a full-blown ideology, while Tijerina was yet to develop his. Elijah Muhammad's claustrophobic ideas about race, communism, the disordered mentality of the white man, the necessity for armed self-defense, an organized security unit, a separate land-base, and even his belief in extraterrestrials—all ideas that occur later in Tijerina's thinking—may have been planted or at least encouraged by the Black Muslim messenger.[45] Whatever the content of these secret conversations, Tijerina returned to New Mexico reinvigorated and ready to proceed with publicity about the crimes committed by the United States against Mexican Americans.

By the end of 1961 Tijerina had returned to Mexico and met with Lázaro Cárdenas, the ex-president of Mexico, regarding the land grant issue. He also arranged a press conference for Mexican journalists hoping they would publicize his views. He spent 1962 stumping among the land grant heirs, circulating a plan for an organization. Up to this point all of Tijerina's efforts were preliminary and theoretical. The reality was that he was unable to incorporate the Alianza because he was still wanted by Arizona authorities. Unable to move around freely in the United States, he took refuge in Mexico with his brother, Cristóbal. Once again he hoped to convince the Mexican secretary of foreign relations to intervene on the behalf of the land grant heirs with the United States over the terms of the Treaty of Guadalupe Hidalgo.[46] And although his efforts at building the Alianza were beginning to show some results, the frequent and lengthy time spent away from his family became too difficult for his otherwise long-suffering wife. Maria eventually filed for divorce and custody of their six children early in 1963. Tijerina's family life, it appeared, was the first of many casualties and injuries that he and his family would endure for the land grant cause. Afraid that his presence before the presiding judge in the divorce proceeding would result in his arrest, he stayed away from the court and threw his energies into preparing for the first Alianza meeting that was being held later that year.

1963–1971: Politics and Action

Tijerina modeled his organization, La Alianza Federál de Mercedes Reales (later, La Alianza Federál de Pueblos Libres) after the much older Abiquiú Corporation. Like the Abiquiú organization the Alianza intended to pursue legal avenues and base their arguments on a combination of American jurisprudence procedures supported by Tijerina's reading of international treaty law and Spanish colonial administrative legal texts. Whereas the Abiquiú organization was centrally concerned with local land grant issues, the Alianza sought to unite the heirs of all Spanish and Mexican land grants throughout the Southwest. Ironically, the incorporation of the Alianza Federál de Mercedes Reales contradicted Tijerina's deep suspicion of institutionalized power and human organization. Indeed, it had been this mistrust of bureaucratic structures and hierarchies that had forced him out of the Assemblies of God in the first place. The incorporation of the Alianza on 2 February 1963, coinciding with the same date that the Treaty of Guadalupe Hidalgo had been signed, was thus a compromise between the Abiquiú Corporation's method of addressing the land grant issue through the legal system and Tijerina's distrust of systems themselves. The Alianza's organizational authority derived not so much from its board of directors, but rested instead on the jurisdiction and sovereignty of the sixteenth-century Spanish *Laws of the Indies*, the Treaty of Guadalupe Hidalgo, and the guarantee of treaty rights set forth in Article Six of the U.S. Constitution—a combination *Newsweek* magazine derisively referred to as "an odd medley of medieval and modern legal lore."[47]

With incorporation of the Alianza accomplished and the expiration of the statute of limitations for his arrest warrant, Tijerina could actively pursue treaty rights. The first Alianza convention was held that October. The meeting was attended by representatives of fourteen land grants.

According to the documents registered with the state, the organization's stated purpose was "To organize and acquaint the Heirs of all the Spanish Land Grants covered by the Guadalupe Treaty. . . . Thus providing unity of purpose and securing for the Heirs of Spanish Land Grants the highest advantages as provided by the aforesaid Treaty and Constitutions."[48]

With a legitimate organization backing his efforts, Tijerina expanded the campaign to publicize the history of land grant injustices against Mexican Americans. He was invited to write a weekly column in a local paper, *The News Chieftain*, that continued into 1965. Under his guidance the Alianza accelerated the stream of letters to officials on both sides of the border on behalf of the land grant claimants, and Tijerina began to hatch an idea to lead a car caravan from Albuquerque to Mexico City to draw attention to the cause. Meanwhile he had taken up residence in the basement of a building at 1010 Third Street in Albuquerque, where Ed Stanton, the editor of *The News Chieftain,* had rented space to the Alianza. It was this building that the Alianza eventually purchased with the money made from the sale of Valle de Paz. Tijerina's busy schedule and minimal living arrangements meant that he took his meals in the homes of his supporters or at local restaurants. This initial burst of Alianza activities began to draw media attention, though to most outside observers the organization and especially their leader were regarded with tolerant curiosity. Reporters began referring to Tijerina as a modern day "Don Quixote," and most often as "El Tigre" or "King Tiger," a pun on the English "translation" of Reies Tijerina.

Alianza activities after 1963 resulted in greater visibility for the land grant issue but sharpened the differences between Alianza supporters and critics. Two years into the effort the organization was engaged in a full-scale letter writing campaign, it sponsored a daily fifteen-minute radio show, "The Voice of Justice" on KABQ, and purchased a Saturday five-minute spot on Channel 4.[49] Tijerina's homiletic training and experience prepared him for a demanding schedule of public speaking. It was about this time that he began to feel that pressure from somewhere high up in the United States government was beginning to bear down on his limited success. In July 1964, during what was becoming a regular annual summer trip to Mexico, Tijerina's itinerary was abruptly cut short by his arrest and humiliating deportation.[50] Shaken by the rough treatment of their leader, the Alianza canceled its plans for the car caravan but proceeded with their second convention a few weeks later in Santa Fe.

By 1965 Tijerina had taken the fledgling organization to a new level of publicity and local notoriety. That year thousands of northern New Mexican Hispanos began to voice anger and frustration over "the harsh, unfair, and capricious decisions by the National Forest Service [over land use issues] that were forcing them to migrate, or seek employment outside agriculture." The Forest Service's decision to ban the grazing of milk cows and sheep while permitting the grazing of riding horses on National Forest lands disguised the fact that Hispanos were the majority of cow and sheep owners, while riding horses for the most part were owned by Anglo ranchers. When appeals to state and federal agencies to repeal the ban were ignored, many Hispanos flocked to the Alianza for support and infused the organization with anger and resolve.[51]

As the Alianza's membership continued to increase, Tijerina grew concerned about his public image and his ability to earn and maintain the confidence of the land grant heirs. In an effort to overcome his outsider status Tijerina had returned to Roman Catholicism in 1961 and remarried in 1963. His return to the Catholic Church, the institution that he had opposed for so many years, became a political necessity in New Mexico. Curiously, he omits this event in his otherwise detailed memoir. His second marriage to Patricia "Patsy" Romero may have also been a part of his bid to ease his way into the local culture. His biographers see his choice for a new bride as cold and calculating. Nabokov quotes an uncharitable comment made by Tijerina regarding his young bride, suggesting that because the Romeros were a land grant family, he was more interested in Patsy's lineage than her love. Tijerina admits that part of his decision to remarry in September 1963 was because it was awkward for him as a single man to visit homes when women were alone and that "fathers and husbands preferred that I had a companion so that they could better trust me." Worried about the damage his divorced status would eventually have on an organization of traditional Catholics, he asked his brother, Margarito, to serve as his mediator and in traditional Mexican rules of courtship ask Patsy's uncles for her hand. He also "consulted the angels that had called him" in his 1956 superdream to confirm that he was making the right decision.[52] Nevertheless, suspicions about Tijerina's motivations still lingered and the

Alianza membership "voted to put Tijerina on a very slim budget which often failed to cover expenses. Sometimes a concerned member would buy his groceries."[53]

In April 1966, Tijerina traveled to Madrid and Seville accompanied by his brother Cristóbal. He went in search of evidences for the Spanish origins of the land grants and to meet with scholars over the legal jurisdiction of traditional communal lands (ejidos). In Seville he examined documents in the Archivo General de las Indias, which houses Spain's administrative colonial records of the New World. He also purchased a four-volume set of *Las siete partidas*, a thirteenth-century compendium of medieval Spanish law that covered all aspects of national life combining Roman jurisprudence with Church Canon law.[54] Tijerina was attracted to the Partidas because they represented the most comprehensive set of laws that governed the largest number of people at the time of their codification.[55] Though he later overestimated the reach and relevance of the Partidas to the Americas, he was nevertheless impressed by the weight of its historical precedent.[56] Before he left Spain he went in search of the 1680 *La Recopilación de Leyes de los Reinos de las Indias*, the administrative regulations for Spain's vast colonial empire. He located and purchased a set of the volumes in Madrid, recalling that written in the Recopilación were "the inheritance titles of my mestizo race."[57]

Most accounts of Tijerina's political activism begin with two Alianza events that occurred in 1966. Tijerina had been moving toward a strategy of direct action when his letter campaign resulted in only a few responses and as the Alianza increased its membership and pent up energy. Inspired by black civil rights marches and César Chávez's UFW protest march from Delano to Sacramento, California, Tijerina called for a demonstration. He tapped into the New Mexican Hispano pilgrimage tradition and prepared to show the public the power of moral outrage. On the Fourth of July the Alianza led a group of about three hundred men, women, and children on a sixty-six mile march from Albuquerque to Santa Fe, the state capital. Led by an old man on a donkey bearing a flag representing the Tierra Amarilla land grant, the marchers walked for three days, enduring catcalls from passing motorists and even a few gunshots. They camped along the route and arrived at their destination to find Governor Jack Campbell out of the state. They regrouped and promptly set up camp at the edge of town and waited. Eventually Campbell met with Tijerina and accepted a petition to President Lyndon Johnson to investigate the land grant issue. The New Mexico state archivist, Dr. Myra Ellen Jenkins, however, advised Campbell against any dealings with the Alianza, pointing out that the land grant issue had been settled decades earlier by the federal government and warning him that the Alianza was only in it for the money.[58] This would be the first of many blockades Jenkins would put in Tijerina's path.

Impatient for positive results the Alianza decided to take more assertive action. Three months later, in October, the Alianza proclaimed that 500,000 acres of the U.S. Kit Carson National Forest were being returned to the heirs of the original San Joaquín del Cañon del Río de Chama land grant.[59] Spain had granted the land to Don Francisco Salazar and thirty-one families in 1806, but now only small sections of the land grant had been officially recognized by the United States Court of Private Land Grant Claims at the end of the nineteenth century. Proclaiming it the sovereign "Free City-State" Republic of San Joaquín del Río de Chama, over three hundred Alianza members streamed past a state police and U.S. Forest Service blockade and proceeded to occupy the Echo Amphitheater campground. When Forest Service rangers Walter Taylor and Phil Smith attempted to collect the entrance fees for the fifty or so cars, an altercation broke out. Seized by the Aliancistas, the rangers were hauled before a panel of elders, presumably the heirs of the San Joaquín land grant. Taylor and Smith were subjected to a mock "trial" for trespassing on Republic land and being a public nuisance. The self-appointed San Joaquín court handed down a sentence and, showing mercy, suspended punishment. They released the two men and impounded their Dodge pickup trucks. The Alianza held a spirited rally and settled in under the watchful eye of government agents a short distance away. A few days later the remnants of the San Joaquín encampment were thrown out of the campsite by federal and forestry officers armed with a restraining order.

Tijerina later admitted that the occupation of the Echo Amphitheater had been more in the spirit of guerrilla theater meant to publicize the land grant situation than an actual secessionist attempt.[60] Chicano activists, however, interpreted this event as signaling a sea change in the direction of their politics and an emergent call to reclaim the homeland. The

Alianza Federál de Mercedes Reales, it appeared, had finally succeeded in proving that it was prepared for more than a war of words. Having tasted victory, the Alianza membership was primed for further actions.

The Alianza spent the winter documenting the ownership of San Joaquín lands while U.S. attorneys under Federal Judge Howard Bratton prepared their cases against the ringleaders of the Echo Amphitheater takeover. The Alianza sent a steady stream of letters and telegrams to the White House requesting an investigation into the disposition of the San Joaquín grant. The organization claimed that the 1891 Court of Private Land Claims had ruled in favor of the grant heirs.[61] Consumed by his cause, Tijerina's first child with Patsy he named Isabel Iris, in honor of the Spanish Catholic monarch who had made Columbus's journey possible, and for the Alianza's logo, the rainbow (*arco iris*).

By now state officials were beginning to worry about the impact and potential violence of the Alianza and its supporters. On 17 April 1967, the Alianza staged a large protest in Albuquerque's Old Town Plaza as a symbolic reminder of the city's Spanish American origins. Later that same day the tireless Tijerina was also in Santa Fe with a large group of supporters occupying the steps in front of the capitol building demanding to speak with the governor. Tijerina's meeting with Governor David Cargo a few days later is reported to have been a tense confrontation with Cargo half-heartedly agreeing to take the Alianza's case to Washington.[62] Over the next few weeks a rash of suspicious fires broke out across northern New Mexico, a sign to state officials that the Alianza was moving swiftly beyond the doublespeak containment tactic of bureaucrats.

In May, District Attorney Alfonso Sánchez ordered the U.S. District Court to obtain the membership list from the Alianza. The request, allegedly a routine matter designed so that Internal Revenue officials could check the organization's taxes, clearly meant to harass and put Tijerina on notice. But Tijerina was not intimidated. Outmaneuvering the government, he immediately resigned as leader of the Alianza and the membership voted to dissolve the organization. They then turned around and reconstituted themselves under the name, La Alianza Federál de Pueblos Libres (The Federal Alliance of Free City States). The new Alianza's first order of business was to announce a strategy meeting for June 3, in the tiny hamlet of Coyote, halfway between the slightly larger towns of Cuba and Abiquiú on Highway 96. Rattling their sabers, they even threatened to retake the Republic of San Joaquín. Meanwhile Tijerina had gone into hiding. Determined to win the escalating move-countermove war the Alianza appeared to be winning, District Attorney Sánchez issued a warning that anyone attending the meeting in Coyote would be subject to six months in jail for unlawful assembly. Caught in the middle of the threats between Tijerina and Sánchez, Governor Cargo attempted to mediate by asking Sánchez to back down on his arrest orders if the Alianza promised to hold a peaceful meeting. In the end, Cargo and other concerned parties were unsuccessful in their attempts to forestall a showdown between the Alianza and the state. Along with the governor and District Attorney Sánchez, the roster of officials caught up in the dispute included State Attorney General Boston Witt, State Police Chief Joe Black, and Rio Arriba County Sheriff Benny Naranjo, whose family headed the local political machine now threatened by the Alianza's popularity.[63]

The Alianza's planned meeting for Saturday, June 3 was set. Sánchez set up blockades on the roads leading to Coyote on the night of June 1 and arrested eleven Alianza officials attempting to pass through. Unable to find Tijerina, state and local police forces spent the next two days questioning locals, entering homes without warrants, and illegally confiscating guns in their desperate search for the Alianza leader. By the end of the weekend, Tijerina was still at large, but tensions over the aborted Coyote meeting seemed to have subsided. Sánchez, it appeared, had won the battle and was roundly congratulated in the press for his victory. A local judge had released most of the arrestees and released on bail those who were bound over for trial. From his hiding place, however, Tijerina decided to move the Alianza meeting to the nearby town of Canjilón and had notified the membership through word of mouth to gather there for a "picnic." Under cover of darkness he then moved to an abandoned adobe house tucked away in a canyon just outside Canjilón, accompanied by Patsy and their infant daughter, Isabel Iris. All through the night and the early hours of Monday, June 5, while District Attorney Sánchez was enjoying his victory, cars carrying Alianza members and their families were arriving at the small ranch where the "picnic" was scheduled.

Early on the morning of June 5, the women of the Alianza were preparing breakfast. Tijerina heard over the radio that Alfonso Sánchez was scheduled to appear at the Rio Arriba County courthouse in Tierra Amarilla. The district attorney was coming to formally charge those eleven Aliancistas caught in the roadblock three days earlier. On impulse Tijerina decided to go after the district attorney. Taking the male heads of the families aside, Tijerina promoted the idea to arrest Sánchez to a unanimous vote. By two o'clock, a convoy of two trucks and three cars rumbled down the highway toward Tierra Amarilla. Packed inside the convoy were twenty Alianza men and Tijerina's eighteen-year-old daughter, Rose. Some of them hid under canvas and they were armed with an assortment of guns and rifles. Tijerina had sent his driver/bodyguard, Moisés Moráles, ahead to scout out the courthouse and report back on the number of armed policemen there. It is unclear whether or not Tijerina planned to use the excuse that he was exercising his right to citizen's arrest in his pursuit of Sánchez. His memoir reveals that upon hearing that Alfonso Sánchez would be in Tierra Amarilla his reaction was visceral and his decision instantaneous: " . . . my heart jumped and I felt a magnetic wave course through my blood and my internal organs. Like being stabbed with a knife, I was assaulted (*asaltó*) by an idea that I least expected: to go to Tierra Amarilla and arrest the symbol of 'anglosaxon justice' Alfonso Sánchez." He recalls:

> The people didn't know what I was feeling in my heart as I was speaking about arresting Alfonso Sánchez. I never told my faithful *valientes* what was going on in my mind that long June 5th morning. My life had been opened like a book. My years underground appeared before me and helped me to remember that the angels of justice and judgment were with me. That day I had asked for a sign. I wanted a sign that might stop my trip to Tierra Amarilla. But, on the other hand, I felt that my duty was to provide an example of valor to the people. The Anglo wanted to squash me so I could not awaken the people. I had known this ever since I had begun to fight for the land in 1956. I felt that this was the moment of decision in the struggle against those who had robbed my people of their land and culture.[64]

When the caravan arrived Rose Tijerina and a few of the men walked into the courthouse to stake out positions. A few minutes later she pushed open the front door and motioned for the rest of the group to enter. Tijerina and his men stormed the building and over the next ninety minutes took possession of the Rio Arriba County courthouse. Although he had ordered that no one was to be hurt, two employees were wounded in the gunfire and confusion. State patrolman Nick Sais was shot when it appeared to the raiders that he was going for his gun. The other wounded man, Eulogio Salazar, the jailer, had been shot while trying to escape out of a first floor window. Other courthouse employees hid where they could and some were forced to lie on the floor. Alfonso Sánchez, however, was not in the building. Sizing up the situation, two of the raiders took Larry Calloway, an *Albuquerque Journal* reporter, and Deputy Sheriff Pete Jaramillo hostage. Other raiders drove back to Canjilón. Tijerina and a handful of men melted into the nearby mountains. Calloway managed to escape and Jaramillo was released shortly after; their captors then joined Tijerina in the mountains.[65]

By all accounts the state's reaction to the courthouse raid was excessive. Overreaction to the Alianza's raid was partially the result and fear of rumors circulating around Santa Fe at the time that "Alianza bands led by Cuban guerrilla experts were moving toward the city, that urban Alianza cells were preparing to revolt, and that enormous caches of heavy weapons were hidden in the northern hills."[66] Four hundred and fifty National Guardsmen who had been put on alert days earlier by a prescient Governor Cargo were mobilized. They brought with them two tanks and several helicopters. Over one hundred local and state law enforcement agencies, including the Apache Tribal police, were enlisted in the search for the bandit Aliancistas and especially their leader who had eluded them for weeks. In Canjilón as many as fifty family members and supporters of the raiders, including small children, were rounded up at gunpoint and held overnight in a muddy outdoor sheep pen without shelter or drinking water. Patsy Tijerina was arrested and held as bait to draw Tijerina down from his hiding place. Four days of negotiations between the Alianza and the state came to a stalemate. Eventually Tijerina was captured hiding in a car en route to Albuquerque. Satisfied that he had finally captured "King Tiger," Sánchez promptly proceeded to file twenty-six criminal charges against the Aliancistas.

The charges against Tijerina and several other Aliancistas for the courthouse raid were seriously complicated by the mysterious murder of

Eulogio Salazar, the jailer who had been wounded trying to escape during the raid. At a preliminary hearing for the raid defendants, the prosecution had seized upon Salazar's testimony that "los Tijerina" had shot him. Choosing to mistranslate the phrase "the Tijerina group" as "Tijerina," the prosecution fully intended to charge Tijerina with assaulting the jailer. Ten days before he was to testify in December, Salazar was found murdered in his car at the bottom of a slope near El Vado Lake. The prosecution, counting on Salazar's eyewitness testimony, assumed that Tijerina's supporters, if not Tijerina himself, were responsible for the jailer's death. There was never any evidence to suggest Tijerina's direct involvement, though he would spend the rest of his life defending himself against the insinuation.

Amidst the legal entanglements Tijerina managed to travel and speak. That October, the Alianza held its fifth annual convention in Albuquerque highlighting prominent black and Chicano leaders. Throwing himself into the national activist frenzy of 1968, he delivered a spectacular address at a Black Congress rally in the Los Angeles Sports Arena. At the 1968 National Conference for New Politics in Chicago he sat on the dais with Martin Luther King, Jr., and other civil rights leaders. Later King appointed him chairman for New Mexico's contingent to the Poor People's March in Washington, D.C.[67] To solidify his connection to the Chicano Movement, Tijerina traveled to California where he met with Bert Corona of the Mexican American Political Association, César Chávez in Delano, and long time activist Ralph Guzmán in Los Angeles. In Oakland Tijerina spoke at a "Free Huey Newton" rally sponsored by the Black Panthers. Pleading for unity between Chicanos and blacks, Tijerina told the crowd, "There is no room for us to fight among ourselves. We both have a common enemy. You need me and I need you."[68] Meanwhile, feeling that they had achieved significant public support, back in New Mexico the Alianza organized the "Partido Constitucionál del Pueblo" and nominated Tijerina as their candidate for the upcoming New Mexico governor's race. However, because of his felony convictions, Tijerina was disqualified.[69]

Eventually the legal system caught up with him. In November 1968, along with nine other Aliancistas, Tijerina faced New Mexico state charges on three counts stemming from the courthouse raid (kidnapping, assault on the courthouse, and false imprisonment). He then stunned everyone by handling his own defense. Prior to the trial, Tijerina had a dream where he saw the presiding judge shedding tears of joy over his acquittal. This he took as a clear sign of victory. This first trial lasted a month and ended in Tijerina's acquittal. In court he displayed what observers noted were "dazzling" legal tactics and brilliant cross-examination questions, eliciting contradictory testimony from hostile witnesses to his benefit.[70] Celebrating a David over Goliath victory against the state, an exultant Tijerina told a crowd afterward that "The revolution of Tierra Amarilla was like Christ entering the temple and cleaning out the Pharisees."[71] In a second trial a year later, however, he was unable to repeat his success and would be found guilty.

Boosting Tijerina's confidence during his legal troubles, the Episcopal Church's Executive Council voted to approve a $40,000 grant to the Alianza as part of its financial commitment to the political and economic development of minority organizations. Tijerina had originally asked the liberal denomination for $90,000 to establish a "community mobilization program," but was opposed by regional Episcopal leaders and state archivist, Myra Ellen Jenkins. Jenkins and regional Episcopal Bishop, The Right Reverend C. J. Kinsolving, argued against monetary support for the Alianza. They pointed to what they saw as the organization's violence, a disqualifying mark against the church's requirement that funded organizations promote nonviolence. The church's Executive Council in New York, however, was not dissuaded by Jenkins and Kinsolving's argument, nor by the media allegations that the Alianza was communist. The Council concluded that "where they found violent acts they saw them as the work of isolated Alianzistas [sic], or they saw them in a mitigating context of provocation."[72]

Around the same time, the United Presbyterian Church, U.S.A., General Assembly was voting to return 20,000 acres of land they owned in New Mexico to land grant heirs. The Ghost Ranch property had passed into the hands of the Presbyterians as a gift from the former owner and was used as a conference site. Because it sat on the Spanish Piedra Lumbre land grant, leaders sympathetic to the land grant movement were willing to give it back. In addition, the Presbyterians were offering a $50,000 grant for development purposes. Like the Episcopalians, the Presbyterians were moved by the spirit of Anglo guilt, invoked by the rising voices of ethnic protest and most recently by the Black Manifesto that charged mainline churches with neglecting their social responsibilities. The Ghost Ranch property was also adjacent to the Echo Amphitheater where the Alianza had staged their takeover in 1966, a fact that no doubt resonated with the good intentions of liberal church members.

Working with the Alianza, Presbyterian Church leaders were prepared to transfer the Piedra Lumbre land back to the heirs through the Alianza. Unfortunately, one of Tijerina's most vocal critics, Bob Brown, the editor of the *Albuquerque Journal*, turned out to also be Presbyterian. He managed to convince the denomination's leadership to bypass the Alianza in favor of handing the land over to local Piedra Lumbre Hispano leadership. But unable to assemble local Piedra Lumbre land grant leaders that were not also Alianza members, the deal fell through. For Tijerina the recognition of his efforts by these church bodies must have given him a sense of private victory over what he had come to believe were corrupt and impotent institutions. In his memory of the Ghost Ranch negotiations he is willing to accept temporary defeat, harboring the belief that "it was better that the church continue holding the land a little while longer, while the Just Judge of all the land brought about a perfect justice."[73]

Tijerina's legal victory spurred him on to other fronts, activities that Nabokov suggests were meant to counter a growing dissatisfaction in the Chicano Movement over Tijerina's leadership. Nabokov writes that Tijerina's "messianic obsessions encouraged the cardinal leftist sin: a personality cult." He describes Tijerina's widening circle of activities as an attempt to strengthen his relevance in the shifting terrain of ethnic politics:

two weeks after the 1968 acquittal, Tijerina cabled General Franco, asking Spain to put the Alianza case before the United Nations since Mexico had refused for "fear of economic reprisal." A week later, he presented the Albuquerque Board of Education with twelve demands, claiming "my people are being skinned alive by remote control. . . . Our children have been controlled, terrorized, and inferiorized . . . when the melting pot melts, it melts white." While petitioning the city of Albuquerque for higher wages for predominantly *chicano* garbage collectors, Tijerina also took on the state, appearing before the Board of Health and Social Services . . . to ask a 25 percent increase in welfare payments. Characteristically, he employed a most non-revolutionary argument: "The rich need the poor as much as the poor need the rich," Tijerina said. "A land without poor people is like a garden without flowers. It is like a home without children. It is the poor that brings balance to society. . . . Finally the poor will lead the rich into salvation, into enlightenment. Not with bullets, not with another war like Vietnam, but in compassion."[74]

In June 1969, during a celebration to commemorate the second anniversary of the courthouse raid and what appeared to be an effort to re-occupy the Echo Amphitheater, Patsy Tijerina set fire to a Forest Service sign at the entrance to the Santa Fe National Forest. When Forest Service agents responded, Tijerina scuffled with one of them. He was immediately arrested and later found guilty of aiding and abetting in the destruction of U.S. government property. And although he had managed to outmaneuver jail time up to then, less than a week later he was behind bars.

While Tijerina sat in jail the Alianza held its 7th Annual Convention in October. In a dramatic shift away from Tijerina's leadership, members who had been inspired by the Chicano Youth Conference in Denver earlier in the spring brought with them a cultural nationalist platform that called for the creation of "La Republica de Aztlán." They passed a resolution to ask President Nixon to permit the independent nation. Up to now Tijerina had successfully kept the Alianza from Chicano nationalist rhetoric and steered the organization toward action based upon the authority of legal documents. But caught up in his own legal worries, the Alianza slipped away from him and the local land grant struggle was co-opted by neo-indigenist and cultural nationalist movement leaders. Angered by this development Tijerina announced that he was against "separatism from the United States." He reminded his supporters that "My motto is justice, but not independence from the government of the United States." From the Albuquerque city jail Tijerina resigned as Alianza president, although his brother, Ramón, stepped in as his replacement. The Alianza's turn to nationalism, however, was inevitable given an emerging Chicano consciousness. Ironically, this new cultural nationalist ideology had taken Tijerina as their model of irredentist militancy. The cultural nationalist cooptation of the New Mexico land grant struggle appropriated the carefully document-based arguments Tijerina had constructed over the years and collapsed them into an ideological defense of the Aztec homelands. The bitter irony for Tijerina was that the Alianza had effectively shut out the infiltration of the organization by left-wing Anglo groups, only to fall prey to Chicano movimiento ideologues.[75]

The tendency to focus on Tijerina's brushes with the legal system and leadership crises, however, does not allow for a full treatment of how other Aliancistas, and especially Patsy Tijerina and the Tijerina children, were harassed and jailed. At one point the Albuquerque police had confiscated more than $4,000 of the Tijerina family savings, which was never returned. There were also incidences of sexual and psychological abuse against Patsy and Tijerina's son, perpetrated by law enforcement officers while Tijerina was in jail.[76] It is also difficult to find an objective account of the events surrounding the courthouse raid because of the partisan viewpoints of the regional papers. Knowlton reports that the *Albuquerque Journal* "carried on a fierce newspaper war against Tijerina in which he was ridiculed, besmirched, and savagely attacked" and "refused to print any items that might reflect favorably on the Alianza . . ."[77] The secondary accounts of how Tijerina was treated by state officials unanimously agree there was "a most determined vendetta" against Tijerina and the Alianza.[78]

Perhaps the most visible example of harassment against the Alianza involved William Fellion, a former deputy sheriff who was caught planting a bomb at the Alianza headquarters in April 1968. According to documents Tijerina later obtained, Fellion, who lost his right hand when the bomb detonated prematurely, was a known criminal and "hired assassin" connected to local officials opposed to the land grant effort. For all of the evidence against Fellion, he was only charged with reckless driving and carrying a deadly weapon, charges that for some unknown reason were dismissed.[79] The Fellion incident, however, was only one of many attempts to bomb the Alianza building. There were also times when rifle bullets were fired into the building during Alianza meetings, homemade bombs lobbed at the headquarters, and members' cars set on fire. Knowlton points out that "law enforcement agencies were singularly lethargic and unsuccessful in finding those involved in any of the . . . criminal attempts against the Alianza leaders and members.[80]

By the end of 1969 the physical harassment, the negative campaign against the Alianza by the *Albuquerque Journal*, and a guilty verdict against Tijerina should have been enough to defeat the land grant effort. On the other hand, Tijerina was certain that the final outcome of the New Mexican struggle for the land would be on the side of justice. And although he would not reveal it at the time, he had maintained an unshakable faith in the power of a divine Judge. He perhaps took some comfort knowing that divine retribution awaited his accusers and enemies. For the time being, however, he faced concurrent prison sentences stemming from the Echo Amphitheater takeover, courthouse raid charges, and the arrest during Patsy Tijerina's arson of the Nation Forest sign. He received two state prison terms of one-to-five and two-to-ten years, as well as a three-year sentence in federal prison.[81] He spent twenty-one months in federal prison, most of it in the Springfield, Missouri, Federal Medical Facility. Suffering from a throat condition that he had managed on his own for years, he was transferred from the Las Tunas, Texas, federal prison to Springfield for treatment. For reasons that are unknown, he was kept in Springfield even after he had been given a clean bill of health. He was incarcerated in the prison's psychiatric ward without any official diagnosis for mental disorder.[82] His ordeal in the Springfield Medical Facility, which he details in his memoir, marks the lowest period in his life. Hundreds of miles away from his family and illegally placed in a facility for the mentally disordered, he struggled against despair, attempts on his life, and thoughts of suicide. The long months in Springfield did, however, give him time to reflect on the larger meanings of his life and reinvent himself. This crucial period in the development of his thinking, and the consequences of his incarceration decades later are examined in Chapter Six.

1972–1978: Erasure and Absence

Tijerina was released from prison on a five-year parole in July 1971. He had survived his nightmarish confinement with the mentally ill. Fully expecting "King Tiger" to come roaring out of his cage, his supporters and Chicano activists across the nation were surprised to find that Tijerina had changed directions in his politics. It was soon clear that prison had radically transformed, and perhaps even broken him. He continued, nevertheless, to move within Chicano activist circles even as the movement itself began to wane in the early 1970s.

Because he was prohibited from holding any office in the Alianza for five years after his release, from the outside it appeared as though Tijerina had lost interest in the land grant cause. He spoke at the Raza Unida Party convention in 1972, sharing the stage with Corky Gonzáles and José Angel Gutiérrez. In a speech that still burned with all of the fire of his preprison days, he made an impassioned plea for party unity and set aside his own agenda to mediate the factionalism between the other two Chicano leaders.[83] He later organized a Chicano Congress for Land & Cultural Reform, but refused to proceed with the conference after the opening session because he felt that La Raza Unida Party members had shown up to take control of the agenda.[84] His postprison activism, while clearly continuing many of the same goals from the late 1960s, however, moved away from the confrontational style of frontier politics in favor of a universal human rights ideology he referred to as "Brotherhood Awareness." This new direction toward reconciliation and the dawning of a new era in human relationships he explained at the first Brotherhood Awareness Conference in April 1972, painting in broad strokes the idea that "Brotherhood should transcend all political, religious, and cultural boundaries." "So let us orient all of our organizations in the path of brotherhood, for peace and justice on our planet," he asked of his audience. So powerful was this emerging consciousness that around him he could see "Men and women [were] becoming more equal every day. Even the most separated men in the world [are] coming together such as Richard Nixon and Mao Tse Tung."[85]

Nostalgic for the "Che Guevara" of northern New Mexico, as he had been called in 1967, Chicano activists were alarmed by the direction of Tijerina's thinking. They blamed the U.S. government for medically altering him in prison, or as one activist newspaper charged, injecting him with cancer.[86] Even Tijerina's rousing conventions became conciliatory gatherings after his change in politics. In sharp contrast to the daughters he had named "Wrath of God," Isabel Iris, and Dánitha ("God is my judge"), in 1973 he welcomed his newest daughter, Harmony, to commemorate the new direction his life had taken.

Though Tijerina had returned to the Alianza as a survivor of the government's campaign of harassment, the Alianza had been unable to withstand the loss of their leader. While Tijerina languished in prison, Alfredo Maestas, who had been unhappy about the financial handling of the Alianza, led a group of about fifty out of the vulnerable organization.[87] Another splinter group broke away in 1972 and revived the "original" Alianza Federál de Mercedes. This Alianza complained that they were unable to work with the parent organization; claiming its mission was to continue "the struggle for heritage, cultural and civil rights." It also emphatically advertised itself as "not involved with the Brotherhood Awareness" conference that Tijerina had planned.[88] Another faction that left Tijerina's organization was led by two of Tijerina's most faithful *valientes* during the 1960s, Pedro Archuleta and Moisés Moráles. These two began a cooperative farming project called La Cooperación del Pueblo and a health clinic, La Clínica. Built on the lessons learned from Tijerina, La Clínica/La Cooperación founded a chapter of La Raza Unida Party in 1973, slated candidates for the 1975 election, and challenged the development of tourism in Tierra Amarilla.[89]

In 1974, still haunted by the events of 1967, Tijerina spent another six months in the New Mexico State Penitentiary for charges linked to the courthouse raid.[90] Weeks before he was taken to the New Mexico State Penitentiary, he was devastated by the news that his twenty-one-year-old son, Daniel, had been killed in an automobile accident. After his release in December, the cumulative effects of his son's death, the tedium of jail, and the disintegration of the Alianza seemed to have finally discouraged him.[91] When he resumed the presidency of the Alianza in 1976 (his parole restriction having been lifted), he was too late to save the hemorrhaging Alianza. In fact, there was nothing Tijerina could have done to save his organization. The internal schism within the Alianza was merely symptomatic of the general decline in the direction and cohesiveness of a national Chicano Movement. Determined to continue research and document land grant ownership on behalf of the *vecinos*, Tijerina's popularity and political capital nevertheless suffered during the 1970s.

Tijerina, it seemed, had abandoned the single identity politics of the Chicano movimiento, when in fact, the movimiento itself had faded. If the Alianza had sounded the call to arms for Chicanos across the west at Tierra Amarilla in 1967, the retreat had begun during Tijerina's incarceration with the massive police attack on Chicano families and the shooting of Chicano journalist Rubén Salazár at the National Chicano Moratorium rally in Los Angeles on 29 August 1970. Rodolfo Acuña writes that Chicanos "staggered into the 1970s—literally clubbed into submission." Little progress had been made by Chicanos relative to others in American society, and Acuña's only conclusion was that the 1970s "restored to the middle class its hegemony over the movement." In addition, the thrust of the Chicano Movement has succumbed to the increasing professionalization of Chicano Studies and the emphasis on individualism at the grassroots.[92] The distance between the now middle-aged patriarch and the next generation of Chicano activists, some of whom had been close to Tijerina, was too great to be bridged by Tijerina's powerful charisma or appeal to ancient documents.

Even as the Chicano Movement dissipated and Chicanos moved into an era of "post-Aztlán" symbolic ethnicity and academic privilege, Tijerina pursued the legitimacy and authority that he still believed were embedded in the Treaty of Guadalupe Hidalgo. For most of the remaining decade, however, he battled the state and the *Albuquerque Journal* over the truth about the murder of courthouse jailer, Eulogio Salazar, enlisting the aid of advocacy reporters associated with the progressive *The New Mexico Review and Legislative Journal.*[93] In 1976, Governor Jerry Apodaca reopened the Salazar murder case. The state attorney general's report after a thirteen-month investigation of the facts of the case cleared Tijerina of any complicity in Salazar's death. Despite a number of possible suspects and several investigations, Salazar's murder remains unsolved to this day. The last grand jury inquiry failed to move forward on new charges only hours before the statute of limitations implicating Tijerina ran out in 1978.[94]

Tijerina's efforts in Mexico over the years eventually came to some success. In 1976 Mexican President Luís Echeverría asked Tijerina to locate and inform Texas land grant heirs that they were owed compensation by Mexico. In 1941 a land-exchange treaty between the United States and Mexico had been brokered, but nothing had ever come of it. Hoping to foster better relations between Mexico and the United States, Echeverría reanimated the process.[95] Despite his Texas lineage and putative status as a land grant descendent, Tijerina had a difficult time with his responsibilities when his authoritarian style and personality clashed with the Texas claimant leadership.[96] A January 1978 meeting between Tijerina and two thousand heirs to discuss the Mexican offer erupted in disagreement over the issue of an admission fee and Tijerina's vigorous speech "attack[ing] the FBI, the news media, and former President Richard Nixon" for the organized harassment of his family.[97] By the end of February the Texas claimants had broken away from Tijerina's leadership and reorganized as the Texas Asociación de Reclamantes.[98] That same month, however, the Mexican government changed leadership, and the newly elected president, Ernesto López Portillo, announced that Mexico would not pay Texas land grant heirs any settlement money over the 1941 agreement or any other treaty arrangement.[99]

Tijerina's relationship with Mexico soured when he publicly lambasted President Jimmy Carter's hypocritical stance on human rights during a 1978 Mexico City press conference. Official feathers on both sides of the border were ruffled when Tijerina alleged that Mexican President Portillo had refused to oppose Carter's laxness in prosecuting police officers who had beaten or killed Mexican Americans or undocumented workers from Mexico.[100]

1979–2000: Religion and Life

In 1979 Tijerina's search for community took an unexpected turn. Dr. Myra Ellen Jenkins, Tijerina's longtime nemesis, accidentally discovered the original Spanish document for the San Joaquín del Cañon del Río de Chama land grant. Finding the document did not result in any legal change of ownership—that had been settled in 1891 by the U.S. Private Land Claims Court. However, the deed did provide an air of legitimacy and documented authority to Tijerina's cause. By then Tijerina, Patsy, and their four children were living in the tiny town, Coyote, which happened to sit within the boundaries of the San Joaquín grant. Preferring to live in the sovereign Free City State of San Joaquín, Tijerina simply ignored U.S. federal, state, and local municipal jurisdictions. For more than two decades Tijerina and the Alianza had played out many of their dramas within the boundaries of San Joaquín, and for him living within the borders of San Joaquín was a combination of a hero's nostalgia as well as his "best protection" against the outside world.[101]

In June of that year the citizens of the Free City State took up arms. A dozen or so armed vecinos erected roadblocks and stopped logging trucks at Mesa Alta, a timber area managed by the U.S. Forest Service near the town of Gallina. Manuél Salazár, the mayor of San Joaquín, charged the timber contractor with trespassing on city-state land reminding them that only citizens of San Joaquín had rights of ejido, common land access.[102] Although he was conspicuously absent from the confrontation (though fully aware of the situation), Tijerina noted in interviews that his presence was no longer necessary. He heartily pointed out that the vecinos had begun to resist the government and continue on their own the efforts that he had started decades earlier. Despite the lack of an organization to back him, Tijerina wrote a bill on behalf of the city-state, asking the U.S. Congress to confirm rights to mineral leases, rentals, grazing permits, and other land uses for San Joaquín. As an indication of his stature and legal abilities, the bill passed successfully in the New Mexican legislature but was killed by conservative interests in committee before its introduction to the U.S. Congress.[103] Clinging to his deep suspicions about the Anglo educational system, he ended the year with a victory in the New Mexico courts over his refusal to send his four children to public school. Once again demonstrating his autodidact legal acumen and rhetorical artillery, he proved to the court's satisfaction that his family was in constant danger and that his children could not be legally forced to attend public schools.[104]

No longer part of the contemporary Chicano consciousness of the 1980s, Tijerina nevertheless labored on. He spent most of his public life speaking on local issues. He also began delving ever deeper into genealogical research. In September 1982, Tijerina appeared at a rally in Taos during an effort by local Hispanos to stop the construction of condominiums in the small village of Valdez, just north of Taos. There had been at least two major controversies over the spread of luxury tourism real estate developments beginning in the early 1970s, and the Valdez "condo war," as it was called, was the front line in the battle for local

Hispano cultural survival. Earlier in the controversy Tijerina had requested permission to attend a public meeting where opposing sides were scheduled to present their cases before the county commissioners. Tijerina was allowed to attend but only under the condition that he not speak. He did not have to. Anthropologist Sylvia Rodríguez, who was studying the controversy, reports that "Tijerina's appearance at the commission meeting heightened media attention and sent shock waves through the business and real-estate community in Taos." Rodríguez's analysis of the Valdez condo war credits "the crystallization of land as a symbol of Hispano cultural survival" to writers, artists, and activists, including Tijerina. His physical presence at the commission meeting had struck the appropriate chords for everyone involved in the controversy.[105] Eventually the citizens of Valdez prevailed over the condominium development.

In 1984 Tijerina traveled to Spain and the Middle East, learning about the Palestinian efforts to create a homeland within the state of Israel. He reports to have successfully lobbied the Spanish government to register the 1493 papal bull, *Noverunt Universi*, with The Hague as a recognized international document. Pope Alexander VI's decree, perhaps even more than the *Laws of the Indies* or the Treaty of Guadalupe Hidalgo, Tijerina considered the earliest Catholic document granting to Spain the rights to explore and colonize the Americas.[106]

The twenty-year anniversary of the Tierra Amarilla courthouse raid in June 1987 was celebrated in Coyote with a reunion of activists and nostalgic media coverage (including a Channel 7 helicopter ride for Tijerina from his home to Tierra Amarilla).[107] Tijerina had begun to refer to the raid as "the Last Civil War," suggesting that he was according it new significance in his developing scheme of history. Signaling publicly that he had indeed turned his mind in a new direction, he preached to the revelers "that Jews were to blame for Nuevo Mexicanos' problems and demanded that reporters not say he was anti-Semitic."[108] Later that same month, he spoke to a group of Mexican and Chicano scholars at the Autonomous University of Mexico (UNAM), where he overwhelmed his audience with a detailed panorama of "3,726 years in 30 minutes." At the event he revealed an unconventional but unmistakable strain of anti-Semitism and a return to his 1950s fear of atomic holocaust.[109]

In the summer of 1988, old land grant tensions surfaced in Tierra Amarilla between an Arizona-based land investment firm, Vista del Brazos, and Amador Flores, a Hispano rancher. With the aid of Pedro Archuleta (who had earlier led a splinter group out of the Alianza) and others calling themselves El Consejo de la Tierra Amarilla (The Tierra Amarilla Council), Flores and his family fortified their property with bunkers and barricades. To demonstrate their resolve they burned a court injunction to leave the property in front of TV cameras.[110] Although Tijerina was not involved, coverage of the event referred back to the Alianza and Tijerina was credited with having planted the seeds of recent rebellion in northern New Mexico.

That same year Robert Redford was in northern New Mexico filming a version of John Nichols's 1974 novel, *The Milagro Beanfield War*. Nichols's tale, centered around Joe Mondragon's attempt to irrigate his beanfield with water belonging to a large corporation, was too similar to the Flores–Vista del Brazos tussle for the press to ignore. Tijerina was pulled into the drama when he filed a lawsuit in Los Angeles against the movie project. Claiming rights to the story, Tijerina charged that Nichols's book was really about the Alianza and events around the courthouse raid. Nichols, however, would only admit that he had "incorporated" all he had learned from working on land and water rights issues in the early 1970s as a staff member for *The New Mexico Review and Legislative Journal*, even though he had penned at least one story about Tijerina in 1971. In addition, the director of the project, Moctezuma Esparza, claimed that there was simply "no relationship between López Tijerina's life story and this book. None." For his part, Tijerina was nowhere to be found discussing the Flores–Vista del Brazos conflict. Many years earlier he and Pedro Archuleta had parted ways and were on opposite sides within an embroiled hostile land grant factionalism that continues to this day.[111]

The 1970s and 1980s were in many ways decades of continued personal struggle for Tijerina and his family. These were also years of retrenchment for the ex-evangelist who returned full circle to a religiously based worldview and apocalyptic philosophy of history. Having finally found his ideal community in the San Joaquín City State, he took his lifetime of experience and learning and began to synthesize a new outlook that had been born in the superdream in 1956 and in his "new science" jail revelations of 1969. By the end of the 1980s the memory of Tijerina's activist years had been pared down to a few paragraphs in Chicano history texts. He had been superseded by a new generation of Chicano scholars and activists whose labors must have seemed far away from the aging movement patriarch. As northern New Mexico continued to battle small farm failures and witness the exodus of its youth to the large cities, Tijerina's neighbors were almost completely dependent upon government assistance. The only jobs available in rural San Joaquín, ironically, seemed to be those funded by the U.S. government.[112] At the height of his land grant activism, Tijerina's following had been primarily among adults and elders who had lived through sporadic waves of Hispano resistance. His main support through the 1990s remained among the adults living within the towns of the San Joaquín del Cañon del Río de Chama grant, and those faithful, mostly Hispanos scattered across northern and central New Mexico. Since 1979 San Joaquín continued its daily round of community life and its rotation of the city-state's judge, mayor, and sheriff positions. When Tijerina and his wife (and the occasional grandchild) were not in residence, they could be found in Albuquerque visiting children and supporters or out of contact somewhere in Mexico.

In 1990, Tijerina was noticeably absent from the program of speakers at the National Association for Chicano Studies conference in Albuquerque. I had been given a grant to visit Tijerina that spring and had invited him to the conference to hear my presentation on his writing. Over the three days of the conference Tijerina was continuously mobbed by students and acquaintances who posed with him for photo opportunities and stopped to converse with the legendary Chicano leader. At one point, Pedro Archuleta, who had been asked to speak at a plenary session on the New Mexico land grant situation, confronted Tijerina and began shoving him. The quick intervention by a local artist demanded that Archuleta show respect and broke up the altercation.

Now in his seventies, Tijerina is far from finished with his work. He has weathered the changes in the political and social landscapes and fully expects to be in the center of events as they unfold as he prophesies they will. In 1990 he had completed two book-length manuscripts and was waiting for "the right time" to release them for publication. Their titles hint at their contents: *La Historia de la Casa de Israel* (The History of the

House of Israel) and a self-disclosing follow-up to his memoir, *My Life, Judaism, and the Nuclear Age.*[113] In 1993 Tijerina's Coyote home and part of his large archive was destroyed by an arson fire while he and his wife were out of town. Throughout the 1990s and into the new millennium, Tijerina moved back and forth among his supporters and residences. Occasionally he accepts the invitations that come to him from colleges and local "heritage" events. His public life is more ceremonial than activist in the new millennium. Or at least it might seem so. Still wary of adversaries, he remains reclusive and continues to dream the future.

Tijerina, who was the subject of an NBC documentary titled "The Most Hated Man in New Mexico" in the 1960s, was hailed as "the most influential person in New Mexico History" at the close of the millennium by the *Albuquerque Journal.* His longtime friend and lawyer, Rees Lloyd, hinted that Tijerina was far from stepping off the historical stage. "Reies has remained true to his cause, his people, and his principles," Lloyd wrote in 2001. He describes Tijerina today as he knew him in the past: "never wavering, never whimpering; ever that valiant champion roaring, like a tiger, not whining, like a mouse, for justice."[114]

3 CLEAN BEFORE GOD

*Yo quiero estar limpio delante de Dios, y por eso hablo en el temor de Dios de
la violencia que la Iglesia hace in estos últimas días: seré culpable si no digo y
hablo lo que mis ojos ven, y los que mis oídos oyen.*
　　　　　—Reies López Tijerina, "Los Enemigos de la Cruz"

[I want to be clean before God, and so I speak of the fear of God,
of the violence of the Church in these latter days: for I will be
found guilty if I do not speak and tell that which my eyes see, and
what my ears hear.
　　　　　　　　　　　　　　　"The Enemies of the Cross"][1]

TIJERINA EMBRACED PENTECOSTALISM FOR A DECADE BEGINNING IN
the early 1940s. His formal membership with the Assemblies of God
denomination, although brief in the context of his long life, trained him
in public speaking and gave him the interpretive reading skills he would
use in his political life. Unfortunately, none of Tijerina's biographers
pause long enough to consider how his evangelical faith pushed him to
the margins of his already marginal life in the United States as an unlet-
tered Mexican American migrant worker. His conversion away from the
Roman Catholicism of his childhood came through the efforts of a
Baptist missionary, yet Tijerina turned to Pentecostalism, which better fit

his assertive charismatic personality and his nascent leadership abilities. Years later, after his expulsion from the Assemblies of God, Tijerina's independent fundamentalist ministry led him far away from the security of denominational sanction and support into a dark and apocalyptic theology. This chapter examines the development of Tijerina's religious thinking in the 1950s and how the decade following his Bible Institute training prepared him for a lifetime pattern of literalist reading of texts and planted the seeds of theological speculations in the closing decades of the century.

Tijerina's ambivalence toward his father's Protestantism and devotion to his mother invariably prejudiced him against the possibility of leaving the familiarity of Roman Catholicism. His initial contact with evangelical Christianity as an adolescent, however, was followed by all the enthusiasm and devotion expected in a new convert. After Samuel Galindo had placed a copy of the Bible into his hands, Tijerina remembers devouring the stories and lessons of the Old Testament.

> I read the rest of the Bible, about Abraham, David, Ishmael, and Moses, who led his people to the Promised Land, and there through the prophets I saw satisfaction for the yearning of my heart for justice and peace. I found the word justice used as many times as words like love. I began to talk to Protestants and especially to Baptists and Methodists there in Michigan, and that was when I began to decide on the religious life and made plans to go to Bible School.[2]

His youthful eagerness and desire to learn more about his newly acquired faith led to conversations with Protestants actively missionizing among Spanish-speaking laborers in Michigan.[3] His decision to train for Christian ministry, however, meant that he was forced to declare allegiance to a particular tradition. While he might have chosen a Christian education at any number of Bible schools between Michigan and California, returning to Texas was his natural choice. Texas was, after all, his home and there were ample opportunities for ministerial training there with most of the large Protestant denominations. Despite its Roman Catholic history as one of Mexico's northern border states, Texas had been fertile ground for the spread of Protestant Christianity since the early nineteenth century.

Prior to the secessionist rebellion by Texans in 1836 to establish the Republic of Texas, Protestant missionaries from the United States had already staked their claims throughout Mexico's northernmost frontier. Mexican law required that all citizens and immigrants to Texas profess Roman Catholicism although enforcement was difficult if not impossible in a region so far from Mexican centers of power.[4] Earlier, when Spain sold Florida to the United States in exchange for the American claim on Texas in 1819, Texas became contested political and religious terrain. Protestant missionaries represented a "fifth column" of sorts for U.S. designs on the westward expansion into Mexican territory.

Protestant Choices

Even before the Mexican-American War, Protestants were well represented in Texas. Their presence and certainly their evangelizing work were, of course, illegal under both Spanish and Mexican flags. Nevertheless, Baptists, Methodists, and Presbyterians of all types were organizing missions, distributing Bibles and tracts, and openly holding camp meetings by the 1830s.[5] Methodists arrived in the late teens and had established a church in 1817. Presbyterian groups organized missionary work in Texas in earnest in the 1830s and continued a steady course throughout the century, although by the time Tijerina was considering his religious options, Presbyterian outreach and education for Mexican Americans was faltering financially and suffering the cumulative effects of unstable leadership.[6] The other limiting factor was that seminary training in the Presbyterian denomination required a prior minimum education Tijerina did not have. Even had he managed to gain a public school education, he would have had to compete for one of five slots reserved for Mexican American seminarians each year. The two-year Presbyterian seminary training in Austin was modeled after traditional theological training and geared toward a middle-class education with little relevance to missionary or pastoral work among the Mexican American population.[7] One Mexican American Presbyterian minister who had attended seminary prior to World War II recalled that Mexican American students were treated differently than the white students. They were forced to live separately from the other students and, when given pastorates, Mexican Americans were paid less than their Anglo counterparts. "And they don't get the best churches," he complained. "At Synod meetings a Mexican American has never directed a study group, said a prayer, or anything."[8]

The Methodist church had also been officially active among Mexican Americans in Texas since 1859, although their presence in the region began during the Mexican period. Unfortunately, the absence of Mexican Americans in positions of responsibility in the various missionary conferences, a prohibition against the use of Spanish at official meetings, and a general paternalistic attitude toward Mexicans meant there were few Mexican American congregations. In 1874 a concerted Methodist missionary effort to reach Mexican Americans was launched, but even fifty years later the Southwest Mexican Conference could report only 6,294 members in an area covering the whole of Texas and part of New Mexico.[9]

Presbyterian, Methodist, as well as Episcopalian efforts among Mexicans were on the whole less successful relative to the Baptist denominations. Owing in large part to hierarchical structures of authority in the "mainline" Protestant denominations, Mexican Americans found it virtually impossible to participate fully or establish themselves comfortably in these churches. Mirroring the patterns of social and economic relationships between Anglos and Mexicans throughout the Southwest, the paternalistic and patronizing treatment of Spanish-speaking converts within Protestantism established in the nineteenth century continued past the middle of the twentieth century.

Mexican converts became a concern for the mainline denominations only after the Civil War revitalized the denominations now split into "northern" and "southern" branches. Previous to the 1848 Treaty of Guadalupe Hidalgo and the disruption of the American Civil War, Protestant missionaries had centered their efforts almost entirely on English-speaking settlers in Texas. In fact, Mexicans in nineteenth-century Texas Protestant congregations were so rare that church officials took great care to note their presence in their records.[10] The spiritual care and feeding of usually poor, rural, and uneducated Mexican American converts from Catholicism, even when earnestly pursued, would never be a priority among mainline denominations more clearly identified with a white middle class.

Moreover, Tijerina had been raised hearing stories of Anglo (read: Protestant) terror and intimidation. The troubled history of race relations in Texas had long been a part of Tejano culture. The fear of white vigilante forces came reinforced through myths about the Alamo, the humiliation of the southern Jim Crow system, the legendary cruelty of the Texas Rangers, and the popularity of Mexican *corridos* (ballads) celebrating resistance to Anglo domination.[11] Tijerina also knew that his father's conversion to Protestantism had been motivated by fear of the Texas Rangers. Religion, like most of Texas society, supported the power and class relations organized around race. Methodism and Presbyterianism, with their segregated hierarchies and middle-class trappings would hardly have been attractive to the ambitious, restless but poor young Reies. As late as 1959, Mexican American Protestants found themselves still subject to the prejudices that they endured outside the supposedly protective walls of mainline Christian churches. A review by the National Council of Churches that year observed:

> In the "Anglo" church, the Spanish American is likely to come in direct and personal contact with people who do not see him as an individual but as a "Spanish American" or a "Mexican." He may not be entirely acceptable because of his physical appearance, his economic status, or his non-Anglo ways. He may be reminded in many subtle ways that he is not really a part of the group and that his attendance and participation is at the sufferance of the Anglo members.[12]

The Baptists, on the other hand, would have been more attractive to Tijerina's enthusiastic faith and nascent leadership. Following the westward movement of the American Republic, Baptists had sent missionaries into the widening frontier as early as 1817.[13] Arriving in the Southwestern missionary field at the same time as the other Protestants, Baptists (and after the Civil War, Southern Baptists) were well entrenched in the battle for Spanish-speaking souls at the beginning of the twentieth century.[14] Along with the close personal relationship to God promoted by Baptist theology, the autonomy of Baptist congregations in nearly all financial and local matters was key to their work among Mexican Americans. Individual congregations were free of the bureaucracy and pyramidal Episcopal and presbytery leadership structures Mexicans found impossible to penetrate. For Spanish-speaking Baptist churches, congregational democracy and independence allowed for smoother assimilation into the Baptist polity. Such freedom gave them power over the day-to-day operations of their churches and allowed natural leaders to rise to positions of authority. So successful were the Southern Baptists among the Spanish-speaking that the El Paso-based Baptist Spanish Publications publishing house established in 1916 grew to become the largest supplier of Spanish language materials for evangelical missions in the hemisphere.[15]

The Baptists, however, did continue a common pattern among many Protestant denominations of maintaining separate white, black, and Mexican congregations.[16] Segregated black and white congregations were already firmly in place in the southern branches of American Protestantism. In Texas separate Mexican and white churches followed this racialized logic among Baptists. When Mexican membership began to increase, steps were taken by the Texas Baptist Convention to organize separate "Mexican missions" sponsored by Anglo congregations. By 1910 the growth in the number of Spanish-speaking congregations warranted the formation of the Mexican Baptist Convention, a separate denominational unit affiliated with the older and larger (Anglo) Texas Baptist Convention.[17]

Between World Wars, aggressive missionary efforts among Mexican Americans by both Anglo and Mexican American Baptists throughout the West and into the Midwest met with a gradual increase in the number of Mexican American congregations.[18] It was one of these Baptist Home Mission Board-sponsored missionaries who led Tijerina into "making a decision" to follow Jesus. Among the Baptists Tijerina would have found the freedom and opportunities to develop his already recognized leadership skills. Furthermore, unlike the mainline denominational seminaries, the Southern Baptists maintained flexible educational requirements for their ministers. In Texas they began sponsoring "preachers' institutes" to prepare Mexican Americans for the pastorate, versions of which evolved into two Baptist seminaries in 1947.[19] The added possibility of ordination without requiring a rigorous program of training should have been attractive to the eager Tijerina. There are, however, good and simple reasons why Tijerina rejected the Baptist options and chose instead to enter the Assemblies of God Latin American Bible Institute at Saspamco, Texas. Even though the modern Pentecostal movement was still in its youth in the 1940s, Tijerina was drawn to its ancient message and archaic spirituality reborn into the modern world.

Pentecostalism as Marginality

Modern day Pentecostalism does not refer to a single organization or unified body of beliefs but to a broad movement. Its roots go back to the first century church, but its contemporary form began to coalesce late in nineteenth-century American evangelical Christianity. With its emphasis on a personal and experiential worship of God, literalist interpretation of the Bible, and "gifts of the Spirit," Pentecostalism in all of its diverse forms has profoundly altered the religious landscape in the Americas.[20]

Emerging out of the confluence of theological innovations at the turn of the twentieth century, the Pentecostal synthesis promoted an immediate experience of God's salvation, and especially the ecstatic physicality of Holy Spirit baptism. Most notably glossolalia, or "speaking in tongues," early on characterized and stigmatized Pentecostal practice. Supported by a bold theology that speculated on the imminent return of Jesus (premillennialism), Pentecostalism rejected the imposition of Church history and theological precedent in favor of a common sense, quasi-empirical Biblical interpretation. Drawing from its Wesleyan roots Pentecostalism required its members to live sober and moral lives. And like its older Holiness and Fundamentalist sibling movements, it rejected most of the secular world as unredeemed and dangerous in favor of a worldview tied closely to church life, family, and an attitude of being "in but not of" the world.[21]

This oppositional and suspicious stance toward culture and society resulted in an uncharitable image of Pentecostal Christians as backward, old-fashioned, and ignorant. Robert Mapes Anderson's analysis of Pentecostalism's earliest adherents of this "folkish," straightforward, and sentimental "old time religion" explains the basis for this "low church" image. With members drawn primarily from a constellation of subcultures associated with remnants of older, rural-agrarian cultures, Anderson characterized Pentecostalism in unmistakable contrast to the liberal, intellectual, and socially oriented religion that has come to typify mainstream Protestantism—or at least, its leadership. Dogmatic, emotional, often intolerant, anti-intellectual, and tribal, the thrust of the old-time religion is diametrically opposed to that of the major denominations.[22]

American religion historian, Martin Marty, similarly observed that

[u]ntil recently, say a generation ago, Pentecostalism was seen as a movement of illiterates, "hillbillies," "rednecks," "snakehandlers," or "holy rollers," who were at the margins of culture but who would remain there without needing or leaving literature of much notice.[23]

Despite these characterizations Pentecostalism's popularity among large numbers of people, rural or otherwise, had less to do with the disappointments of liberal Christianity than it did with the ability to provide an entire worldview, lifestyle, and supportive "tribal" community.

The landmark 1906 Azusa Street revival in Los Angeles "renowned among Pentecostals ever since as the center from which their movement radiated around the world" had in fact been characterized by its broad appeal across different races and classes. Quoting sources at the time of the Azusa revival, Anderson described the diversity of the new Pentecost:

Ethiopians, Chinese, Mexicans, and other nationalities worshipped together. Other ethnic groups represented at one time or another in those early days were Portuguese, Spanish, Russians, Norwegians, Frenchmen, Germans, and Jews. One of the Azusa leaders estimated that more than twenty different nationalities were represented at the meetings. "It is," said an eyewitness of the work, "noticeably free from all nationalistic feeling. . . . No instrument that God can use is rejected on account of color or dress or lack of education." The ethnic minority groups of Los Angeles found themselves welcome at Azusa, and some would discover there the sense of dignity and community denied them in the larger urban culture.[24]

The initial enthusiasm that swept through the early years of Pentecostalism after Azusa Street eventually blossomed into a harvest of denominations seeking to prepare Christianity for Christ's return. In their premillennial zeal the earliest leaders in the Pentecostal movement were slow to form denominations, though the bureaucratization of loosely organized congregations was nevertheless inevitable. Mexican Americans present at the origins of Pentecostalism heeded the urgent call to redemption and made the most of the movement's openness to multiracial and shared gender leadership. Within a decade of the miraculous Holy Spirit fires on Azusa Street, Pentecostal missionaries and organizations spread the flames of this charismatic and millennial faith east across the United States, into Canada, and all the way south into Latin America. What was to become the largest of these budding denominations, the Assemblies of God, organized and was aggressively seeking converts by 1914. As a result, the Assemblies witnessed a phenomenal growth in the United States in the first half of the twentieth century: from 50,400 members in 1925 to 400,000 in the mid-1950s.[25] It was this organization that Tijerina chose for Christian ministerial training.

Religion along the *Frontera Quemada*

The Pentecostal message arrived in Texas in 1906, along with political, social, and economic upheaval along the Mexico-U.S. border. Between the late 1880s and the 1920s, the border region in Texas witnessed the dispossession of Mexicans from their land and massive migration during and after the 1910 Mexican Revolution. The rapid growth of corporate agriculture on the U.S. side of the border at the turn of the century, soon dependent upon the cheap labor of Mexicans and Mexican Americans, turned the lower Rio Grande Valley into one of the most productive regions in Texas.[26] Yet this dependence upon Mexican labor did not ameliorate the already existing cultural and economic caste system that had developed in the decades following the American Civil War. Besides the vertical tensions between Mexican and Anglo, the rapid influx of Mexican nationals who were fleeing the ravages of the Mexican Revolution threatened the stability of Mexican American communities that had been in Texas for generations.[27]

Accompanying the rapid demographic changes and economic transformation were the efforts of Protestant missionaries who up to now had all but ignored Mexicans and their "pagan" Catholicism. Alarmed at the inability of Protestants to penetrate the masses of Mexicans, one El Paso church official observed in 1913 that "there are several denominations working there, but only the border of the population is being reached by these agencies. . . . [F]rom our survey of the city we know that not more than one out of thirty is brought within the influence of the gospel. Four of the principal churches for the Spanish work are within three blocks of each other, leaving a great mass towards the river and towards Juarez and on the Mexican side, without any gospel agency whatsoever."[28] By 1925 the superintendent of the Latin American Mission of the Methodist Episcopal Church had quantified the religious affiliation of "Latin Americans" above the border as

(1) Roman Catholics claim about sixty percent, made up for the most part of the women, the aged, the ignorant peons, and the old patrician families . . .

(2) The positivists, or freethinkers, number about ten percent, made up of the men who have read or listened to the ubiquitous French philosophy . . .

(3) The *Evangélicos*, or Protestants make up some ten percent. They are handpicked, awakened people, most of them from the middle class and many of them young people. They form a gallant array of leaders who are the products of missions and mission schools. . . .

(4) Various fanatical, diverse sects number about ten percent. . . . They usually exceed the bounds of their respective sects in extravagance and bigotry. They include Pentecostal groups, New Thought followers, Mormons, Spiritualists, Russellites, Christian Scientists, Holy Rollers, some "Faith Missions" members, *Independientes*, and some extreme Protestant groups as difficult to combat as to classify . . .

(5) The socialists, atheists, and anarchists number about ten percent. They are also handpicked and leavened people who have no easier lot than the Protestants. They are almost exclusively adult men of the middle and lower class.[29]

Amidst such religious diversity, the folk religious practices of Mexican Catholicism, and the ministrations of famous folk healers like Don Pedro Jaramillo and Niño Fidencio, marked Mexican and Mexican American religion at the time.[30] In the context of rapid changes along the Texas-Mexico border from the 1890s to the 1920s, religious activity on both sides of the border suggest that it was a "burned-over" border, or more appropriately, a *frontera quemada*. In ways reminiscent of the religious revivalism that swept western New York at the turn of the nineteenth century, the Mexico-U.S. frontera quemada refers to the vigorous proselytization by Protestants and sectarians and the eruption of vernacular Mexican Catholicism refreshed by the massive arrival of northward-bound immigrants.[31] This effervescence of religiosity along the southern Texas border region had been prepared by decades of political and cultural readjustment between Mexican Americans and Anglo Americans after the power shift following 1848. Matovina notes that by the turn of the century, resistant Tejano Catholic culture was being threatened by popular practices brought by waves of new Mexican immigrants, and the combined incursion of Protestant and sectarian evangelists.[32] The combined effects of sectarian proselytization, indigenous innovations, and vernacular Catholic practice only served to further weaken the fumbling official Catholic hierarchy's attempts to "Americanize" their Mexican congregations and divest them of their "pagan" practices. Unprepared to deal with their large Mexican flock, the Catholic Church unwittingly opened the door to recruitment by Spanish-speaking evangelical and Pentecostal missionaries.

The borderlands provided fertile ground for Protestant mission work, sectarianism, and religious innovation. In the context of enormous population movement and resettlement, the Mexican Revolution, World War I, worsening race relations in the border region, the gaps between Anglo and Mexican and between Church hierarchy and parishioner changes in religion and culture were inevitable. Although exact numbers of Mexicans moving across the border are unknown, San Miguel quotes a government labor agent who estimated that in 1926, the year Tijerina was born, over 200,000 Mexican laborers had passed through the San Antonio area.[33] Remy has pointed out, however, that the energy expended by Mexican immigrants during this time was toward "attaining economic stability, with little left over for religion."[34] Between what was "left over for religion," presumably Catholicism, and their marginal acceptance within the American Catholic community, Mexican immigrants and Mexican Americans were ripe for Protestant and sectarian persuasion. In this mix Pentecostalism proved to be particularly adept in the great south Texas spiritual harvest when it arrived. Unlike other evangelical and Protestant groups that arrived with the main intention of reaching the potential Anglo convert, Pentecostalism early on targeted Mexican Americans for conversion and did better than almost all of its competitors.[35]

In 1916 Henry C. Ball, a Methodist convert to the Assemblies of God, began to preach and organize Mexican farm laborers in Kingsville, Texas. Other, mostly Anglo, Pentecostal missionaries had met with resistance in their work among whites and so began to target Spanish-speaking communities.[36] Under Ball's tutelage a separate "Latin American District Council" in the Assemblies of God was organized in 1929 to concentrate on Spanish-language evangelization in the Southwest (and eventually to Puerto Ricans on the East Coast). From humble beginnings in 1918— seven ministers, six churches, and one hundred members—the Latin American District increased to 174 ministers, eighty churches, and 4,500 members by the time Tijerina joined them in the 1940s.[37] Although Ball, referred to as "Hermano Pelota" ("Brother Ball") by his Mexican American associates, and other non-Latino Pentecostals have often been credited with bringing the movement to Mexican Americans, the great expansion of Pentecostal churches among Latinos was guaranteed by the immediate evangelistic successes of Mexican American, Mexican, and Puerto Rican leaders.[38] Almost from the beginning of the Pentecostal effort in Texas, the leadership of Francisco Olazábal, Antonio Rios Morín, and others multiplied the number of Mexican converts. Despite the hard work of Anglo missionaries, de Leon reports that Mexicans preferred Latino leaders, especially Francisco Olazábal, because "the very presence of H. C. Ball made some of the ministers feel they were controlled by the 'gringos.'"[39] Under competent and dedicated leaders Mexican American Pentecostalism in Texas and California encompassed a number of sects and quickly drew in sizable numbers of converts.

This early rapid growth of Pentecostalism among Mexican Americans has yet to be fully measured. Recent work by Gastón Espinosa, Daniel

Ramírez, and Arlene Sánchez Walsh have challenged the received history of early American Pentecostalism, noting the early presence of and active leadership by Latinos.[40] The scholarship indicates that the institutions, organizational structures, evangelizing efforts, and membership numbers in the Latin American District were substantial enough to account for a steady rise in church growth following Ball and his students' work beginning in the early 1920s.[41] Recalling the early effort, Ball notes that

> [p]eople came from as far away as 15 miles to hear and see what the Lord was doing. Soon our people were scattered all over South Texas to pick cotton. Wherever they went they held services at night. Soon I was receiving letters to go and meet the new believers in several South Texas places. These believers from different towns requested me to supply them a pastor. Since we had no men to act as such, we simply appointed the best qualified men to lead the small congregations.[42]

It is clear following Ball's description that the power of the Pentecostal movement among Mexican Americans came not from administrative Home Mission boards or attractive church buildings, but through the powerful oral tradition of the gospel message established by the first century Christians. Unable to meet the demands for educated ministers, early Pentecostal leaders placed their faith in the power of the Holy Spirit to direct the willing, but otherwise untrained men they sent to serve as pastors.

There can be no doubt that the success of the Assemblies of God among Mexican Americans was due in large part to the straightforward, vernacular style of Pentecostal theology and practice. For many Mexican Americans who had worshipped in the American Roman Catholic Church under German and Irish American (and the occasional French) priests since the 1850s, Protestant conversion, and especially evangelical and Pentecostal conversion, provided more than a simple spiritual rebirth. Unlike the Catholic Church, which tended to treat Mexican Americans with contempt and as second-class citizens of the Kingdom, evangelical and Pentecostal missionaries actively went out among Mexican Americans, frequently learned Spanish, and granted them power over their own congregations. Pentecostalism lifted the veils of mystery about God and theology from their eyes of faith, put the living word of God into their hands, and encouraged them as individuals to experience the awesome power of the Holy Spirit.[43]

Even though Mexican Catholics, Baptists, and Pentecostals occupied the lower end of the socioeconomic ladder, Pentecostalism held obvious advantages, and thus appeal to potential converts from Catholicism. The use of colloquial Spanish in church services, active participation by members in church decisions, access to scripture and its interpretation, and a supportive, usually small church family all proved irresistible to many Roman Catholics.[44] Pentecostalism's focus on restoring authentic Christianity as revealed in the Bible released former Roman Catholics from the burdens of arcane theology and tradition. Uncomfortable with the liturgical forms of American Catholicism, Mexican Americans were demeaned by Church officials for their inability to become good "Mass and Sacrament" Catholics. In turn they retreated into their *domus* oriented popular Catholic traditions.[45] Access to the Bible and the visible evidences of salvation and healing in Pentecostalism offered Mexican American Catholics something unavailable to them in the Catholic church: agency and control in their religious lives.

The cultural difficulties between the American Catholic Church and Mexican American Catholics are partially responsible for the turn to Protestantism. Lacking an indigenous leadership, Mexican Americans remained "dependent Catholics" well into the second half of the twentieth century.[46] As outsiders in their own tradition, however, most Mexican descent Catholics were nevertheless comfortable as "nominal" Catholics, living out their faith within the cycles of family and community life (baptism, confirmation, marriage, etc.).[47] On the other hand, conversion to Pentecostalism meant a radical and willful leap of faith. Pentecostalism required a break with strong cultural traditions and ties with family and friends. By the time Tijerina was "born again" into Pentecostalism, Mexican Pentecostal congregations had established a second generation of supportive familial structures to receive him. Evangelical theology notwithstanding, these churches nevertheless retained both a strong Mexican ethnic identity and traditional male leadership. In these intimate worlds one was surrounded by *hermanas* and *hermanos*, brothers and sisters, all under the watch of a loving God and the reassuring warmth of the Holy Ghost's fire.

Tijerina could only have chosen between the Baptists and Pentecostals.[48] In the early 1940s, the Southern Baptist faith had been firmly planted among Mexican Americans in his home state. The Texas Baptist Convention even created a bureaucracy to handle the nettlesome and perennial problem of racism in their ranks.[49] Southern Baptists and most of the Pentecostal groups shared a common theology that leaned toward fundamentalism in matters of Biblical interpretation and soteriology. Both shared democratic and autonomous congregational polities; they were identified with lower socioeconomic populations and were actively proselytizing among Mexican Americans. The one organizational advantage Southern Baptists had over the Pentecostals was the financial support of their missionaries through the cooperative giving of a large national convention.[50]

Texas also was home to seminaries run by the Southern Baptists and the Assemblies of God. These seminaries were open to Mexican Americans, pragmatic in their education, and flexible about educational prerequisites. The Assemblies of God did not require its ministers to hold seminary degrees, and made allowances for the ordination of pastors in the informal manner of the New Testament. As early as 1917, the Assemblies had recognized the "privileges of the mature local church" to ordain qualified ministers as they saw fit. De Leon confirms this, noting that a theological education was not a prerequisite for Mexican American ministers during the first decades of the Pentecostal movement. As Ball's description of the earliest evangelizing among Mexican Americans noted, the call for Spanish-speaking pastors was great, necessitating *ad hoc* training for ministers already in the field through Bible and ministers conferences. However, de Leon remarks, "very few of the [Mexican/Mexican American] preachers had seminar training; in fact, in the thirties, the young man who attended the Bible institutes was shunned by the congregation."[51] So zealous were some congregations in pursuing the experience of the Holy Spirit that they felt no need for "human teaching," arguing that "the Bible schools quench the Spirit." At the extreme end, "some went so far as to forbid the reading of the Bible itself, saying that the Holy Spirit would teach us all we need to know."[52]

"The outer boundaries of the religious world"

Tijerina's decision to join the Assemblies of God speaks to the marginal nature of Pentecostalism. His recollection of conversion corroborates Robert Mapes Anderson's analysis that Pentecostalism's vision was a powerful attraction for the disinherited in society. Among all of his Protestant options, Tijerina chose Pentecostalism because it suited his socioeconomic class. He was also attracted to the racial diversity of the Assemblies' organization, and the conferred authority that could not be granted through formal education, material wealth, or political office. "When I went to Bible school, that was the outer boundaries of the religious world," he recalled.

> The center of religion was—like the Islamic world, the Catholic world. They had powers! Then comes the Protestant; the organizations are small—a hundred, or two hundred years old. So I was in the outer boundaries of the religious world. And I grabbed onto it because that's where I was! I was very poor. I was brought up a migrant. We never owned a house, not even a one room house. We never owned a lot, property, nothing. So that was the best I had at that time. But that was good enough to lead me and move me on to my life, my dreams. . . . The Protestants, they had found, you know, a conversion. They had a better religion than the Catholics.[53]

Tijerina's attraction to Protestantism from the outer boundaries of poverty and marginality substantiates traditional sociological views about the stratification of Protestant denominations according to differences among members in a society. In his classic study of how structural differences in American society mirrored religious affiliation, Niebuhr noted that "disinherited," "immigrant," and racially marked minority populations were coextensive with "sectarian" religions. "In Protestant history," he explains, "the sect has ever been the child of an outcast minority, taking its rise in the religious revolts of the poor, of those who were without effective representation in the church or state and who formed their conventicles of dissent in the only way open to them, on the democratic, associational pattern."[54] Niebuhr's observation is echoed in de Leon's assessment of Pentecostalism's attractiveness to Mexicans early in the century. In 1916, when Ball began to preach to Mexicans in Texas, "most of the Mexican population in the Southwest were political refugees. The majority were displaced people who had been victimized by the fast changing governments and the indiscriminate destruction by the armies of revolution [in Mexico]."[55] On the American side of the border, race relegated Mexicans to the lower end of the social, economic, and religious spectra.[56]

Also confirming Niebuhr's sectarian template, sociologists Thomas O'Dea and Renato Poblete found that among recently arrived Puerto Ricans in New York in the 1950s, Pentecostalism's strength rested with the reinforcement of meaningful social relationships for converts in response to geographical and cultural dislocations. A sense of group membership, individual responsibility, and unspoken support by others in the group were key elements in holding and increasing the number of converts. A crucial qualification that these researchers make, one which helps explain Tijerina's choice, is that group solidarity seen from the convert's point of view appears "not as a loss of individuality, but rather as a chance to develop his own personality—to experience a worthwhile fulfillment."[57]

Their structural subordination in American society allows Pentecostals to symbolically invert their social and economic contexts. As Mexican American Catholics were shut out of leadership roles, Pentecostal ideology proclaimed its members equals in the "priesthood" of all believers and promised direct personal access to God. As agricultural laborers, miners, tenant farmers, or service workers, Mexican Americans found themselves trapped at the bottom of the caste system in the labor market. In Pentecostalism Mexican Americans were "born again" as heirs to the Kingdom of God.[58] Faced with a hostile world by virtue of race, language, education, and socioeconomic status, Pentecostalism provided safe passage through these states of powerlessness, creating a new identity, supportive community, and individual agency.[59]

In the 1940s, there were specific transformations in the Southwest that threatened the advancement Mexican American communities might otherwise have made. As part of the large multiracial mobile labor force that followed the booming agricultural miracles in the western states and the needs of wartime industry, Tijerina and his brothers were firsthand witnesses to the worsening conditions of Mexican Americans. As David Montejano and David Gutiérrez have both detailed, Mexican Americans throughout the Southwest were caught between the arrival of thousands of Mexican *bracero* laborers and competition among different ethnic groups for limited labor opportunities in both agriculture and urban industries.[60] Everywhere Mexican Americans looked, finding and keeping a job was becoming increasingly difficult. Beginning in the early 1920s, agricultural labor had become dangerously competitive among Filipinos, Japanese, Chinese, Sikh, and later, dust bowl "Okies," and eventually bracero Mexicans. When mechanization of farm labor forced thousands of Mexican Americans into the industrializing cities beginning in the mid-1930s, they competed with others driven from agriculture, and later, with African Americans who had migrated west, and with women, both groups drawn into the labor force by the wartime industry.

The Tijerina brothers' labor migration during the 1940s illustrates this precarious labor market and explains why they were beyond the Texas borders harvesting crops in the Midwest and working in Michigan automobile plants. In fact, "Texas-Mexicans," according to a government commission on migratory labor, emerged in the 1940s as the largest domestic group of migrant workers "within Texas and into the Mountain and Great Lakes States."[61] After two years in the Assemblies' Instituto Bíblico and without institutional support, Tijerina was forced to continue this pattern of temporary migratory employment as he labored for the Lord. As an itinerant Mexican American Pentecostal evangelist, he was at the outer boundaries of both the religious and secular worlds.

Tijerina's difficulties with the authorities at the Bible Institute, and later the Assemblies of God denomination, reveal that his zeal exceeded structures of authority or organization. Even with its liberating salvation message, the socially restrictive ethics of Pentecostalism could not keep Tijerina from a prohibited friendship with a female student, Vicky Rivera, at the Bible Institute. Doctrinally, Tijerina had begun to forge his own theology prior to his expulsion from the Institute in 1946. Kenzy Savage's comment that he remembered Tijerina as "fanatical" and "peculiar" in his thinking suggests that Tijerina was filtering what he was learning through his experience and testing the limits of Pentecostal orthodoxy.

There is some confusion as to whether Tijerina was officially diplo-maed from the Instituto and under what credentials he served as a min-ister of the Assemblies of God. While some of his biographers concur that Tijerina graduated and earned a denominational license to preach, others indicate that he was refused his diploma over the Rivera affair but managed somehow to gain a ministerial license. This murkiness sur-rounding Tijerina's credentialed status with the Assemblies reveals a tension between his need to have legitimate/legal permission by the organization to preach and a strong desire to reject the structure of the Pentecostal organization. Stating that he had fulfilled the requirements for graduation but was refused the diploma, Tijerina blames the institu-tion and absolves himself of any wrongdoing.

The issue of licensing is remembered in a similar way. There is no rea-son to doubt Kenzy Savage who says that he and Tijerina doubled up for an evangelizing tour of the Santa Fe area.[62] Although superintendent of the Bible Institute, Savage was probably responsible for expelling Tijerina from the Assemblies. Nevertheless he praised Tijerina's preaching style, which he claimed had "alot of spunk and spirit."[63] Tijerina's statements about having his ministerial license revoked by the Assemblies of God in 1950 are curious given that he was expelled from the Institute and denied a diploma. In addition, he preached with Savage on occasion and was given charge over at least five Assemblies congregations through 1950, at which time his "credentials" were revoked. Tijerina's biographers all accept the confusion and ambiguity of his credential status because his religious affiliations and concerns were supposedly behind him by the late 1950s. Tijerina's own explanation of the situation as he remembers it decades later, however, does little to clear up the confusion but reveals something of his attitude as a student:

> they refused to graduate me. My diploma was kept. And they still have it. When after . . . 1950, I went through there—I was an evan-gelist; a Protestant evangelist—[Savage] offered. He says, "Reies, the graduation is pretty soon. Why don't you stop in Ysleta and we'll give you your diploma."
>
> "No!" I said. "No! Let that monument there speak for itself . . . about who and what happened and who I was." . . . So I refused it.

Later on they have spread the fact that my preaching license was suspended. Never! I never had licenses. Never did ask because I was arrogant. Very proud! And I wouldn't take no license from them because I thought they were wrong. And all the other little groups, you know, Protestant groups, including the Church, of course—the Catholics. [T]here are books that say that they suspended my credentials. I never had any! That's the truth.[64]

At the time his biographers were writing, Tijerina had publicly rejected "religion" in favor of a moral ideology based upon civil rights and international treaty law. Having diplomas, licenses, and credentials was unimportant to the larger tasks at hand. Tijerina's motivations as an evangelical missionary derived from the very center of Pentecostal theology, being "called" and "chosen" by God for the work. Authority to preach could have been granted him by a local congregation. Thus the existence of a diploma (which is apparently still at Ysleta) granted him a measure of legitimacy, which meant that there was *something* to be revoked by denominational officials in 1950.

By the time the Assemblies of God expelled him, Tijerina was preaching a hardened theology that was fundamentalist in its literalist hermeneutic of the Bible and sectarian in its apocalyptic urgency. In his ministry he began to tell congregations to give their money to the poor as commanded by Jesus (Mark 10:21). And late in the 1950s, he and his male followers donned white robes and refused to shave following the Biblical prohibitions in Leviticus (19:27) and Deuteronomy (14:1). His son, Reies H. Tijerina, remembered that during this itinerancy, "I was hitchhiking before I could walk. People who used to feed us were winos and hobos."[65] According to Clark Knowlton, between 1950 and 1955 Tijerina was "disoriented" and settled for a time in Tierra Amarilla, flirting with anti-Anglo organizations. Tony Hillerman reports that Tijerina was in New Mexico trying to pull together a religious sect.[66] Had Knowlton, Hillerman, and others examined Tijerina's book of sermons, they would have found that he spent the first half of the 1950s pursuing evangelistic missions across the country. Preaching a radical return to the fundamentals of what he knew to be true Christianity, the theology he developed on the road he preserved in his sermons to which we now turn.

¿Hallará Fe en la Tierra . . . ?: "Great big chapters on justice"

Tijerina's collection of sermons *¿Hallará Fe en la Tierra . . . ?* marks his career transition from Pentecostal preacher to land grant activist. When George Grayson, Jr. interviewed Tijerina in the Santa Fe jail in 1967 and asked him to describe the book, Tijerina replied that *¿Hallará Fe en la Tierra . . . ?* was "about religion: just plain religion, with great big chapters on justice."[67] Nabokov's jail interview notes reveal the book's genesis came early in Tijerina's religious life when, Tijerina recalled, he "noticed the word 'justice' [was] used as many times [as] words like love" in the Bible.

> so I wrote later on this Book, I don't have many copies left [because] I gave most of them away, "Hallará Fe en La Tierra?" "Will there have . . . ," no, "*be* faith on earth?" You see, it's a question.[68]

Speaking behind prison bars days after the courthouse raid in 1967, Tijerina downplayed the significance of his collected sermons to his journalist interviewers. *¿Hallará Fe en la Tierra . . . ?* represented a life that must have seemed much further away than the dozen or so years since he had thundered from behind a church pulpit. Yet between the lines of this slim volume the seeds of all his later work—the Valle de Paz settlement, the land grant struggles, his memoir, and his apocalypticism—were sown.

In its tan paper cover and stapled spine, *¿Hallará Fe en la Tierra . . . ?* has the appearance of an extended religious tract with its compact, single-spaced typeset. Tijerina's poverty and the nomadic character of his ministry meant that he could have only printed and carried a limited number of copies. Written throughout the early 1950s and printed in the spring of 1954, the chapters/sermons in *¿Hallará Fe en la Tierra . . . ?* came spontaneously through the portable typewriter Tijerina bought after leaving the Instituto Biblico.[69] Despite the stereotype that Pentecostals were an illiterate lot (how much more so Mexican American Pentecostals!) the Assemblies of God had early on promoted Spanish language tracts and regularly published a magazine, *La Luz Apostolica*, to aid in their evangelistic efforts and sustain their Spanish-speaking congregations.[70] Though it must have been difficult and expensive to produce, Tijerina's sermons should be seen as the continuation of his familiarity with Pentecostal literacy and tract production. His inspiration may also have been related to a renewed national interest in religious books at the time. Popular inspirational texts like Charles Sheldon's *In His Steps*, Harry Emerson Fosdick's *The Man from Nazareth*, E. Stanley Jones's *Abundant Living* daily devotional series, and Peter Marshall's *Meet the Master*, among others, were all best sellers during the time Tijerina was wandering the countryside.[71] Writing at a time prior to the rise of evangelical radio and the advent of televangelists, Tijerina's small book would not have seemed out of place or unusual, except, of course, that it had been written by a Mexican American.

His title, printed in large red letters on the cover, is taken from the parable of the unjust judge in Luke 18:7–8:

¿Y Dios no hará justicia á sus escogidos, que claman á él día y noche, aunque sea longánimo acerca de ellos? Os digo que los defenderá presto. Empero cuando el Hijo del hombre viniere, ¿Hallará fe en la tierra?

(And shall not God avenge his own elect which cry day and night unto him, though he bear long with them? I tell you that he will avenge them speedily. Nevertheless when the Son of Man cometh, shall he find faith on the earth?)

Beneath the open question Tijerina answered with a passage from Psalms 85:10,11.[72]

La misericordia y la verdad se encontraron; la justicia y la paz se besaron. La verdad brotará de la tierra; y la justicia mirará desde los cielos.

(Mercy and truth are met together; righteousness and peace have kissed each other. Truth shall spring out of the earth; and righteousness shall look down from heaven.)[73]

Read together, Tijerina suggests that when the Son of Man returns at the end of human history the faithful will be known through their mercy, truth, justice, and peace. This remnant will be borne through the horrors of the Great Tribulation. Reversing the standard Christian logic of reading prefiguration in the Old Testament followed by fulfillment in the New Testament, Tijerina here tests authentic Christian faith through appeal to Old Testament statute.[74] This strategy in the title reveals his theological preference for measuring the claims of Christianity against the foundations set in the Hebrew scriptures. As Tijerina observed organized Christianity around him, what he perceived as the apostasy of the churches was anything but mercy or truth.

On the inside cover this cynical view of the modern Christian church is evident in the epigraph:

> The Church that today leads the peoples, at one time possessed the law and salvation; at one time cherished God's wisdom; at one time had eyes to perceive good from evil. But now, its eyes are closed, and it is not privileged to see what is coming; its eyes cannot see the evil that awaits it. Now the things that are to come are hidden. You have fallen into the hands of tyrants, O people of God; they have deceived you with great lies, and covered your eyes so that your end so sad you do not see; You have fallen into error O people, and until now you have not been raised up, until this day you remain prostrate on the ground. Your days are finished, and your season is passed; and who will give you your recompense? Those who teach and indoctrinate you: they have hidden the law of Salvation; they have broken the commandments of God eternal, those which were revealed through his Son; O, if only the people knew, the evil that awaits them, and the end of their days.[75]

¿Hallará Fe en la Tierra . . . ? is written in the baroque vocabulary and style of the Reina-De Valera Spanish translation of the Bible (akin to the English King James translation in its archaic style). Its forty-three sermons appear in no discernible chronological or thematic order, arranged between an introductory stern first sermon ("The Clamor of the Earth"), and Tijerina's condemnation of the United States (" . . . is there any nation more immoral than this one?") in the final sermon ("The Good Considered Evil"). Tijerina's florid style incorporates common scriptural features as the parallel structure of phrases, the familiar plural (*vosotros*), and vocative admonitions (e.g., Woe unto . . .). Such affected rhetoric flows naturally from a preacher whose main textbook in seminary was the Bible in the Reina-De Valera translation.[76] The deployment of archaic

vocabulary and scriptural verse fragments indicate Tijerina not only relied heavily upon the Bible's form and content for his first writing experience, but that he sought to legitimate his claims by applying and invoking the authorizing power of sacred language.

The sermons portend God's juridical retribution against false religion, pride, mercilessness, and materialism. Six sermons indicate when and where they were written revealing that Tijerina, then in his late twenties, and his family evangelized from New York City to southern California between May 1953 and November 1954.[77] It is useful at this point to examine one of these sermons to reveal how far Tijerina had moved beyond the Assemblies of God and to look for hints of his future race consciousness and taste for politics. "The Provokers of Judgment" sermon in particular reveals the roots of his transformation.

"Los Provocadores del Juicio"

"The Provokers of Judgment" is one of the longest sermons in the collection. It is among the more interesting texts in its complaint against American society juxtaposed or combined with judgment against institutional Christianity. Written sometime between 1952 and 1954, the cultural and political context for this sermon is apparent in Tijerina's reformulation of Cold War rhetoric and the reminders here and throughout the collection of Japan's devastation from the atom bomb. Positioning himself as narrator and actor within the text, Tijerina takes on a prophetic role in the modern era; first as the one labeled by the enemies of God as "rebellious and a fanatic" and then as the "prepared instrument" "raised up" by God to "do his will among his butcherous people." In an earlier sermon he had taken upon himself the burden of prophetic vision:

> I do not ignore the many names that will be given me for speaking and placing myself against the works in the last days. Murmurer, they will call me; faultfinder will I be called by others, and fanatic and stupid others will call me; but I know that all the prophets and those that feared and fear God will know and recognize my spirit . . . I know that the ancients will not call me a fanatic, neither a murmurer; and of hypocrisy I will never want to take

part; because I know that God will bring all works to Judgment, and nothing will remain concealed.[78]

Tijerina begins "Provokers of Judgment" with a grim introductory curse that preserves the oral quality of a text written for the evangelist's pulpit:

> A mighty and dreadful curse is proclaimed against those who rebel against God. Mankind is not unaware of this for God has declared it through his holy prophets and has made it known across the ages. For God it has cost the blood of many righteous men to declare the truths of the future. The righteous were loathed and abused because they announced the ruin and destruction of the rebellious who, against God, rebelled. And to these same ones were given death. Unfortunately the people of God have always been a rebellious people. Because the people, blind and ignorant, do rebel, they know nothing of the law of God. But it is the people of God that, having known the good and will of God later rebelled, forsaking the Law of God and following the law of men, being clever in order to deceive. And to gain glory and riches they decree unrighteous decrees: in which are found neither good nor justice, not even for the poor, nor refuge for the widows and the oppressed.

Modeled after the revelations of the Hebrew prophets, Tijerina faults the Churches for ignoring divine law. The vocabulary and tone he uses to describe the declension of the modern Churches—he uses a form of the word "rebel" no less than six times here—indicates close attention to the vocabulary of the opening chapters of the prophets (Isa. 1, Jer. 1:7–19, Ezek. 2:3–8, Zech. 1:2–6). Unlike many of the other sermons, "Provokers" makes few chapter and verse references to the Bible because Tijerina assumes that the churched reader is familiar with its numerous scriptural allusions and biblical lore.

Tijerina compares the apostasy of the modern Christian churches with ancient Israel, offering up Israel's chastisement as a warning of God's sober judgment. Tijerina reminds his reader that Israel, God's "chosen treasure" for whom God "labored and suffered," was guilty of "imprudences and follies." Constructing Old Testament texts into a grisly montage, he recounts the destruction of Jerusalem in 586 BCE as a warning to the contemporary Christian church of God's response to Israel's sins.

> God chastised and scourged and crippled and delivered them into the hands of the most harsh people. He sold them into the hands of a government most cruel and without mercy; he forgot them completely for a space of seventy years. Upon them fell the most harsh and cruel curse that history has ever known.
>
> When the enemies of this people (once again called a "Chosen Treasure") fell upon Jerusalem, City which before had been the city of Peace and blessing: They slew the men, raped their wives, and dashed the innocent children upon the stones. They slew the sons of the king before his very eyes, and put out his eyes, and so he died blind in a strange land, living off of the crumbs of the king whom God had raised in order to humble his people Israel. God is the same yesterday, and today, and forever.[79]

Tijerina's "Biblesque" text here contains at least eighteen identifiable fragments of scripture including the curious appellation "Chosen Treasure" that combines Deuteronomy 7:6 ("chosen") with Exodus 19:5 ("peculiar treasure"). Moving from the Old Testament prefiguration to New Testament fulfillment by way of his rephrasing of Hebrews 13:8 ("Jesus Christ, the same yesterday, and today, and forever"), Tijerina goes on to detail the numerous and reprobate actions that "we" the new chosen people of God have committed. We have learned nothing from the disciplining of ancient Israel. In "Provokers" the similarities between the Old Covenant with Israel and the New Christian Covenant are enumerated negatively. Both are guilty of disobedience to law and commandment. The failure of the churches to demonstrate the Christian virtues of love and mercy compels Tijerina into his role as prophet. What is certain in his reading of Christendom's rebellion, is the coming judgment in a New Covenant. "Everything gives testimony" in American culture he observes, "that we are a rebellious, gluttonous, ignominious, blind, and despotic people. Our people speak it, our clothing stores and food markets testify to it. The roads and streets where we walk proclaim our violence and stupidity."

Alerting us to the dangers of America's excesses, Tijerina reminds us that God chastised ancient Israel's sins through other nations. He aligns himself with the prophet Jeremiah who "took the side of the Chaldeans" against Israel, and he lauds the virtues of Soviet communism in comparison to the excesses of American culture. Careful, however, not to endorse the Soviet Union, Tijerina is drawn to what he understands to be the equality, dignity, and honor of Russian culture under communism. His portrayal of a system where citizens dress "humbly and with honor and decency" and live inexpensively he contrasts with America's ostentatious wealth, superficiality, and vanity. "[M]any of their worthy customs should be imitated by so called Christians," he admonishes. "I say this because in Russia there is greater dignity and honor (even if it be only humanistic or moral honor)."

At the climax of his jeremiad he raises the specter of the atom bomb as the "greater work" of communism. Tijerina completes his analogy between the destruction of Israel by the Babylonians and fall of Christian America, lamenting that nothing can prevent its inevitable destruction.

Before all [the world], Christians cooperate to build the atom bomb, to build airplanes, to fortify war's defense. And who among us cries out? Who can put an end to the building up of arms that shall come upon us? Everyone is dulled and blind like beasts and brought to deception and to the brink (*abismo*) of the end of our rebelliousness. There is no one to cry out and rebel against the deadly work that occupies the people who profess to fear God. Fathers and sons, mothers and daughters, husbands and wives, the old and the young, good and evil, all are busy unto a single end, which is: to fulfill the will of God, our downfall. Because we have forsaken him, he has forsaken us.

"Where?" Tijerina laments, "are the wise in the land? Where are the counselors to instruct the people? . . . Why do they not spare this people, who like blind cattle are led to the altar of burnt offering (*holocausto*)?" Tijerina's choice of the term holocausto here refers to the atoning offerings of sheep and cattle on the sacrificial altar as described in Leviticus 4:22–26. He also clearly means to warn his reader of God's judgment brought about through nuclear holocaust, both meanings linked to the double meaning of the word abismo, which translates as "brink" or "hell"/"inferno." Both glosses of holocausto (unavailable in the King James English translation) and perhaps even its reference to the genocide of the Jewish people are carried through his question and reveal Tijerina's preaching skills.

By the end of his tirade Tijerina has seen the coming ruin of both the Church and the nation. The Church and the state have busied themselves creating the weapons of their own destruction, falsely worshipping the outward appearances of religion, and turning aside from the love of God. He condemns both, acknowledging their surface differences but accusing them of being moved by the same spirit of "arrogance, envy, selfishness, and vainglory." In prophetic fashion he exhorts the reader to depart from the "life of deceit," "Babylon" (one of his favorite epithets for the United States), and the "powers of pleasures" in favor of loathing evil and vanity. He urges true Christians to give away their possessions to "remove judgment" that hangs over the heads of lukewarm Christianity. Returning to the theme of holocaust he writes that just believers during the coming judgment will be "refined"; their sins and false religion burned away. Finally, at the very end of his sermon, Tijerina can only conclude that the impending fall of the United States to the godless Russians is the result "of a rebellious world like the one we, the children of God have made." "Communism" he concludes sadly, "has come to do a greater work than our [so called] love."

In style and construction "Provokers of Judgment" is representative of the other sermons in ¿Hallará Fe en la Tierra . . . ? The invectives against the contemporary Christian church are consistent throughout the collection, and for the most part the inventory of the peoples' sins are interchangeable. In particular, the major themes of faithlessness, false religion, lawlessness, dishonor within the family, and the seductions of Babylon the Whore are ubiquitous. The net effect of his rhetorical strategies, however, is numbing.

The juridical quality of Tijerina's sermons is rooted in the dark and brooding language of Old Testament covenant and retribution. Here in

"Provokers of Judgment," as in all of his subsequent writing, he adopts a legal terminology borrowed from ancient law meant to endow him with the authorizing voice of "Justo Juez," the God of Judgment. His adoption of Old Testament prophetic formulas and types of address further enhance the deployment of Biblical phraseology and language. Claus Westermann's analysis of the tripartite structure of prophetic judgment-speech in the Old Testament is useful for demonstrating how closely Tijerina followed the rhetorical structures of his Hebrew prophet heroes. Recognizing that prophetic judgments against a nation in the Hebrew Bible follow a regular pattern, Westermann suggests a sequence that involves (1) the reason/introduction to the message, including an accusation against the listener; (2) a "messenger formula" that moves from the introduction; and (3) the announcement of judgment.[80]

"Provokers of Judgment" begins with the opening declarative curse ("A mighty and dreadful curse is proclaimed . . ."), followed by the accusation of Israel's rebelliousness as the cause for God's anger. Tijerina embellishes this theme, employing Israel as a typological model for the failures of contemporary Christianity and the United States. The "messenger formula" ("Therefore, 'Wait!' saith the Lord") is located in the last paragraph and does not function so much as an introduction to an announcement of judgment as Westermann positions it, but as the assurance that God will intervene and save the faithful who endure. Unlike the ancient precedent of total destruction of the nation, however, here the Christian eschatological idea of a saved remnant allows Tijerina to imagine himself and those who follow him as the truly faithful. Finally, the announcement of judgment finds its expression in the threat of nuclear holocaust. Whether or not Tijerina consciously reiterated the patterns of prophetic judgment-speech in his sermons, it is clear that whatever the amount or quality of his formal Bible training, he was intimately and intuitively familiar with the prophetic tropes. In many of the other sermons Tijerina liberally sprinkles them with "woe oracles," a Hebrew Bible rhetorical device that, with one single exception, is found exclusively in the prophetic books and employed to address groups.[81]

"Provokers of Judgment" is also representative of the other sermons in its handling of Cold War political themes cast in the framework of a pessimistic Pentecostal premillennialism. His readers in the early 1950s would have been familiar with hyperbolic warnings of the twin dangers of atomic fission and the looming shadow of Soviet communism. As with other American Christians Tijerina reversed his opinion on the benefits of modern science and scientists after the horrors of Hiroshima and Nagasaki. In another sermon Tijerina depicts the industry of war and legions of scientists lying awake in their beds at night imagining new weapons of mass destruction.

> Day to night, men are preparing for war; day and night arms are being manufactured; everyone works hard, everyone is busy in the great work, factories and plants powered by giant electric motors; everything cooperating for the grand end. In large cities around the world industry is on the move, men are hurrying; their bosses make haste, crude iron is thrown into ovens of fire, all done for one sole end; even the women, day and night, work in the factories, in the plants, fashioning mighty instruments, powerful apparatuses; scientists, busy in their laboratories, thinking, even as they lay in their beds, and then creating right away; inventing powerful instruments and projectiles.[82]

In another sermon he would write, "Woe unto those who are united with a mighty nation; woe unto those who put their trust in atomic energy." He then goes on to describe the citizens of Hiroshima and Nagasaki as being less "astonished" than the wicked of today who will fall under the "wrath of the Lamb."

To his title's question "Will faith be found on the earth?" Tijerina thundered his reply in the harshest language of Biblical legal authority in 115 pages of numbing jeremiad. Writing spontaneously and inspired by the truth of his vision, he accused organized Christianity of hypocrisy in a theological legalist vocabulary before an Old Testament God of Judgment. In his later political tracts and the memoir, this Biblically derived legal lexicon remains basic to his writing, although reinscribed through the secular documents of Spanish land grant deeds, international treaties, and even the founding sacred documents of the United States.

From Pentecostalism to Nondenominationalism

Tijerina avoids the details of his Pentecostalism in his public life. In his sermons, interviews, and memoir he omits any discussion of his association with the Assemblies of God or denominations he may have passed through between the Bible Institute and his return to Roman Catholicism. Over the years he has repeatedly referred to his itinerant evangelist career as "nondenominational" or simply "Protestant."[83] It is tantalizing and curious that in his sermons and memoir there is no emphasis on the Holy Spirit, defense of the "gift of tongues," divine healing, or other doctrines specific to Pentecostalism. In fact, a close reading of *¿Hallará Fe en la Tierra . . . ?* without the knowledge of the writer's Assemblies of God training would not betray his Pentecostalism. For example, the sermons studiously avoid the term "Holy Spirit" (*Espíritu Santo*), choosing instead the phrase "Spirit of God" (*Espíritu de Dios*). Tijerina never defines the Spirit in the context of "gifts" or denominational affiliation but rather in relationship to justice and faith: "The Spirit of God is not against him who loves justice, is not against him who pardons his brother; nor against him who does good unto his neighbor, to the poor, the needy, the orphan."[84] What then accounts for Tijerina's eventual departure from organized Pentecostalism, or from any denominational affiliation? It is likely that Tijerina's disenchantment with the Assemblies of God occurred during changes within the Assemblies organization itself, sectarian challenges to the bureaucratization of Pentecostalism, and perhaps the unmet promises of intense spiritual experiences.

Tijerina was beyond the boundaries of established Christian denominational affiliation by the time he had completed *¿Hallará Fe en la Tierra . . . ?* His rejection and judgment of American Christianity guaranteed that he would never return to even the most marginalized Pentecostal congregations. His years spent wandering across the country and "provoking the preachers" confirmed everything he had come to detest about complacent and compromised Christian life. And even though he eventually rejected its institutions, Pentecostalism had burned in his mind a restorationist vision of a pure, original Christianity and a desire in his heart to enact those ideals.

Tijerina's sermons intend to restore the spirit and simple truths of the early, "primitive" church. They reveal the restorationist impulse in Pentecostalism that stressed the unity of Christians, the perfection of the

Christian life and the premillennial expectation of Christ's imminent return.[85] *¿Hallará Fe en la Tierra . . . ?* called for sweeping reform in the churches. It ordered a puritanical lifestyle for true believers, chastising the faithless with its dark premillennial view of the future. In fact, Tijerina's positions on such matters appeared to be extreme to the point of fanaticism, and so the observations about his "peculiar" and "unorthodox attitudes."[86] A reference in "Provokers" to shaved faces as stumbling blocks to faith ties Tijerina to an unnamed group of bearded sectarians he appears with in a photograph late in his ministerial career. This group directly influenced at least the outward appearance of Tijerina and his followers when they appeared in New Mexico in the 1950s, the men bearded and wearing flowing white robes.[87]

What Tijerina's sermons do reveal even as they lack a distinctive Pentecostal "spirit" is an intense restorationism and chastising of the existing Christian orders. His sermons suggest that he may have been influenced by "Latter Rain" Pentecostal sectarians emerging near the time of his unorthodox and "fanatical" ideas. In reaction against the Canadian Assemblies of God in 1947, the "Latter Rain" schism emphasized prophesy, spiritual gifts, and the wholesale rejection of denominations in favor of the local congregation.[88] As these sectarian ideas moved south from Canada into the United States, it reinvigorated Pentecostal congregations worried about falling into the routines and organizations of Protestants around them. The urgency of Latter Rain millennialism, focused on its leaders as prophets and apostles, as well as "rereading the New Testament with a stress on contemporary restorationism" spawned a number of new movements. These reform efforts emphasized orthodoxy in Pentecostalism while simultaneously disrupting the development of older denominations like the Assemblies of God.[89]

Latter Rain congregations were everywhere along Tijerina's migration route in large cities like Detroit and in small towns in the upper Midwest. George Hawtin, one of the founders of the schism, had denounced complacent Pentecostalism. In language strongly reminiscent of Tijerina's sermons, Hawtin pointed out that "all sects and denominations from Paul's day till now exist because of Man's carnality."[90] Accompanying an urgent theology about the fall of the Spirit in the latter days, it was common for Latter Rain evangelists in the 1940s to fast and pray in preparation for the

Spirit's outpouring, practices that Tijerina would take up at key points in his own ministry.[91] Tijerina's experiences of getting locked out of churches and demanding that congregations live by New Testament standards suggest he was influenced by the torrent of Latter Rain restorationism of the times. The Latter Rain controversy, along with several other important "heresy" issues at this point in the Pentecostal movement, survived in various sects and forced the Assemblies of God to revisit its original message. Whether Tijerina was directly involved with Latter Rain congregations is not really the issue; what is certain is that much of his invective against "the Church" and lazy Christians was not uncommon for Pentecostals resisting the pull toward the spiritual dryness of middle-class denominational respectability.[92]

Contributing to Tijerina's move away from denominational affiliation was the reconciliation of the Assemblies of God with her fundamentalist sisters. Putting aside old animosities between Pentecostals and Fundamentalists, the Assemblies General Council's vote to join the National Association of Evangelicals (NAE) in 1943 signaled their desire to move closer to the mainstream of American evangelical Christianity.[93] It was the Assemblies' capitulation to the status quo that sparked schism and seeded the Latter Rain movement. No doubt it contributed to Tijerina's condemnation of organized religion in his writing. He had entered the Assemblies-sponsored Bible Institute with all the fire of the newly converted, only to have the flames doused by the organization's move toward the center of American evangelicalism. The Assemblies had fallen victim to its own routinization, proving Weber's observation about the "continual decay of pure religion" and the inevitable institutionalization of sectarian charisma.[94] One lay minister who had led a group of California believers out of the Assemblies during this period explained:

There is no difference between our church and the Assemblies of God except that we believe that the spirit has the right of way. The [Assemblies of God General] council has tightened down, and are becoming formalized. Back East they are still free, but here many of the churches have tightened down. Educated ministers and college students who were stiff shirts came in and some of the people fell for it.

One member of this minister's congregation added that they had left the local Assemblies congregation because, "they set you down—they won't let you get up and shout when you get the spirit, and that is not right."[95]

Finally, it is also possible that the absence of the Holy Spirit's work in Tijerina's writing reveals that he had waited and hoped for the experience of the Spirit's baptism, but was in fact never "slain." The most visible mark of Pentecostal faith, glossolalia, may have eluded him despite his ardent faith, fasting, and prophecy. By the 1940s, de Leon reports,

> many members of the Hispanic Pentecostal church had not received the Holy Spirit Baptism. Some Hispanic Pentecostal preachers, in an effort to revive the desire anew for the Spirit baptism, began preaching "that without the infilling accompanied by the speaking in tongues, Heaven would be denied them." Many began searching their hearts for sin. Some prayed and fasted for days. The end result was good: many received it. But some joined the ranks of the "sanctified" only.[96]

Maybe without the witness of visible gifts of the Spirit, Tijerina turned instead to the restorationist and millennial aspects of Pentecostalism so prominent in his sermons. There are hints that Tijerina aimed his most stinging criticisms against organized Pentecostals, indicating that the "fruits" of the Spirit were superior to the "gifts" of personal Spirit baptism:

> The Pharisees had an image of flesh and idol: the letter (law); but they did not have the Image of God, the Spirit who works Justice and Judgment. For this reason Christ accused them, for they had abandoned Justice and Mercy and Faith: for in these things does one see the Image of God; and he that has these things does the will of God, and does good unto others, including his enemies. *Christ promised that all who kept his holy commandments, would receive the Spirit of God who would lead them to all truth and to all Justice. The Spirit whose fruit is charity, joy, peace, patience, kindness, goodness, faith, meekness, and self-control.* When these things were lost, the earth was divided by the false view of self-interested men (*hombres alquilados*). The

Pharisees were fools (*hombres animales*), and so did not see the things that were of the Spirit of God; being like those in the present generation, thinking that they had the law and the Spirit of God . . . (emphasis added).[97]

By the mid-1950s Tijerina was independent of any organization. He was free from the bureaucratic expectations of the Assemblies and the mid-century controversies over dogma that divided and subdivided Pentecostals. Thus he was able to boast that "I speak of God, and not from men; my payment (*salario*) is in heaven; and though I may not be receiving a [money] salary, this allows me freedom to speak, for we should always serve God without other interests: for my interest is Christ, and my salary is life eternal. Woe unto those who sell the word of God and exchange judgment and justice for bread that spoils."[98] For Tijerina there would be no return to any of the Pentecostal sects, or other denominations: "Why condemn the Baptist? Why condemn the Pentecostal? Why condemn the Adventist? Why condemn the denominations?" he had posed in one of his sermons. Of course, he knew precisely the reason: they were all hypocrites and deceived by false teachers.[99]

During his years as a "nondenominational" evangelist, Tijerina began to confront and negotiate the tensions between his world-rejecting theology and his experience as a Mexican American. Up to this point in his life, and despite a childhood full of reminders of racial inequality, issues of race played almost no role in his theological thinking. The Assemblies of God had been a multiracial organization from its origins. Although the separation of congregations by race eventually occurred, it is his poor, working class status that is expressed in his sermons' critique of wealth and ostentation. In the sermons racism or ethnic differences are absent, reflecting the relatively easy race relations in Pentecostalism where, at least theologically, "there is neither Greek nor Jew, circumcision nor uncircumcision, Barbarian, Scythian, bond nor free" (Col. 3:11).[100] In fact, race and culture do not become significant in Tijerina's work until the late 1950s when he begins to uncover the history of the New Mexican land grants. Kenzy Savage mentioned the land grant theft by Anglos to Tijerina during the 1940s, but it would take more than a decade for him to move beyond the universalism of Christian doctrine. In 1950 Tijerina recalls having been approached by Spanish-speaking members of a land grant organization in northern New Mexico, but noted that

> I didn't know anything about it then. I was preaching "heavens" at the time. You know, up, up, up in the spiritual world and I didn't care . . . I was not interested in earthly things.[101]

By the middle of the 1950s, however, Tijerina had taken the first step away from his preoccupation with "heavens." In the process of detailing the sins of a faithless nation in his sermons, he became convinced that he was ready to see himself and his followers through the impending final holocaust as the remnant of the true spiritual Israel.

From Theory to Praxis

Tijerina spent all of his young adult life searching for the best way to live out authentic Christianity. Even though he later publicly repudiated his career as an evangelist, his Pentecostal spirituality that bordered on the mystical had a profound influence well beyond the 1950s. By his own admission the outward disappearance of his religious life by the time of the Alianza's incorporation in 1963 reflects a deliberate distancing from what he saw as a defiled and fallen American Christianity.

> Since my people were in need of justice more than in need of religion, I decided to give up so-called religious doctrines and dedicate myself to their more immediate needs. There are too many preachers. People are tired of empty religious ceremonies, they [the preachers] are no longer like the hard-feeling warm-teaching religious leaders of old.[102]

As early as 1947 Tijerina had begun to question the value of his ministry and the ends it served. Walking out of a Dallas church one Sunday morning where he had been invited to preach, he was approached by a man who offered to feed the poor guest preacher and his family. Tijerina recalls this man telling him that "there's no mercy in the churches, no justice in religious people."

And he said to my face, "I don't like preachers, they take advantage of the people; what I think you should do is quit teaching religion, what the Spanish American people need is a Spanish American politician, you may be that." I learned then that deeds of love are found in men who don't teach.[103]

Although the strength of his religious conviction sustained him in even the most impoverished and difficult periods in his ministry, a growing awareness of his status as a Mexican American during a period of great changes in American society would become another driving force in his life. Eventually the combined and sometimes competing ideologies—Pentecostalism and race—would force him to choose between the two communities at the outer boundaries.

His unwillingness to work within the bureaucracy of the Assemblies of God and his suspicion of Roman Catholicism had much to do with his eventual rejection of organizations going into the 1950s. Equally important and problematic for Tijerina was the failure of Pentecostalism's focus on individual salvation over and against the communalism of Mexican Americans reinforced by and made meaningful through Catholicism. He would eventually forego the emphasis on individual salvation and search instead for community through his Valle de Paz experiment, his land grant work, and eventually in his genealogical theories. In the 1940s, however, and particularly at the end of the 1950s, mediating between his religious faith and a primordial attachment to language and culture became too difficult.

Yet Tijerina did find a natural affinity between Pentecostalism and his Mexican American identity. His religious life and his race both shared social and economic marginality in American society. When Tijerina eventually broke away from his religious bonds and focused on his ethnic community, he chose "Mexicanness" over "born again" as his locus of self-identification. He had always been aware of his racial identity, but in the theology of the true Body of Christ, racial identity was unimportant where salvation was concerned. As the 1950s wore on he would find it impossible to ignore the immediate material needs of his followers. Eventually he would come to see that the spiritual justice and judgment for which he clamored in his sermons had flesh and blood relevance in the contexts of racial conflict and the land grant struggle.

Tijerina struggled for another decade to recreate an authentic Christianity. By the late 1950s the power of racial ideology required him to reinvent himself and refashion the prophetic message that he had so effectively wielded in his religious life. His break with his religious career and his entry into identity politics would not come until the limits of his restorationist vision were met in his Valle de Paz experiment. *¿Hallará Fe en la Tierra . . . ?* with its doomsday predictions and world rejection stance appeared the year before Tijerina and a small group of families went in search of a place to build the perfect Christian community. The sermons in *¿Hallará Fe en la Tierra . . . ?* voiced all of the arguments for withdrawing from the world and trusting God to save but a small remnant of the faithful. Indeed, when Christ returned, he would find true faith only on a 160-acre tract in the central Arizona desert. When Tijerina finally turned to the things of the world it would be at the far end of the Valley of Peace.

4   VALLE DE PAZ:
TEXTS, VISIONS, AND LANDSCAPES

Pero a los pequeños de la tierra; a los que temen a Dios si quiero aconsejar,
porque ellos conocen la voz del buen pastor: decir ellos conocen cuando es la pal-
abra de Dios; y al oirla la obedecen, porque ellos temen a Dios; y ellos están
listo a hacer todo lo que el alto Dios mande.

      —Reies López Tijerina, "El Entendido Entenderá"

[But to the meek of the earth; to those that fear God I want to
counsel, because they know the voice of the good shepherd: they
know when it is the word of God; and when they hear it they obey,
because they fear God; and they are prepared to do what the Most
High God commands.

      —The Discerning Will Understand][1]

LIKE MANY VISIONARIES BEFORE HIM TIJERINA WITHDREW FROM THE
world. Leaving behind the years of wandering and preaching his ascetic
version of the gospel, he gathered around him followers who over the
years had come to trust him completely. Tijerina led them into the desert
wilderness and proclaimed their new home the Valley of Peace. Modeling
the community after the first century Christian church, he drew strength
from the primitive Church's example where "all who believed were
together and had all things in common; and they sold their possessions

and goods and distributed them to all, as any had any need" (Acts 2:44–45). Tijerina meant to restore true Christian faith in a world at the edge of judgment. The Valley of Peace would prove that he was in fact following the voice of the good shepherd and putting into practice his belief that God had chosen him for a special purpose. Experience had brought him to the realization that the world was beyond the pleas of his preaching. "I saw and heard so many things in those years that I was preaching from place to place that I can't remember them all, only the ugliness and hopelessness," he told Richard Gardner, "a man could preach the word of God forever and never change a thing."[2]

The story of Valle de Paz has yet to be told. Most of what is known about this short-lived communitarian experiment comes from the opening pages of Tijerina's memoir and in a few paragraphs that his biographers devote to the mysterious decade of the 1950s. Tijerina's account is revealing but is also an obscuring one, retold through the hindsight of two decades, political struggle, and changes in his religious thinking. The half-buried remains of the colony, now weathering in the desert, give no hint to the power of a religious vision that required whole families to leave their homes, jobs, and relatives to start the world anew. The Valley of Peace, like so many other utopian communities in the nation's past, was short-lived and quickly forgotten. Unlike the others, however, Valle de Paz is the only known Mexican American religious utopian experiment in North America. Buried in the desert, passed over in Tijerina's biographies, and ignored in Chicano history, this chapter uncovers what happened at the Valley of Peace, how it came to be, and why it failed. It is an extraordinary tale about the power of religious vision, the margins of religious experience, and the struggle of competing utopias in the American west.

Tijerina lists nine men and their families as his loyal followers coming out of the shadowy opening years of the 1950s.[3] Between his break with the Assemblies of God and his exodus into the Arizona desert, Tijerina and his family had continued to live on the road and on the edge of abject but purifying poverty. On occasion he would leave his family and wander off on his own,

teaching, talking to the other people . . . farmworkers, in the towns going from one church to another where I was invited. I would sleep under bridges, or in the open. Drunkards and poor people would invite me to their homes to eat. It was a training period. My beliefs were greater than my experience.[4]

Eventually the "ugliness and hopelessness" that he had spent almost a decade combating wore him out. It was time for him to put into practice what he had up to now only known to be true in his heart. He put away his evangelist's tent and with his closest followers began to look for a suitable location for his experiment in truth.

Calling themselves the Heralds of Peace, Tijerina and his followers purchased a tract of Arizona desert for less than nine dollars an acre within a triangle bounded by the small towns of Casa Grande, Eloy, and Coolidge (approximately fifty miles south of Phoenix on the way toward Tucson). Tijerina tells us that his first choice for the community had been somewhere in Texas near where his mother was buried, but the rich agricultural land prices there were prohibitive. Gardner quotes Tijerina's explanation that he chose "the wildest spot I could find so that we wouldn't trouble others and wouldn't be bothered ourselves." In his memoir he remembers that Valle de Paz was a way to rescue his family and those who wanted to "withdraw from the system of the 'church' and corrupt society." He describes how he and his farmworker followers spent a backbreaking summer in 1955 thinning, weeding, and blocking sugar beets in Colorado. Pooling their wages at the end of the season, the group bought the property. Still smarting from his dismissal from the Assemblies of God, the 160 acres of chaparral gave him the opportunity to create a community in defiance of organized religion. "I had fought with the 'church' (with all religion) for ten long years, trying to get them to take the side of the poor in their struggle against the rich, but had failed," he remembers. The Assemblies "threw me out and I was convinced that my struggle (against them) was useless."

Here in this desert my soul found the peace and safety that I longed for. We decided to call this virgin land, Valle de Paz. Here neither the church nor the school would be able to condition the minds of our children. We were far from danger, from temptation, from the influences of the monopolies, and we would remain happy.[5]

Acting on the suspicion of the world written into his sermons, Tijerina led the Heralds of Peace to their refuge in the Santa Cruz Valley's stark desert. Surrounded by dramatic saw-toothed mountains and isolated from their rancher neighbors by the thick desert scrub, they were far from the corrupting cities. Building homes appropriate to their poverty and desert landscape, he writes,

> Like ants, we began to remove the earth. Each family settled temporarily beneath a tree while each *valiente* dug a pit. From the city dumps of Casa Grande and Eloy, Arizona, we took car hoods and trunks for roofing our subterranean homes.

In addition to the earthen homes, they built a church, school, and a small storage facility. To keep the settlement afloat, the Heralds of Peace worked in local agriculture during the weekdays and returned in the evenings to the community to excavate their homes and resume their community life. Material existence in the Valley of Peace was a simple one. The women made all of the clothing and cooked in converted gas tanks retrieved from local city dumps. Evidence from the site indicates that the utopians brought with them the bare necessities from their former lives such as eating utensils, beds, medicine, and domestic farm animals. Food was shared in common. Parents were held responsible for their children's socialization and education. The long growing season in central Arizona translated into plenty of work, and the nearby small towns supplied any necessities that the Heralds of Peace could not make themselves or rig. "We created what we considered to be a paradise," Tijerina recalls. "Everyone was happy. No one spoke of returning to their previous lives. For the first six months we enjoyed the peace and freedom that we had been looking for."

Tijerina's charisma and vision of communal existence notwithstanding, the tiny community appears to have replicated a rather conventional Mexican patriarchal family structure. Tijerina's memoir, for example, indicates that throughout the life of the community the men made all of the decisions, and on occasion he would leave with several male valientes ("braves") to transact business for the group. Outside the Valley of Peace there was only mild interest in what was referred to as the "gypsy camp" over at Peter's Corner.[6] Despite its best efforts to escape from the noise and corruption of the outside world, the Valley of Peace and their charismatic leader eventually attracted notice. Drawn to Tijerina's personality and his growing advocacy on behalf of his community, outsiders, and in particular, Mexican and Mexican American farmworkers, local Native Americans, and blacks began to appear in the settlement. "Many of them revealed to us their problems and grievances," Tijerina explains. "Soon after helping the first one out of jail I was unable to handle them all. Mothers, fathers, spouses, and other relatives came to see me in order to get their loved ones out of jail."[7] Eventually, Tijerina would be unable to keep the outside world from his utopia; but through the fall and early winter of 1955, the Valley of Peace functioned as well as he might have hoped.

The Valle de Paz experiment is the first event Tijerina records in his memoir. That he does not begin with his childhood or the Tierra Amarilla courthouse raid reveals how central religion and the search for community operated in his life and how he chooses to remember his history. His account of what happened at Valle de Paz demonstrates that even as he actively distanced himself from organized Christianity, he was nevertheless tied to the narratives of the Bible. However, unlike his dependence upon the archaic language of and allusion to the Bible in his sermons that served to confer authority, his narration of the Valley of Peace takes as its organizing principle significant events in the lives of Old Testament patriarchs and prophets. Beginning and ending with Moses as his framing figure (leading his followers into and then out of the desert), the rise and fall of the Valle de Paz community is told as a recapitulation of events drawn from the stories of Adam, Noah, and Jacob. Writ large, Tijerina's story is about the battle between good and evil, between the God of justice and the demonic forces of injustice and the modern world. Here at the beginning of his memoir direct biblical quotation and style give way to primordial symbols and acts of creation.

Nowhere is the combat between good and evil better demonstrated than in Tijerina's account of his daughter's birth in the spring of 1956, an auspicious seven months after the creation of the community. The story of his daughter's birth and her naming happens in four short paragraphs but it is heroic in its symbolism and cosmogony:

On the 18th of April, the first inhabitant of Valle de Paz was born. I helped my wife with the birth, the child was born in the subterranean home that I had built with my own hands. I was thirty years old and this was the first house that I had ever built. It cost me sixty days of work, but not a single cent. When my wife gave birth (*dio a luz*), I took into my hands the child I named Ira de Alá. But when I stood up, I saw a rattlesnake wrapped around the headboard of the bed where my wife lay. I moved my daughter and wife away and killed the snake.

It had been ten years since the United States had started to manufacture atomic bombs; continuing day and night without ceasing. And I had already been convinced that the Church had damaged humanity more than any other organization on the Earth.

I knew that if there was a God of Justice, he had to be angry and very unhappy with those who ran the government and religion here on the earth.

And for this reason I gave my daughter the name Ira de Alá (Wrath of God); I was also very unhappy with the way men were running things.[8]

Religious myths and symbols arranged in binary oppositions of good versus evil pervade this short account. The snake, cosmogonic symbol of evil in the Bible, appears here in opposition to the birth of a female child named "Wrath of God." Suggesting the enmity placed by God between Eve and the serpent in Genesis 2, here Tijerina writes himself into the role of (pro)creator and protector. He is the agent of the serpent's defeat in the triumph of good over evil, bringing order over chaos, and implying the final routing of Satan by Christ at the end of time. The place of action, the subterranean home created through Tijerina's own hands is more than mere reiteration of sacred space and time. It also reflects a deep Mexican connection to the physical earth, traditional family values of patriarchal control, and a gesture to indigenous concepts of genesis and emergence from the womb of the earth. Here, beneath the profane surface world of humanity, out of the normal measurements of time and history, the incarnate "Wrath of God" is born. The child is not the incarnate Word of God that the Gospel of John describes, but rather, the enfleshed "wrath of the Lamb" from Tijerina's sermon. The Wrath of God is the first child of a new cosmic order born from the first parents Adam/King ("Reies" = King) and Eve/Mary (Maria). The cosmogonic quality of the story is also revealed in the Spanish idiom for giving birth: to give light (*dar luz*). There are two simultaneous acts of creation and salvation here: the original creation in Genesis with its promise of God's victory over the serpent, and its typological reenactment at the beginning of the new Eden, the Valley of Peace.

The magical realist quality of Tijerina's narrative about the birth of his daughter suggests that it is fiction, or an attempt at allegory. Yet its matter of fact telling denotes that the event is merely witness to an unfolding pattern of triumphant divine justice on the microcosmic, personal, one might say, daily level of humble human existence. The story is all the more astonishing because of Tijerina's casual attitude about the event. His response to an interview question about the symbolic flavor of the story was simply to remark, "Yes, yeah, you know, we found that rattlesnake coiled, on top of our heads. He was there inside of our dugout house. . . . Well, we saw it."9

"I the Lord will make myself known unto him in a vision, and will speak unto him in a dream"—Numbers 12:6

Seven days after Ira de Alá was born, Tijerina left Valle de Paz for southern California accompanied by two of his closest valientes, Manuel Mata and Rodolfo Mares. Unable to completely abandon the pulpit he had been invited by a church in Visalia to preach. While away a violent spring rainstorm swept over the tiny Valley of Peace flooding out its residents. Guadalupe Jáuregui, whom Tijerina had left in charge, called him in California. "The news was bitter," he recalled.

> Added to the injuries and scorn I had endured during those last years a great rain had now destroyed my home.
> "Your wife is living beneath a tree," Guadalupe told me, "because the underground [house] is full of water." This news crushed my spirit. . . . That night I could not sleep . . .

Now that his family was homeless and he was too far away to help them, Tijerina was forced to rethink the wisdom of his withdrawal into the desert. He was thrown into despair, afraid that he had led his followers into disaster. That evening, tired and distraught, he spent a fitful night sleeping outside his host's home. "That night I had a vision."

Tijerina's vision, or *supersueño* ("superdream") as he refers to it, changed the course of his life and has ever since led him in search of its meaning and fulfillment. The details of the superdream/vision are dramatic and vivid. Its symbols and images are drawn from the reservoir of his evangelical worldview and supported by the Mexican Catholic tradition of belief in the prophetic nature of dreams (*sueños*) and visions (*visiones*). From his handwritten manuscript:

> That night I saw in a vision the figure of a man descending near my small hut. After him, another descended and landed to the right of the first man and looked around; then, a third man, the same as the others, landed. They were seated on something that resembled a cloud and they spoke to me. My wife was with me and followed. They said that they had come from far away to get me and take me to an ancient kingdom. My wife interrupted, "But why my husband? No one else?" They replied, "There is no one else in the world able to do the work. . . . We have searched the earth and only he can do it."
>
> At that moment I asked, "What work?" To which they replied, "Secretary," and immediately I was pulled up, or rather, I was lifted onto an unknown apparatus that was [moving] so fast I fell back on my haunches. I could see clearly that I was flying; I was taken quick as lightning and set down in a dark pine forest. Others were walking alongside me but I did not know who they were or how many there were.[10]
>
> Realizing that I was in that dark forest, I was seized by a horrible fear.[11] I had never before felt such strange terror. At that moment I could think only of the grave; of how to escape and get out of that place. I ran quickly looking for a way out and then suddenly I was before a graveyard full of standing frozen horses.[12] One of them came to life and approached me. Without thinking I mounted it and it took me away. One of the beings on the apparatus jumped down and grabbed me at the waist because he was

unable to steady himself on the horse. The horse did not touch the ground and seemed to fly.

In a flash, I arrived at an ancient kingdom. An ancient wall circled this great city.

I was received with praises and applause. Carried aloft I was surrounded by a huge crowd. To the being that held me by the waist they said, "You have no business here and cannot enter." I wanted to get down, to be free of them, but to no avail. Upon entering the city I saw at a distance an old man dressed in loose white clothing that reached the ground. I intuitively knew that this ancient was the chief of the old kingdom. I was afraid. I believed that there had to be a mistake.

Finally, he ordered the multitude to let me down. As I approached the old man, the wrinkles on his face began to slowly fade and when I reached him his skin was like that of a child, although his great age was still evident.

Behind the old man were maybe six or seven figures of authority. These watched me with an envy and jealously that lit up their faces. When I approached the old man of many years, he said to me, "Speak that we may know who you are." I felt a respect mixed with terror. I replied, "Yes, sir, gladly . . ." but he did not let me say anything more. "Enough," he said and gestured with his hand and then took out a great silver key. With his other hand he pointed to the majestic kingdom and said, "You shall be over all of this kingdom," and added, "And over you, only me," and then he put the key into my hand. He then turned, looked me in the eyes and said, "Let us go," pointing far off into the distance where a great throne was set in the middle of a majestic place.

Then I opened my eyes. The sun was shining. Although the night had been very cold and I was outside, my body was hot. I thought this strange but was completely certain that I had a revelation, vision, or a superdream.[13]

Gardner records that Tijerina initially responded to his dream in spiritual terms "because, you see, I was still clinging to my religious feelings. I thought the dream was of heaven, the kingdom of God and things like that."[14] In the 1970s, however, Tijerina explains that at the time he was still unsure about the meaning of the dream. At first he told only his trusted traveling companions because he was afraid of what the others might have thought of him.[15] Later, when discussing with his valientes the possible meanings that the dream had not only for him, but for the entire Valle de Paz community, he concluded that the dream was responding to "the invitations that the people of Tierra Amarilla had made in 1945, 1951, and 1952." Eventually he came to believe that the ancient kingdom of his dream was New Mexico and the frozen horses the Spanish land grants.[16]

The importance of the superdream on Tijerina's life has been over-looked. Because of the focus on his land grant activism in the late 1960s, we tend to ignore the event itself and focus instead on its obvious connection to Tijerina's New Mexican activism. However, the details of the dream and the role of dreaming in his religious life offer tantalizing hints about the complexity of dreams, visions, and their relationship to his leadership.[17] The inventory of Christian images (a trinity of religious figures, kingdoms, heavenly cities, apocalyptic horses, etc.), and especially the dream narrative of the prophet Zechariah, are obviously employed here. Evident as well are the residues of Tijerina's daily life and the expression of his anxieties. In hindsight the surface dream content and message coincide neatly with what we know will occur later in New Mexico, veiled here in the metaphors and symbols of his religious life. A psychoanalytic analysis here would note the sensations of falling, flying, other intense physical action and movement, expressions of wind, water, fire, and quasi-human animals (angels? aliens?) indicative of a "titanic" or "big" dream that substantially altered the course of his life.[18] It is also tempting to play with the metaphors, puns, slips, and archetypes in Tijerina's dream as he reports it over the years in the hopes of unlocking the door to the various rooms in his mind.[19] We know Tijerina had an active dream life since early childhood that appears to culminate in this 1956 superdream. His deep, "false death" sleep at the age of four (where he dreamt he was walking with Jesus) initiated a pattern of "big" dreams extending beyond even this superdream. Later dreams and revelations would bring to him the meaning of the 1969 NASA moon landing and dark apocalyptic prophecies in the 1990s.

"Big" dreams, visions, and other supposedly supernatural, magical events are common among Mexicans and Mexican Americans. Mexican

American Catholicism originates in the miraculous appearance of the Virgin of Guadalupe in 1531 to a humble Indian. More importantly, she continues to reappear wherever people of Mexican descent reside. Mexican American children are raised to believe in "La Llorona," the tragic revenant who weeps for the children she herself drowned. And along the border the Mexican Day of the Dead elaborates the Catholic All Saints Day with the expectation that the dead souls of family members return to altars laden with gifts of their favorite foods and drinks left by their loved ones.[20] Although the experiences overlap, dreams, visions, and their messages as they occur among Mexican Americans (religious or otherwise) are not viewed with suspicion as they are by Americans of Western European descent.[21] In his research among various ethnic populations in Chicago, anthropologist Emile Schepers found that "the experiencing of 'visions' and 'voices' [was] a common phenomenon in non-psychotic individuals in [the Mexican American] community." Schepers concluded that the "Mexican-origin equivalent experiences [of so-called "psychic phenomena"] . . . seem to be more frequent and more taken for granted, and also, more importantly, to involve more specific and clear auditory and visual impressions, sometimes in 'broad daylight.'"[22] Discussing his dream with his followers afterward, Tijerina's experience confirms the "natural" place of such occurrences in Mexican American culture regardless of religious affiliation.

Tijerina's recounting of the superdream in his memoir (which probably mirrors closely his journal entry at the time) is a remarkable moment in his biography. Analysis of the dream's symbolism and latent meanings based upon either an archetypalist reservoir of symbols or Tijerina's singular psyche is tempting. More fruitful for our purposes, however, is to consider how this particular dream is connected to his Biblical literalism and his Mexican American identity at the time of the event. Unfortunately, the scholarly treatment of Mexican American dreaming (most of it from the perspective of psychological dysfunction or left uninterrogated as simply a part of the "folk" culture), is not particularly useful for understanding Tijerina's experience.[23] There are, however, a few other recorded examples of Latino Pentecostal dream/vision experiences, two of them from male Mexican American narratives at the beginning of their involvement with Pentecostalism. One of these is from Miguel Guillén, an important figure in early Latino Pentecostalism. The second is a short dream reported by the actor Anthony Quinn. Both of these two dream/vision narratives share uncanny similarities with Tijerina's dream, suggesting that there may be patterns and themes common in Latino Pentecostal dreaming.[24]

It is helpful to compare Tijerina's dream with the vision recorded by Miguel Guillén, an early leader of the Concilio Latino Americano de Iglesias Cristianas (Latin American Council of Christian Churches).[25] In his account of the rise of the Concilio Latino Americano, Guillén includes his 1917 vision experience that took place along the frontera quemada between Brownsville, Texas, and Matamoros, across the border in the Mexican state of Tamaulipas. Late one night Guillén was walking home from an evening church service in the hamlet of El Alta Mira. His Bible tucked securely under his arm, he followed the dirt road toward his home. He recounts:

> That night, the moonlight was very bright. After having passed the wooded hill and coming to the plain, I began to feel an emotion, like when one feels the presence of the Lord; each moment the emotion became more and more intense. Suddenly an inexplicable fear entered me; a fear that was unbearable, so terrible that I wanted to flee towards El Alta Mira to escape this fear. But thinking that I was too far to turn back. I then intended to run with all my might to Los Limones, but I knew that was also impossible. It seemed to me that I was running in circles but I was not sure exactly what I was doing. Out of such terrible anguish I started to pray and ask the Lord in a loud voice and with all my strength, "Lord! I cannot bear this, nor do I want to see anything!" I said this several times. While I was praying I saw at the top of the trees in front of me a rectangle full of a white milkiness, white like snow but without the sparkle, a pure stainless whiteness.
>
> From out of that whiteness, I saw someone rise from inside the rectangle and whose hair covered the face; like when someone sinks into water and then comes straight up and the hair spreads out on all sides; I could not tell if it was a man or a woman. Without knowing who it was, I extended my hand and took theirs and held it behind me. Then, out of the whiteness appeared

another being, the same as the first one. I turned to extend my hand, felt that I had their hand . . . and put it also behind me, but I didn't turn around to see any more.[26]

Suddenly Guillén found himself back on the road, Bible still under his arm, and facing in the direction of his home. Despite the experience, he remembers feeling "very calm and without any fear, as if nothing had even happened." He later remembered that earlier that same evening he had mysteriously lost his voice during prayer before dinner and wondered if that had been a premonition.

Tijerina's dream and Guillén's vision are not exact matches, but they do share the features of dark forests, nighttime flying objects, unknown extraterrestrial beings, spatial displacement, intense fear, panicked flight, and a postexperience serenity. Not surprising, both Guillén and Tijerina interpret their experiences through the Bible. Guillén writes that although the real significance of his vision might forever elude him, over decades of pondering a bizarre incident he recalls in perfect detail, he prefers to understand the vision through the Book of Acts (10:9–20). In the Biblical account, the disciple Peter has a vision of a large sheet descending from heaven filled with various creatures. The vision is followed by an invitation to preach to the gentiles and the speaking of tongues among those who hear him. Looking back over half a century and still trying to interpret the vision, Guillén came to the tentative conclusion that the two mysterious figures he saw represented the two branches of Latino Pentecostalism: the Assemblies of God and the Concilio Latino Americano. For Guillén, his experience was meant to fulfill the prophet Joel's statement that "the young men will see visions" (2:28), and he records that he could only hope that God would someday give him clarity on the odd occurrence.[27]

Unlike the Mexican Catholic repertoire of visions and appearances of the Virgin of Guadalupe, the Saints, and the miraculous mediations of the heavenly hosts, Pentecostal dreaming and visions (based, admittedly on two accounts written decades after they occurred) remain tied to the Biblical text. Less familiar (comfortable?) with the details of Biblical narratives, and certainly less centrally concerned with the Bible as sole religious authority for Christian belief, Mexican Catholic dreaming and

visions can and do range over the hundreds of years of saintly martyr-
dom, an elaborate mariology, and visually rich worship and veneration
practices. The Roman Catholic confluence of heaven and earth, seen for
instance in the complementarity of sacramental theology, locates the
authority of visions and miracles within a creation permeated by and
coextensive with the sacred. For Mexicans and Mexican Americans an
indigenous spirituality is also active and coextensive with Christianity, creating a distinctly Latino form of religion.[28] In this arrangement the miraculous is not only possible but essential to the belief that spiritual forces
populate the world.

But can Latino evangelicals support this view of the world when they
are saddled with the materiality of the fallen creation and bound to the
common sense Word of God? For Mexican American Pentecostals and
evangelicals, spirituality and the experience of God are derived primarily through scripture. Visions and dreams are permissible only when
there is a scriptural precedent (as with Guillén's interpretation), and if
they do not contradict New Testament theology. Consistent with their
repudiation of Catholicism and its visual spiritual universe, Latino evangelicals and Pentecostals take their dream and vision residues from text
rather than image.[29]

Yet dreams and visions do not hold as central a place in Anglo
American Pentecostalism as do glossolalia and healing.[30] However, Latino
Pentecostals and evangelicals like Tijerina and Guillén—as Mexican
Americans—are comfortable accepting and sharing with others these
experiences as meaningful and prophetic. Guillén's vision is different from
Tijerina's superdream in that he is at the beginning of his preaching career
and thus anxious to test the content and message against Biblical precedent (Acts 10). In hindsight Guillén is almost certain that his experience
previews the fulfillment of God's work through two branches of Latino
Pentecostalism. Tijerina's superdream, on the other hand, comes after his
career as a nondenominational evangelist, and so ranges freely across the
Christian imaginary, leading him away from the Bible toward his new work
in land grant politics. Five years later, for instance, he was convinced that
the beings in his dream were "angels of justice and judgment."[31]

An analysis of Tijerina's superdream and Guillén's vision would be
incomplete without discussing the alternative interpretation that both

men had a "close encounter of the third kind." In fact, Tijerina has left open the possibility that the beings in his dream were "interplanetary" messengers or agents.[32] In my interview Tijerina added the following details about the flying apparatus in his dream:

> I was picked up by this flying thing . . . like, it looked like a cloud. . . . I don't remember going in. But when I was in, I remember seeing little windows, looking out. And there were [other] people in there, and I saw a car [from the window] . . . and then the car . . . the image of the car went like this [pulls arm close to body] . . . from big [quickly pulls arm out and away] to— sshheeoo!—tiny! But in a, you know, a fraction of a second.

His vivid account of what can be portrayed as a trip in a flying saucer seems obvious. What is intriguing about Tijerina's account is its context. His superdream/vision occurs precisely when the post-1947 UFO phenomenon begins to accelerate in the United States. His description of the three beings as having long dress, loose hair, and no shoes, and Guillén's long-haired beings, are consistent with beings described in the late 1940s and early 1950s by people claiming to have come into contact with extra-terrestrials. Tijerina also admits that he used the term "angel" for lack of a better description, indicating that he was not connected to the American occult or Theosophical interpretations of such beings as the Ascended Masters or Space Brothers.[33] In addition, the combination of evidences that are common among abductee claimants are present in Tijerina's and Guillén's accounts: bright, blinding light; missing, or stolen time; a feeling of dread prior to the experience; frozen surroundings; and an overlay of positive feeling and reassurance after the experience.[34] Tijerina's memories of his earliest vivid dreams—walking with Jesus in a beautiful field, and the terror of seeing a driverless black car—are in fact common themes in the abductee literature.[35] Finally, the transformation in Tijerina's thinking from religion to politics, from preaching to activism, conforms to the narratives of contemporary abductees, many of whom devote their postcontact lives to pursuing positive societal change.[36]

In both cases Guillén and Tijerina interpret their experiences within what they would have determined to be in accordance with appropriate, scriptural models of dreaming and visions.[37] For Guillén, interpreting his dream as not unlike Peter's vision in Acts meant that any lingering doubts about the puzzling details (for example the mysterious appearance of the beings) were irrelevant. The stereotypical inventory of Tijerina's superdream, drawing directly as it does from the Old Testament prophets and New Testament apocalypticism, confirmed the legitimacy of his land grant activism as a sacred duty. Later his return to the prophet Zechariah would initiate even more startling visions. Ironically, it was this new sacred commission that signaled the demise of Valle de Paz, his own attempt at God's Kingdom on the earth. After his superdream Tijerina realized that God was not ready for him to find the perfect beloved community he so desperately craved. But until that realization occurred, he would try and rescue the community. Awakened from his extraordinary dream, he began "to see new things and to understand other things that before I could not have understood." Later that same morning he and his companions bid farewell to their hosts and drove back to Arizona.

The Collapse of Valle de Paz

The rainstorm that had destroyed Tijerina's home in Valle de Paz prefigured the colony's demise. Having at least one commission revealed to him in his dream, Tijerina's enthusiasm for his world-renouncing vision in the desert faded when trouble with his rancher neighbors arose and local and federal officials began to harass them. As if to signal this turn for the worse, a series of tragedies occurred that Tijerina read as dark omens. Vandalism by neighborhood teens on horseback went uninvestigated by the local sheriff, a child was abducted and raped, and an air force jet that crashed on the property drove an old woman in the community insane. A pregnant girl lost her child. Multiple charges of theft against Tijerina and his brothers eventually forced the leadership to consider abandoning the settlement.[38]

The financial condition of the community began to deteriorate. By May of 1956, the entire community was forced to return temporarily to the Colorado beet fields. In June Tijerina was in New Mexico with a handful of his male followers, drawn there by the connection between his dream and memories of earlier trips he had taken there. An acquaintance, Zebedeo

Martínez, began to explain the loss of the Tierra Amarilla land grant to him and introduced him to the aging members of the Penitente brotherhood. In his recollection Tijerina describes these men similarly to the ancient "priest" in his dream ("Old mestizos: the truth and sincerity shone in their faces . . . these humble elders had a holy, just and sacred cause").[39] The Penitente stories of how the Spanish Americans had been cheated out of their lands convinced him that perhaps Mexico held answers to questions about the land grants. Three months later he was in San Antonio, Texas, where he left Maria and their five children with his brother Ramón. On his thirtieth birthday he left alone on a quest to Mexico.

Tijerina spent three inspiring months in Mexico visiting archives and touring historical sites. It was there that he learned about ancient Spanish legal documents and held in his hands a fragile copy of the *Recopilación de leyes de las Indias*, a text that would replace the Bible for a time as his guiding text. He thrice visited the pyramids at Teotihuacan, the last time climbing to the summit of one of them and meditating on recent events. "I felt like a stranger on this planet," he recalls, "[a planet] so old and I don't even know the history of my own people, much less the world." That night Tijerina had another dream whose meaning he pondered for days: "I found myself among the magnates of Mexico and the continent. But the way we treated each other was with the trust that can only exist between brothers of the same family." Tijerina was now convinced that his mission was to work on behalf of his people.[40]

The final blow to Valle de Paz came from the U.S. Department of Education, whose agents had arrived to investigate truancy. Tijerina claims to have obtained permission from the Arizona Department of Education to homeschool the community's children, and they had devoted three months to building a one-room schoolhouse. But along with the vandalism of the subterranean homes, the school had been damaged and burned by neighboring teens. He argued forcefully with the state for an exemption under the First Amendment Free Exercise clause, citing the Mennonite, Quaker, and Amish exemptions to mandatory public schooling.[41] But this final attempt to salvage the integrity of the community's sovereignty failed. Even his attempts to get his side of the story told in the Arizona press failed. "We had left our home states, sacrificed our families and left the world in search of peace. And now they denied us the right to educate our children," he fumed. "We were forced by threat of jail and guns to accept a foreigner's education. . . . They closed all of the doors. I asked for counsel from the invisible forces, but there was no solution or alternative to the Anglo threats and violence."[42]

It is at this point in Tijerina's memoir where we see the shift from a theological emphasis on faith to a more activist focus on justice. He had tried to answer the question, "Will faith be found on the earth?" by building Valle de Paz. Now the question, "Where is liberty in this free world?" he wrote into the mouth of one of his valientes. Harassment by the Department of Education was an obstacle the Heralds of Peace neither expected nor were finally able to overcome. "They didn't bother us about religion, invite us to their churches or force us to their gatherings. But they wanted our children in their school. And they decided to teach them by force."[43] Besieged by powers and principalities beyond their control, the majority of utopians decided to flee the Valley of Peace late in 1956. A deadline for placing the children in local public schools had been set as an ultimatum by education officials. To stay and refuse would mean facing criminal charges. Conveniently, pressing difficulties with the local Pinal County sheriff's office over charges of stolen property found in the community made the decision to abandon the settlement an easy one. The defeated Heralds of Peace decided to leave behind adult members of the community without children to protect and care for the property. In the cold first days of February 1957, the experiment came to an end. Tijerina led a caravan out of the Valley of Peace and the remnant of the Heralds of Peace headed toward New Mexico.[44]

Larger Landscapes

The Valle de Paz community was a Mexican American sectarian utopian experiment based upon an evangelical millennial ideology. Notwithstanding Tijerina's later claims that the community was not religious, the model and principles directing the group were undeniably the outcome of his Pentecostal/fundamentalist suspicion of the secular world he had excruciatingly detailed in his sermons. By the end of the experiment, Tijerina's religious worldview had remained intact, but the world around him (the county sheriff, the nearby ranchers, U.S. Department of Education agents, etc.)

forced him to set aside his personal beliefs on behalf of the immediate needs of his followers. It is here in the desert crossroads between the metropolitan areas of Phoenix and Tucson, amidst a patchwork of Native American reservations and the northward migration of Mexican nationals in search of work where race difference and class antagonisms erode the spiritual vision of the perfect community.

Tijerina's move into the Arizona desert in the mid-1950s had been partially motivated by the growing nativist and Cold War xenophobia. Chicano scholars have summarized the crushing effects postwar changes in the American economy and culture had on Mexican Americans as they struggled at the bottom of the labor market.[45] Tijerina's wanderings through the Southwest, the Midwest, and across the U.S.-Mexican border brought him into contact with an endless cross-stream of bracero, temporary contract workers, and illegal *mojados* under constant surveillance and threat by Anglo labor unions and the Immigration and Naturalization Service's deportation programs. Tijerina's distrust of the "the system" was everywhere confirmed as he watched Mexican Americans moving into urban areas and suffering job discrimination and de facto racial segregation. To the south of Valle de Paz, the Mexican American community in Tucson saw a decline in their jobs with the Southern Pacific railroad industry and the rise in competition for low and unskilled labor.[46] To the north, a growing Mexican American awareness of the power of numbers began to translate into incremental gains in eliminating racist housing covenants, literacy tests for voting, and segregated schooling in Phoenix.[47]

Information about the work and economic life in rural Pinal County in the late 1950s offers insight into the context for how the Valley of Peace was able to survive from day to day. Valle de Paz was located in the western, agricultural area of the county, allowing the Heralds of Peace to find plenty of work in the rapidly growing cotton industry. The long growing season of the central Arizona desert coupled with the miracle of modern irrigation initiatives had transformed the largely chaparral covered valleys into one of the nation's top cotton producing regions. In 1956, the first full year of the Valle de Paz settlement, Pinal County was a relatively new farming region, yet it already ranked third in the nation for cotton production.[48] Ample agricultural employment lay just off the community's property, with some 350,000 irrigated acres near the farming and mining cities of Casa Grande, Eloy, and Coolidge. As with other agricultural paradises, more than half of the cultivation and harvesting of cotton at the time was performed by seasonal workers supervised by labor contractors and crew leaders. The majority of laborers, or "Drive Out" crews as they were called, were strategically housed at a labor camp aptly named 11 Mile Corner, because it was a convenient eleven miles or so to any of the three cities in the agricultural triangle. The Arizona State Employment Office notes that at the time the farm labor force was "comprised of Negroes, Spanish-Americans, Anglo-Americans, Pima, and Papago Indians." To supplement the fall cotton harvest an additional multiracial labor force was hired. In 1956, augmenting this diverse workforce was a large population of "bracero" Mexicans (3,794 in October of that year, only a sliver of the total 276,900 braceros nationwide that month) who were vulnerable to the vicissitudes of local and national labor markets.[49] Incoming bracero labor, welcomed as temporary workers during World War II, crested to an all-time high nationally the year Tijerina set up his community.[50]

At one point the Valle de Paz community harbored a group of braceros who came to Tijerina with complaints about the withholding of wages by ranchers and violence against them.[51] Beginning in the early 1950s Arizona became increasingly dependent upon bracero labor for the agricultural boom. Unfortunately, the weaknesses in a system that paradoxically denigrated Mexicans but was almost completely contingent upon large numbers of them as workers allowed for their exploitation because "short-run, carefully controlled labor migration" was preferable to permanent immigration.[52] Valle de Paz, a Spanish-speaking community skeptical of the world beyond their 160 acres, became a sanctuary for undocumented laborers. For many of them the path to El Norte crossed through the desolate Sonora desert along the lifelines of Highway 84 and the Southern Pacific railroad tracks that passed the northeast corner of the community's land. Making their way through the desert, migrant and undocumented workers and their families had to contend with searing heat and lack of water. In addition, they had to hide from an increasingly militarized INS and avoid falling into the hands of Native Americans hired as "Operation Wetback" bounty hunters who could earn $2.50 to $3.00 for each undocumented Mexican apprehended on reservation lands.[53]

The local economy's dependence upon a racialized agricultural labor force and the process of taming wild desert landscapes into disciplined and productive rows of cotton set the larger context for Valle de Paz. In some ways, these realities were simultaneously responsible for the physical survivability of the community as well as its inevitable doom. Led by Tijerina's charismatic power and propelled by the sheer determination of its members, Valle de Paz negated the need for a deportable, migratory, ethnic Mexican labor force and stood in the way of the encroaching vision of well ordered highways and city streets.

For as long as it lasted Valle de Paz served as a defiant refuge for the marginal. To the Heralds of Peace it was a taste of the coming Kingdom of God. For Mexican immigrants and braceros passing through the desert it offered safety and even life itself. Local blacks, some Native Americans, and others down on their luck sought out Valle de Paz's fearless and capable leader for material and legal assistance. The Heralds of Peace, however, were neither from the closely-knit Mexican American communities in the area, nor part of the mobile transient Mexican national agricultural labor force.[54] Their middle position between these two sets of ethnic Mexican populations (the ones that are usually the focus of study) surely worked against them at times, but it also assured them their isolation, served to reinforce community bonds, and tied them closer to their powerful leader.

Valle de Paz as Frontier Utopia

Valle de Paz is regarded as nothing more than a curious footnote in Tijerina's career from doomsday Pentecostal prophet to enthusiastic land rights activist. This view, preferred by his biographers and Chicano scholarship, however, overlooks a defining moment in his life and conceals the power of his community's collective spiritual vitality. The uprooting of families from their kinship networks in response to Tijerina's millennial call required not only the courage of conviction, but also the transcending of traditional, conservative Mexican American cultural identities and values. Following Tijerina into the middle of the desert with families in tow and with only the barest of material effects, the devotion of his followers through the obstacles over the life of the colony speaks to the intense power of Tijerina's charisma. If at any point in his religious life Tijerina fit the classical model of sectarian head, it was here during his leadership of the Valle de Paz community. The power of his restorationist vision amplified through his overwhelming personal magnetism and quick mind explains in large part why he was able to attract and convince his fold to follow him into the wilderness. Withdrawing from the world they awaited the inevitable apocalyptic end their leader predicted would soon come.

Scholars of religion since Max Weber have pondered the character of religious leadership in sectarian movements, and certainly Tijerina's rhetoric and restorationism locates him among religious visionaries in American Christianity. Like so many others before him, Tijerina perceived what he thought to be a better way for Christians to live in the world. He was inspired by the rugged ancient Hebrew prophets and patriarchs and found solace in the eventual triumph of the first-century Christians. These models and principles we see in his writing and in the very character of the Valle de Paz community. What is less accessible in the texts and interpretations is his powerful charisma, more than the sum of his physical stature, ardent faith, piercing hazel-green eyes, animated gestures, and electrifying public speaking. This *extraordinary* quality that so marked Tijerina's religious charismatic leadership of the Valle de Paz, however, is different from the symbolic leadership *imposed* on him by the Chicano Movement as we have seen in Chapter One.[55] Unwilling to abide by any authority other than God's—whether in dreams or in the ancient texts of the Bible—Tijerina rejected American Christianity, insulating his followers from the corrupt churches and isolating them from the corrosive Americanization occurring around them.[56] Like sectarian movements before and after it, the Valle de Paz experiment reveals the hallmarks of what Robert Fogarty categorizes as "charismatic perfectionist" colonies. "Such communities were charismatic in one of two ways," he explains. "They were based either on the personal sanctity of the membership as a whole and/or on the personal sanctity, special gifts, or power of a forceful leader. They were perfectionist in their promise that the perfected life could be led within the confines of a community and that the community was the way to perfection. Such communities quite often served immediate religious and spiritual goals within a millennialist or spiritualist tradition. Their concern for social questions was secondary to their concern for the personal and religious development of their members within an evolving set of collective goals outlined by the leadership."[57]

The Heralds of Peace, however, were unable to disconnect entirely from the world. Fogarty's description of perfectionist sects, in this instance, has to take into account the hard facts of race and the labor market if we are to make sense of what happened to the Valley of Peace. Despite their willful spiritual withdrawal from the world, and separate from any personal religious belief, the realities of day-to-day survival must have been rude reminders for them that the Kingdom of God on earth would be long in coming. Religious faith might have compensated Tijerina for his structural subordination in the real world as a Mexican American migrant laborer, but there were no real world gains to be had even when surrounded by his fellow saints. When any of the Heralds of Peace stepped outside the border of the colony, the world regarded them as cheap Mexican American labor. Clinging desperately to their convictions the forces of the world literally came crashing down on them as neighboring teenagers on horseback raced recklessly over their homes and burned their buildings. Thunderstorms washed them out, and state and local governments began pressuring them to conform. The combined disorder and chaos of the world eventually overcame even the power of Tijerina's charismatic leadership and vision.

The other part of the Valle de Paz story is the larger context of which, as we have already noted, corporate agriculture is only one facet. The immensity of the central Arizona desert, where geographer Stephane Quoniam suggests one could "look for truth at the edges of infinity," must be considered integral to the narration of the utopian experiment.[58] The Valle de Paz landscape with its cave-like pit houses and make-do structures begs for a type of salvage archaeology, or hermeneutic of space. Making sense of what happened there means accounting for the relationships over time between geography, built environment, race relations in industrial agriculture, and a people transformed through religious ideology. To do so reveals how this square of desert space was simultaneously "a social product (or outcome) and a shaping force (or medium) in social life."[59] The Arizona desert has always provided fertile stages for utopian dramas. The same year that the Heralds of Peace were digging into the desert earth, the Italian visionary, Paolo Soleri, was carving a prototype earth house for his futuristic community of Arcosanti out of the northern desert near the ancient ruins of Tuzigoot. Inspired by a philosophy that imagined urban architecture and ecology as a single interwoven process, Soleri's utopia would fall victim to the hard realities of an uncomprehending public.[60] A decade later and east of where Valley de Paz stood, the scientific visionary community, Biosphere2, attempted to transform the desert by collapsing the opposing utopias of garden and city by encapsulating nature inside a bubble of technology—protecting it, ironically, from the natural world itself. Like the Valle de Paz, Biosphere2's origins lay in the powerful visions of a charismatic founder, John Polk Allen, who placed his faith in ideas at the margins of scientific orthodoxy rather than at the margins of religion.[61]

Only miles from Valle De Paz, the remnants of the U.S. government's experiment in farming, Valley Farms, had also been drawn to the promises of the open landscape and the miracles of desert irrigation. Initiated by no less a person than Eleanor Roosevelt, Valley Farms was to be a modern agronomy utopia in central Arizona, a witness to the blooming desert. Valley Farms would prove the American agricultural myth of the Garden as true, but it would be completely dependent upon the availability of cheap migrant labor. The nearby remains of the Gila River and Poston Relocation Centers, that housed hundreds of interned Japanese Americans in the 1940s,[62] and the quilt of surrounding Native American reservations are also part of the Arizona desert heterotopia, posing the rhetorical question, "Whose utopia?"[63] Like these utopian and dystopian experiments, the elusiveness and eventual loss and erasure of Valle de Paz as a once viable, but now lost "living set of social relations in a specific physical setting" is captured by Allen Pred's haunting notion of "lost wor(l)ds": people, places, events, and conversations now lost to us.[64]

Like other utopias in American religious history known and forgotten, the tiny but valiant Valley of Peace collapsed and was lost to the transformations in the economy and local geography. In 1960 interested parties offering to buy the Valle de Paz property had contacted Tijerina. Discovering that Rockefeller money was being poured into the planning of a retirement leisure development less than three miles from the defunct colony, Tijerina paid the back taxes on the land and waited for a better offer.[65] Tijerina's utopian desert experiment, named as an extension of the natural world (Valley) and suggesting a return to Eden, was to be replaced by the man-made utopia of cities and economic relationships.

In its short and troubled life, Valle de Paz, a utopia of primitive nature and escape, gave way to Arizona City, a utopia of technology, bureaucracy, and capitalism. Poised at the southern edge of the expanding postwar Phoenix metropolitan area, Arizona City would incorporate the comforts of urban life with the slow pace and beauty of the desert, what Dolores Hayden defines as a "Fat City." Such imagined perfection, she notes, synthesizes the best of both an urban and a rural life yet fails to capture "the quality of either in exchange for the material benefits of both."[66] Pursuing this vision of dual benefits, Arizona City would boast: "a low crime rate," a "wide choice of recreation," including an "18-hole championship golf course," and "over 90 miles of paved wide congestion free streets." And to underscore the blessings of its synthesis, the planned community's promotional literature would entice potential converts with its easy access to "Two factory malls, over 85 stores" strategically located in the heart of a Golden Corridor between Tucson and Phoenix. [67] The final obliteration of the tiny Valle de Paz community came about with the construction of Interstate Highway 10 in the 1960s. The promises of Golden Corridor boosters left no room for the radical theology of the small colony. Arizona City conceals the wor(l)ds lost to speculative capitalist development and the domination of desert landscapes by the booming Arizona 1950s sunbelt economy. Eventually, the fragile desert between Phoenix and Tucson would be overwhelmed by an ever expanding horizon of fat cities and "edge cities" built for retirees and "snow birds" seeking out the desert Edens of Sun [City] and Leisure [World].[68]

Dreaming, Landscape, and Memory

Cultural geographers compare the social construction of landscape with the creation and interpretation of texts and theatrical production. These metaphors of the stage and the linear script can also applied be to what happened at Valle de Paz.[69] What geographers less often describe is the alternate text sectarian religious vision has played out on the stage of place. Even though it was viable for only a year or two, Valle de Paz was directed by a Biblical script and charted by a heavenly geography super-imposed over the county registrar's maps.[70]

In his memory, Tijerina is imprecise about the exact location of the settlement, hinting only at nearby roads and locations as backdrops to the drama of the landscapes that lay just beneath the visible surface and in the nighttime forests and kingdom of his superdream. In ways important to the daily struggle of the Heralds of Peace, Tijerina's heavenly land-scape existed simultaneously with and floated above the worldly theater of agribusiness, regional planning, and the demands of government edu-cation bureaucrats.[71] The texts that ordered and instructed Valle de Paz were ancient Greek and Hebrew ones not easily translated into the artic-ulations of capitalism and the post-World War II consumerist environ-ment being set up around them. In 1955 Biblical narratives produced the dreamscapes upon which Tijerina built his future. Laid over the narrative of Valle de Paz's rise and fall, the religious impulse of dreams and prophecy choreographed the Heralds of Peace's entry and exit out of the wilderness. In Tijerina's textual reconstruction of what happened at Valle de Paz, he interiorized the texts of Genesis and Exodus. He literally pop-ulated the Arizona desert with the mythic recapitulations of Adam in the Garden, Noah escaping the flood, Jacob's dream and struggle with the angel, and Moses leading his people into the wilderness and to the edge of the Promised Land. Tijerina's narration of what happened in the desert could only make sense through the sacred Biblical dramas he knew intimately and understood as scenes in a larger, meaningful plot. As Michel de Certeau might have described this process, Tijerina "made his voice the body of the other; he was [the text's] actor."[72]

When the last car carrying the Heralds of Peace turned off the dirt road and onto the highway leading toward New Mexico, they left behind a desert palimpsest over which ideologies of various sorts had written themselves out for more than a thousand years. Less than five miles away, the ancient Hohokam had built the multistoried Casa Grande as a fortress to protect their way of life against the encroachments of cultures to the south. Centuries later Spanish explorers would pass through in search of fabled cities of gold. They bypassed the hostile desert, but left missionaries with the native people there. In 1862 conflicts that were meaningless to nearby residents erupted at Picacho Pass in the only Civil War battle fought in Arizona. And in 1883 James Addison Reavis was settling into his mansion in nearby Arizola, having just filed fraudulent documents that proved ownership of the whole of central Arizona and part of eastern New Mexico.[73] The rise of cotton production brought with it the accouterments of American civilization to the region, even as it overlooked the exploitation of its racialized labor force. But like other rich farmlands in the twentieth century, the cotton fields eventually gave way to numbing suburban development. In the context of such overweening designs, Valle de Paz's impact on the land is negligible but remains in Tijerina's memory a "monument of our rebellion against the corruption of this nation."[74]

Valle de Paz has been erased from historical memory for half a century. Today it is mostly buried beneath the desert. Its borders are invisible on today's maps. What is left of the property forms a diamond sandwiched between the old two-lane highway and the newer six-lane Interstate that cuts cleanly across the desert. To the northwest and southeast, numbered freeway exits with self-serve gas stations and fast food restaurants only add to the anonymity of that particular stretch of desert. There is no historical marker or mention of it in the local tourist brochures. Motorists speed past the property, unaware of its existence. There is nothing left to see of the Valley of Peace, only burned out shells of the subterranean homes that once held the promise of a new world.

5 🐆 Mi lucha por la tierra:
A STRUGGLE FOR VOICE

AS I ARGUED IN CHAPTER ONE, CHICANO HISTORY SCRIPTED A MASTER narrative assigning Tijerina the role of an armed Mexican revolutionary. In this chapter, I examine Chicano literature for its production of movimiento images, myths, and narratives coextensive with Chicano history. Even as Chicano history imprisoned Tijerina, Chicano literature's assumptions about community and cultural struggle would require the erasure of Tijerina's memoir, *Mi lucha por la tierra*. In his analysis of the annual prize for the best Chicano novel by the publishing house Quinto Sol, literary critic Juan Bruce-Novoa observed that into the mid-1970s, "the criteria for canonization [in Chicano letters] was tied to political ideology in the attempt to mark out well defined Chicano cultural boundaries." Explaining that the Quinto Sol prize intended to "create a Chicano consciousness, if not create a Chicano culture," Bruce-Novoa characterized the earliest celebrated Chicano novels as "by and large those that lent themselves to allegorical readings of society that the movement desired."[1]

By the 1980s, however, Bruce-Novoa detected a trend away from the closed, controlled movement literature. As Chicano literature matured and increased, it reached a wider public and included several genres. If Chicano history was still bound by its cultural nationalism, Chicano literature appeared to have escaped its ideological origins. Such developments allowed Bruce-Novoa to declare an end to the era of ideologically restrictive canonization. Freed from its narrow definitions, Chicano literature could move forward, rediscovering works by relatively unknown authors and texts published since the mid-1970s.

Luís Leal, the don of Chicano literature, expressed a similar desire for the recovery of texts. In particular, Leal was interested in the retrieval of self-disclosing narratives (*memorialistas*) and their role in assisting a "comprehensive history of Chicano scholarship."[2] The proliferation of Chicano texts since the movement period, the reprinting and recovery of early and unknown texts, as well as the professionalization of Chicano literary criticism are all affirmative responses to the postmovement calls for an open, diverse body of Chicano texts. The appearance of popular but heterodox texts, especially Richard Rodríguez's *Hunger of Memory* (1982) and Gloria Anzaldúa's *Borderlands/La Frontera: The New Mestiza* (1987) are possible, so Chicano literary critics would have it, only after the erasure, or at least the reconfiguration of Chicano literature's borders. The broadening of the Chicano literary canon into a more palpable "Hispanic" or "Ethnic" one resulted in its recognition by dominant American culture.

This being said, the proliferation and success of Chicano texts does not necessarily indicate the end of an ideological current. What counts as "authentic" or "traditional" representations of Chicano culture persists despite the mainstream acceptance of Chicano writing. The lack of reception and critical commentary of Tijerina's memoir in Chicano literary criticism confirms that problems of exclusion and canonicity have not been overcome since the earliest years of the Quinto Sol prize competition. Indeed, the absence (exclusion?) of *Mi lucha por la tierra* from the critical scholarship on Chicano literature, like the omission (repression?) of events or details of Tijerina's life in Chicano history, suggests a strong link between them.

Measuring this silence is an easy task. A survey of standard sources on Chicano literature and autobiography produced within the ten years after the 1978 publication of Tijerina's memoir reveals a complete absence of its mention.[3] Only Marquez lists *Mi lucha por la tierra* in his bibliographic compilation of New Mexican Hispanic literature. Although given the marked differences between Tijerina's text and the conventions of the Catholic New Mexican Hispano literary tradition, the problem of genre and the memoir's connection to a distinctly regional tradition is raised. A similar review of extant periodical or monograph Chicano scholarship reveals the same absences even where analysis and comparisons among Chicano autobiographies are the focus.[4] The only attention given *Mi lucha por la tierra* even twenty years after its publication has been from Mexican scholars. Graciela Phillips's gracious review for a Mexican trade journal appeared almost immediately after *Mi lucha por la tierra* was released, and sociologist Jorge Bustamante lists Tijerina's text in a bibliography on "Chicano Social Movements." Bustamante, however, was well aware of Tijerina's memoir because Tijerina had asked him to write the introduction for it.[5] Tijerina's publisher, Fondo de Cultura Económica, republished excerpts from the memoir in Tino Villanueva's Spanish-language anthology on Chicano history and literature, but like the memoir this has received no critical response. References to *Mi lucha por la tierra* do appear, however, in nonliterary Chicano scholarship. Up to now historians and social scientists have made spare use of Tijerina's version of events in the collective history, selectively mining it for corroborative evidence but otherwise ignoring it as a text in its own right.[6] In short, Tijerina's lengthy text has been all but ignored by Chicano scholars. Most, if not all, information about Tijerina continues to come from Peter Nabokov's and Richard Gardner's books on the Tierra Amarilla courthouse raid.

An extraordinary example of the convenience these two texts provide is the collection of studies on the rhetorical worlds of the "Four Horsemen" by Hammerback, Jensen, and José Angel Gutiérrez.[7] In their analysis of the movement patriarchs' communication styles, these scholars rely almost completely on Nabokov and Gardner for their chapter on Tijerina, "The Tongue of a Latin Moses: The Rhetoric of Reies Tijerina." Not once do they reference Tijerina's verbal style preserved in his memoir. Mention of the memoir is tucked away in a bibliographic essay at the end of the book where the authors refer the reader to "Tijerina's recollections."[8]

Why is *Mi lucha por la tierra* absent in Chicano scholarship? The silence surrounding Tijerina's memoir in large measure mirrors Chicano historiography, expressed most visibly in the influence and popularity of texts like Rodolfo Acuña's *Occupied America*. Tomás Almaguér's observation that Chicano historiography has "unwittingly obscured the complexities of Chicano history" by adhering to longstanding assumptions about Chicano authenticity and tradition is applicable to the obscuring of *Mi lucha por la tierra* in Chicano literature.[9]

In the memoir Tijerina revisions himself through a framework outside an established collective Chicano historical memory. Compiled ten years after the courthouse raid, the memoir's overt religious language and obsessive and dark conspiratorial narrator clearly threaten the ideological balance of the Four Horseman trope. The threat to this Chicano mythology looms even larger given that it is one of the Horsemen trampling over the heroic, seamless master narrative. On the other hand, Tijerina's four Anglo-authored biographies penned at the precise historical moment when he is at his most heroic became the authoritative sources for the preferred version of the charismatic leader's life. With enough variation and slant among them to satisfy a variety of readers, their synoptic treatment of Tijerina's life and work relieved scholars from having to wade through his difficult memoir. Accounts of the Chicano Movement as recently as 1996 still prefer these secondary sources to Tijerina's own observations.[10] My argument here is that *Mi lucha por la tierra* continues to undermine a nationalist Chicano sacred history that has yet to be overcome.

Mi lucha por la tierra is not, however, the only problematic text that challenges Chicano history and identity. Other self-disclosing narratives have posed serious challenges to Chicano tradition and authenticity. In particular, Rodríguez's *Hunger of Memory* and Anzaldúa's *Borderlands* both jeopardize idealizations of the Chicano family, disrupt the mestizo racial synthesis, and poke large holes in the fabric of Chicano unity. Articulate and precise in their critiques of Chicano cultural values, Rodríguez and Anzaldúa have nevertheless been contained by layers of Chicano literary commentary. Ironically, issues of transgressive sexual identity in their texts pulled them into the center of attention when Chicano studies was transformed in the 1990s by feminist, gay/lesbian, postmodern, and postcolonial scholarship.[11] Eventually both texts were co-opted and promoted as examples of Latino literature's evolving complexity and multivocality. It is interesting to note, however, that the religious content in *Hunger of Memory* and *Borderlands* continues to be ignored or dismissed as cultural anomie (Rodríguez) or a hindrance to self-realization (Anzaldúa). I will return to these texts later in the chapter.

Poised against the ideological, mythological, and symbolic demands of Chicano history, it is not surprising if most readers of Tijerina's memoir agree with Gomez Quiñones's characterization of it as rambling. The immediate impression is that there is no clear emplotment to his memory other than to provide a singular voice on events in the past. Both the jeremiad style and circular digressions in the text, strategies Tijerina perfected in *¿Hallará Fe en la Tierra . . . ?*, are deployed in the memoir to serve a larger purpose and vision than simply reporting the past.

The transition from *¿Hallará Fe en la Tierra . . . ?* to *Mi lucha por la Tierra*, about twenty-four years, is bridged by a corpus of short and ephemeral texts including correspondence to government officials, newspaper columns and editorials, at least two open letters from prison, and political tracts. These documents, and in particular a pamphlet Tijerina produced for the Alianza land grant effort in 1966, "The Spanish Land Grant Question Examined," reveal that he was still wrestling with his Pentecostal restorationist worldview even as he was fashioning himself into an evangelist for political causes. As a measure of his thinking, the twenty-one-page pamphlet links his two larger texts, working forward and away from the moralistic and sober religious vision of *¿Hallará Fe en la Tierra . . . ?* and anchoring the memoir securely to the style and flavor of the ominous theology of Tijerina's Pentecostal eschatology. It is helpful to take a brief look at this transitional work, as well as one of his letters from jail, before moving into the memoir itself.

"The Spanish Land Grant Question Examined"

The Alianza Federál de Mercedes Reales/Pueblos Libres grew out of Tijerina's advocacy on behalf of the vecinos in northern New Mexico. Although his detractors would see the organization as a front for his personal self-aggrandizement and financial gain, the Alianza played a pivotal role in fostering a regional consciousness about the legal tradition that supported the land tenancy of Spanish-speaking New Mexicans. Tijerina's devotion to the land grant issue led him to scour archival collections in three countries. His dogged research produced proof of illegal land appropriation by the United States federal government in violation of the 1848 Treaty of Guadalupe Hidalgo and by unscrupulous Anglo land speculators.

As he tells it, Tijerina began his research in the late 1950s listening to elder members of Spanish land grant descendants. Eventually he also turned to the documentary evidence bringing to light the injustices wrought against Alianza constituents. Focusing his attention first on the Treaty of Guadalupe Hidalgo, he intended to demonstrate the legal superiority of international treaty law over and against U.S. federal claims to legal land ownership. His argument was a simple one: the Treaty guaranteed certain rights to land use and ownership by deed holders. Unfortunately, Tijerina was faced with the difficulty that Article X of the original Treaty, explicitly guaranteeing land ownership rights to former Mexican citizens, had been removed by the American administration prior to Guadalupe Hidalgo's ratification. In addition to the vagueness of the Treaty's explicit meaning of guaranteed "rights" in other sections of the document, a tangled history of confusing federal and state attempts at adjudicating land grant claims had to be learned, digested, and countered. Tijerina's ability to rise to the challenge—without the benefit of legal training or funded support—has forever transformed our understanding of land grant issues in the American Southwest.[12] In his study of the legal and historic documentation, Tijerina attempted to circumvent the limitations of the Treaty of Guadalupe Hidalgo by arguing precedence in earlier texts that appeared to legitimate Hispano land grant claims. "The Spanish Land Grant Question Examined," written sometime during the late spring of 1966, represents a culmination in Tijerina's attempt to argue the Alianza's case through the combination of authoritative texts.

The tone and presentation of legal evidences in "The Spanish Land Grant Question Examined" clearly derives its animus from Tijerina's sermons. In addition, it is connected to the baroque but somber legal text, *La Recopilación de Leyes de los Reinos de las Indias* (*The Laws of the Indies*), a sixteenth-century codification of laws governing the Spanish colonies. Tijerina had learned about *The Laws of the Indies* on one of his trips to Mexico in the 1950s and had traveled to Spain in 1966 specifically to trace Spanish legal precedent and purchase an edition of the multivolume *Leyes*. In his desire to reach further and further back in defense of Spanish land grants in the American Southwest, Tijerina found in the 6,500 *Laws of the Indies* the basis for arguing his position.

Why *The Laws of the Indies*? In his memoir Tijerina writes that the *Leyes de las Indias* "gave form and character to the Mexican people" because it had been, at least in theory, enforced in the New World for over three hundred years.[13] Throughout his speeches and writing Tijerina makes frequent reference to Books Four and Six of the *Leyes de las Indias*, sections dealing specifically with Spanish discoveries and the administration of native populations in the Americas. At the time of the earliest New Mexican settlements in 1598, the ponderous machinery of Spanish colonial bureaucracy had extended Castilian royal prerogatives over the new lands as a monopoly of the crown. Within decades of the Columbian encounter, the well-oiled apparatus of Iberian legal tradition had moved colonial administration from a single minister to the crown, to a dual administrative bureaucracy concerning temporal and spiritual matters. At each level of the colonial administration members of the Church hierarchy were matched with civil bureaucrats as a strategy to ensure that the religious responsibilities of New World discovery were guaranteed. For instance, the Spanish king bridged both civil and religious realms at the top of the administration, as he was both the pope's temporal representative and political sovereign. At the bottom of the bureaucratic pyramid parish priests were paired with the *alcaldes ordinarias* (local magistrates).[14] Thus conceived, the colonial administration of newly acquired lands and peoples assumed continuity between secular and sacred functions in the colonization of the Americas. In "The Spanish Land Grant Question Examined," Tijerina restores this medieval relationship in his appeal to both legal and religious texts of authority. Finally, and conveniently, *The Laws of the Indies* "read" like the authorized Reina-De Valera translation of the Bible, a rhetorical style comforting and reassuring for the ex-preacher. His frequent citation of Book, Law, Title, and Section from *The Laws of the Indies* rolled off his pen like Bible chapter and verse.

"The Spanish Land Grant Question Examined" is organized into five sections: an Introduction, three Chapters, and a Commentary. The Introduction lays out the issue of property protection rights as "prior vested and paramount." This entitlement to property forms "a basic foundation of our society." Unable to break free of his natural inclination toward Biblical reference, Tijerina includes in his argument a paraphrase of Matthew 5:

Therefore, every person has a vested interest in seeing to it that not only his but his neighbor's property is being adequately protected, so that the thieves will not inherit the earth.

Also consistent with his previous writing is the imitation of official, authorizing language appearing here as legal terminology, case history citation, and a "legalesque" style. Given his lack of formal education or legal mentoring, Tijerina's negotiation and deployment of legal writing is impressive. This rhetorical ability, or even "gift," is noted by all of his biographers and would be displayed more than once in New Mexico courtrooms. In "Chapter I" of the pamphlet Tijerina cites no less than fourteen legal cases and documents supporting his argument that the Treaty of Guadalupe Hidalgo guarantees the rights of Spanish land grant heirs as stipulated by the prior Spanish and Mexican legal systems.

Marshaling sections from the U.S. Constitution, the New Mexican State Constitution, Supreme Court rulings, and *The Laws of the Indies*, Tijerina's purpose is to overwhelm the reader with a display of legal authority. In the next two chapters of the pamphlet, he proceeds with detailed discussions defining land grant *pueblos* (townships) and the provisions under Spanish law for their governance. Arguing that the Spanish land grants were prior and valid at the level of international law in relationship to the Treaty of Guadalupe Hidalgo, he points out the obvious contradiction with the U.S. treaty with Mexico:

> It is well settled that there cannot be at the same time within the same territory, two distinct corporations exercising the same powers, jurisdiction and privileges. This rule is based upon the practical consideration that intolerable confusion instead of good government almost inevitably would obtain in a territory in which two corporations of like kind and powers attempted to function coincidentally. *This is bad government; . . . away with bad government.*

The Commentary section at the end of the pamphlet is marked by a strong moralistic tone. Tijerina returns to the tools of his religious training, persuading through ethical appeal to Anglo supporters and hinting at potential violence as the consequence for their lack of response:

The days of hopelessness for the Spanish people of New Mexico are numbered. The Anglos should read this handwriting on the wall and make allowances for it in their hearts and lives. For the justice and just cause of the Spanish people, is their struggle to restore authority vested in the community, the natural unit of society, and down with all Anglo anarchists. All Anglos have a vested interest in and a moral obligation to help these pueblos and their townsmen to regain their ancient rights and heritage. For if this struggle of the Spanish people to restore their birthright to its proper place in the community is throttled, before it can be realized, why then the people will lack direction and see the futility of it all and seek other roads to follow. The Anglos should not forget the "Mano Negra" movement in New Mexico earlier this century.[15] Vigilance Committees and venadetta [*sic*] movements are always terrible for both sides. The Alianza Federál de Mercedes has been endeavoring to guide the Spanish people into an enlightened course of action towards a solution of this century old problem of these pueblos. But if the Alianza loses the confidence of the Spanish people, and can no longer guide them upon a proper course of action within the law to recover their rights, then the Anglos should realize that the failure of the Alianza is their failure also.[16]

Here Tijerina threatens the reader with Hispano covert resistance. A decade earlier he had wielded the divine "wrath of the Lamb" over the heads of hypocritical Christians in his sermons. Now, however, his writing makes clear the racialized division between "the Spanish people" with "authority vested in the community" and English speakers, "Anglos," who are either "anarchists" or need to fulfill their moral obligations to the authority of history.

The closing statements in the pamphlet indict the corruption of human institutions. Having established the authority and precedence of Spanish laws over the U.S. and New Mexican State governments, Tijerina declares the system and the officials incompetent to interpret or exercise legal control over the land grants. By locating Spanish colonial law in the daily practices and understandings of the humble Hispano land grant heirs, the arrogance and disgrace of the American legal system's blindness to the truth is heightened. Finally, resurrecting his preacher's techniques he creates a sense of urgency, hammering his reader with questions whose answers are readily apparent:

> How many of the judges of these courts are required to possess knowledge of the laws of the Indies, which is the local law of New Mexico? . . . How can people have confidence in such courts, wherein the judges are not required to have even a rudimentary knowledge of the local laws?[17]

"The Spanish Land Grant Question Examined," written twelve years after the collection of sermons and twelve years before the memoir, moves from a closed religious worldview into the rough and tumble world of land grant politics. Tijerina's obsession with text-based authority (as the word of God, or established, prior legal precedence) remains at the core of his land grant arguments. He has only to unleash the authority of these texts through a literalist reading of them. Earlier in his life he had learned to read the prefiguration of the Christian gospel in the Hebrew scriptures, Tijerina now locates the truth of the New Mexican Spanish land grants in the most ancient of Spanish legal texts. His trust in Biblical authority is not diminished, rather the earthly authority vested in the *Recopilación de Leyes de los Reinos de las Indias* has supplanted it. By cleverly pairing the Bible with the *Leyes*, Tijerina not only doubled his claims to authority; he also reinstated the pairing of sacred and secular in the administration of the Spanish colonies. Although Chicano revisionist history would remember him as a revolutionary nationalist, "The Spanish Land Grant Question Examined" clearly indicates that Tijerina believed in his rights of due process and equal protection as a citizen of the United States. His respect for and appeal to authority present in the Bible, *The Laws of the Indies*, or the U.S. Constitution nevertheless appear contradictory to his critics and observers.

Tijerina believes that behind all of these texts is the God of Justice. He is here in the text expressed as moral obligation, the "general public's welfare" and medieval codes authorized by the Roman Catholic Church through the Spanish monarchs. Supporting the prophetic voice in all of Tijerina's writing is the power and sovereignty of the God of Justice making possible and logical Tijerina's shift from theological sovereignty to territorial sovereignty. Building a spiritual community in the 1950s now gives way in the 1960s to protecting and regaining the New Mexican earthly domains established by Catholic Canon Law and worldly legal authorities. Later Tijerina would combine theology with international treaty law as he probed deeper into his relationship to the divinity he would call Justo Juez, the Righteous Judge. He would also discover that the struggle to "restore" the Spanish New Mexican birthright went beyond mere legal conflict. But before he could reach those conclusions there would be more revelations.

"I, Reies López Tijerina . . .": Letter from Prison

Tijerina's October 1969 prison letter was written from the New Mexico State Penitentiary.[18] Writing near the time of the Alianza's 7th annual convention in October, Tijerina was in good health and in good spirits even though he was in the southernmost part of the state, far from his family and supporters. His court hearings and trials, however, took place in the north, and as a consequence, he was shuttled back and forth across the state and between the Albuquerque and Santa Fe jails from June through October. He was tangled in a web of judicial bureaucracy and appeals but remained optimistic despite having already spent almost four months behind bars. In fact, his letter has a celebratory tone in his description of his incarceration:

> But for the first time in my life, I feel a deep satisfaction and conviction that I am serving my people with all my energy and strength of my heart. . . . Here in my prison I feel very content— I repeat, very content and very happy because I know and understand well the cause I defend. My conscience has never been as tranquil as it has been during these days in prison, because, as I have said before and now repeat from prison: For the land, culture, and inheritance of my people I am ready not only to suffer imprisonment, but I would, with pleasure and pride, sacrifice my life to bring about the justice which is so much deserved by my people— the Spanish American people.[19]

The purpose of this letter is not only to assure his supporters that he is well, but also to reiterate the Alianza's position on the land grant cause. The letter moves on to a defense of the ejido, shared community land that accompanied Spanish colonial settlements by decree of *The Laws of the Indies*.[20] As such, the ejido was open to anyone from the pueblo for grazing, harvesting timber or taking other resources of benefit to the community. Predictably, Tijerina argues in his letter that New Mexican ejido lands are still protected by Spanish legal authority. He places their importance at the center of the land grant issue. "Without our ejidos, there can be no justice," he writes. "And without justice in New Mexico, our culture and our language will never be respected."

Following the strategy of "The Spanish Land Grant Question Examined," he parades his legal texts. Speaking from moral high ground, he argues that all citizens of New Mexico would benefit from the recognition of Hispano land grant claims. "Progress in New Mexico," he asserts, "depends upon the solving of the problem of the land grants; thus progress depends on the rights allowed the Spanish American." Responding to the criticism that he is profiting personally from his leadership he ends the letter pointing to his imprisonment as proof of his intentions: "My imprisonment has also resolved what to me has been an enigma—"

> the fact that many of my adversaries continually accuse me of robbing my people and working for my own interests. . . . But now that my people see me imprisoned and at one time on the point of dying in the gas chamber,[21] they are convinced more than ever that I was not and am not a fraud, that I work with goodwill and an honest heart for their benefit.
>
> Prison has made me feel more worthy of my people and much stronger than before in offering my life for the protection and advancement of their rights.

This prison letter is clearly written for as wide an audience as he could hope to reach. On the face of it, it is not particularly interesting or informative. Tijerina's optimism, his appeal to legal authority, and the martyr's tone are predictable and probably the reason the letter was reprinted in a popular anthology of Chicano texts in 1971. There is, however, another feature here in the letter that is absent up to now in his other texts. Scattered throughout the letter Tijerina begins to hint that he is moving toward a different kind of politics. Unlike his political tract written three years earlier, here there is no mention of the "Mano Negra" or vendetta. Except for a bravado swipe at crooked politicians, his call for justice now reaches across racial lines in startling statements such as:

> In spite of the fact that in New Mexico it is the Latin and the Indian who have suffered injustice and wrong, I must say that the desire for justice knows no boundaries of race or culture.
>
> I think that if another race were the victim of oppression, I would defend it as I now defend my people.
>
> We want to see schools and high schools in New Mexico where the Hispanic, the Anglo-Saxon, and the Indian cultures are equally studied. Only thus shall we have future harmony and friendship between the United States and South America.

Here Tijerina tempers his earlier position that Hispanos must reject the mindset produced by Anglo education, and widens his concern for oppression beyond the narrow focus on the land grants. There is a larger, universal project in the letter that extends beyond the northern New Mexican Hispano struggle. What accounts for this slight but definite shift toward reconciliation with Anglos and "future harmony and friendship"? Only a few weeks earlier he had penned an angry thirty-page open letter to his supporters in the spirit of his political tract, but without the legal trappings. There he hammered away at the injustices perpetrated against the Indo-Hispano people by the Anglo United States government.[22]

After his acquittal for the courthouse raid the previous year, he told reporters that he was "writing a new science" and that he believed that Mexican Americans could be the healing bridge between blacks and whites.[23] What exactly this "new science" was he did not elaborate. Now, in the late summer of 1969, as he sat in jail awaiting his second trial for the raid, Tijerina had a stunning vision/revelation giving substance to his quest. Quoting again from Nabokov's description of his last conversation with Tijerina during the second trial:

Tijerina grabbed at me and whispered in hisses:

"I tell you Pete. In that prison cell, forty days after the moon-shot, I had this dream, this experience, the most fantastic thing. I was laughing and crying when I awoke. I was afraid to reach out and touch the walls for fear my hand [would] go right through them." His arms were out, penetrating imaginary concrete. His hazel-green eyes caught hot points of light. His mouth widened into an enthusiastic grin. "You see, now the land grants are so much of my attention," he pinched his fingers in the Mexican gesture for *a little*, "but the Middle East is so much," he threw out his arms.

"I saw in that dream that time and space are barriers to com-munication, and I was shown a new language, a universal language, the fourth-dimensional language. Then I looked in the Bible and read it all in a new way, and it all checked out. The Arab and Israeli peoples are both the sons of Abraham. So I am going to petition U Thant to send me alone as a civil emissary to the Middle East and bring these warring tribes together."[24]

This startling dream occurs between the first, angry letter from the Santa Fe jail and the second, New Mexican State Penitentiary's conciliatory one. This change in tone might be explained as the simple difference between his intended audiences (the first to his Hispano supporters and published in the unofficial Alianza paper, *El Grito del Norte*), although there are enough differences between them to argue that his jail revelation reported by Nabokov accounts for the drift toward racial reconciliation in his second letter. Here in this dream of a new, fourth-dimensional science are the seeds of what he would later call "Brotherhood Awareness." Leaving a discussion of the connection between the NASA moon landing and a "fourth-dimensional language" for the next chapter, it is sufficient here to indicate that Tijerina was compelled to reevaluate his perceptions of religion, science, and the scope of the commission he had been given in his 1956 superdream. It is important to observe here that even though he saw a radical new physics, he was nevertheless bound by his Christian faith to corroborate this new knowledge in the Bible: "Then I looked in the Bible and read it all in a new way, and it all checked out."

Once again, he had opened himself to the Old Testament God who had spoken through the riddles of his "dark speech" (Num. 12:8).

As a transitional text between *¿Hallará Fe en la Tierra. . . . ?* and *Mi lucha por la tierra*, the second letter from prison combines the legalistic trappings of his sermons and political pamphlet, while enlarging his quest for community rights. He had traveled a great distance since his days of imitating the Bible's florid vocabulary and phrases. In the letter from prison he was already evolving out of the image that the Chicano Movement had erected after the courthouse raid. No one would recognize this transformation, however, until his release from prison two years later. In the fall of 1969, he could still afford to be optimistic as he awaited the court's decision on his various appeals and legal countercharges. By the time he would write his memoir, the most optimistic intentions of this "new science" revelations would be crushed by his experiences in the Springfield prison hospital. What remained, however, was a greater conviction that he had access to divine knowledge from God reserved for only a very few.

Mi lucha por la tierra: A Problematic Text

Reading *Mi lucha por la tierra* is difficult. Finding Tijerina's distinct voice requires some detective work as it is obscured by layers of expectation about genre, questions about its place in Chicano narrative, the text's editing, and language. The oral quality of the writing presents a nonlinear subject and is chiefly responsible for its characterization as rambling. Framing these formal issues is Tijerina's own understanding and selective memory about himself. How and why he writes must be understood through his deep reverence for the written word, and especially his dedication to the scribal task required of him by angelic visitors in his superdream.

Readers of *Mi lucha por la tierra* expecting to find the heroic patriarch of the Aztlán nation are quickly disappointed. Not, however, for any failure on Tijerina's part to reveal himself, but because the gap between Tijerina the icon and Tijerina the narrator remembering the past has not been bridged by Chicano history. Although the narrative follows a strict chronological sequence and is, in some sense, historical, Tijerina begins the memoir with the 1956 events surrounding the founding of the Valle de Paz, summarizing the first thirty years of his life in the opening paragraphs. The reader who looks for childhood clues and adolescent excess that might aid in revealing the man behind the lofty title "King Tiger" is instead plunged immediately into the swirling waters of an unconventional text. Because a detailed critical reading of the entire memoir is beyond the scope of this chapter, my analysis of *Mi lucha por la tierra* considers three problematic aspects of the narrative that work against its own reading: genre, the production of the text, and the underlying religious impulse that requires a virtuoso reader.

The Problem of Genre Expectation

The issues involved in defining and defending self-disclosing narrative genres (autobiography, as-told-to biographies, memoir) are legion, particularly when addressing problems of subjectivity, author/narrator disjuncture, memory, fiction, and historical context.[25] Formal criticism of autobiographical forms, concerned with questions of subjectivity and the predicaments posed by postmodern fragmentation, continues to produce, as James Olney has observed, "more questions than answers, more doubts by far (even of its existence) than certainties."[26] The vast production of autobiographical critical commentary, especially on those self-disclosing narratives by racial minorities, women, and other marginalized perspectives in the United States, is further complicated by the demands of a strategic canonicity accompanying the emergence of discrete, paradigmatic schools and styles of ethnic literatures (such as "Chicano literature," "Native American autobiography," "Black Women's novels," etc.).

Chicano/a autobiography, like Chicano/a identity itself, is the product of politics and the search for communal authenticity. Conceptualization of what constitutes Chicano autobiographical discourse was jump-started by the urgent need to respond effectively to ideologically threatening voices. Richard Rodríguez's *Hunger of Memory: The Education of Richard Rodríguez* appeared at the precise moment when the conservative Reagan administration began to dismantle liberal social programs. *Hunger of Memory*'s conservative narrator represented an affront to progressive Chicano ideals in matters of identity, family, Affirmative Action policies, and bilingual education. Rodríguez's text required that progressive political and literary commentary match his well articulated, formidable, and politically astute arguments. Even decades after its publication, *Hunger of Memory* is defused in Chicano scholarship by treating it tendentiously and reading it comparatively against other texts.[27]

At the end of the 1980s, Gloria Anzaldúa's *Borderlands/La Frontera: The New Mestiza* would again threaten canons of Chicano narrativity. But unlike the nostalgic and tragic narrator in Rodríguez's text, *Borderlands*'s critique of patriarchal, heterosexist Chicano culture was contained by appeal to the lyrical quality of the text. In addition, *Borderlands* celebrated a post-modern fragmentation of the narrator and welcomed a strong Chicana lesbian feminist voice into the literature. Neither Anzaldúa nor Rodríguez, however, come into their narratives as established, historic personalities in the Chicano consciousness as is the case for Tijerina.

The consensus on Chicano autobiography reveals that such narratives are shaped and controlled from within the context of community identity and the constellation of familial relationships.[28] How subjects speak to these issues, as reinforcing community ties or rejecting familial and ethnic community relationships, gauges "successful" or heterodox Chicano narrations of self. Canonized texts such as Oscar Zeta Acosta's picaresque *The Autobiography of a Brown Buffalo*, Ernesto Galarza's *Barrio Boy*, and, of course, *Hunger of Memory* and *Borderlands*, all wrestle with the core issues of community and family central to Chicano discourse and to mainstream definitions of autobiographical narration. Acosta's irreverent gonzo confabulation about his activist politics fits comfortably within the shared space between autobiography and fiction. In this way, it demonstrates the hallmark of autobiography's predicament, that is, the suturing of memory to a linear plot construction. Galarza's classic immigrant voice bears out the true marks of the autobiography in the transformation of the subject from childhood to adulthood, chronological organization, and the maturation of self-identity.[29] Rodríguez and Anzaldúa, on the other hand, reject the "normal" assumptions about Chicano community and family, but fit quite easily into the simplest definitions of autobiography as self-disclosing texts told from the first person.[30] Unfortunately for the critics of Chicano literature, Tijerina's text differs from all of the aforementioned texts structurally and from the narrative strategy employed by the speaker. Rather, *Mi lucha por la tierra* does not submit to any clear definitions of (Chicano) autobiography, historical narrative, or the novel.

Mi lucha por la tierra is better understood through the form of the memoir, and the memoir subgenre of Mexican autobiography.

Marcus Billson, who champions what he refers to as the "forgotten genre," clarifies the confusion between the sometimes overlapping autobiographical and memoir forms. While both types of self-disclosing narratives are concerned with viewing the world from the subjective "I," in the memoir the subject does not undergo the radical personal identity transformations characteristic of the autobiography or western *bildungsroman* tradition. Instead, the memoir presents the self as already formed. The memorialist, Billson notes,

> derives his personal identity, not from a sense of himself as a developing emotional, intellectual, or spiritual being, but rather from his posture among men, his role in society. If the memoir's story concerns the author's participation in life, then the memoir narrates the process of being-in-the-world rather than becoming-in-the-world.[31]

Referring specifically to the Mexican version of memoir, Richard Woods offers a similar distinction between autobiography and the memoir.

> The creator [of the memoir], perhaps egotistically concerned that his role in an historical event be recorded, finds the memoir with its limited self-portrayal as a natural vehicle. . . . Autobiography proper, the patterned reconstruction of a whole life from the perspective of age, incorporates a constantly changing self over a long period. . . . The key delineators in this difficult form are "entire" and the "changing self," and their impositions on Mexican autobiography relegates almost all of the examples [in my research] to memoirs.[32]

This crucial difference between the autobiographic self in transformation and the memorialist "being-in-the-world" is that the memorialist is unhampered by the continuing struggle to know and learn about self. The memorialist is free to interpret, reconstruct, and fashion the past from the privileged vantage point of a complete and utterly confident hindsight. Billson refers to this narrative strategy as a moral act of "reconfronting and reappraising" memories, which in turn "hypostisizes the very act of bearing witness to them, affirming their significance and meaning for the future."[33] From such a supervisory position the memorialist "defamiliarizes" history, retelling it so that the "common experience of the past" is transformed and made new in ways that satisfy the narrator's memory and purposes.

The memoir as a literary form is usually understood as a narrative that recounts past events, eras, or great historic figures. However, it continues to be overlooked in the critical literature because the narrative voice in relationship to "objective" history is unreliable. In addition, the memoir fails to capture the reader's interest because it denies the naive voice of the autobiographic subject viewed as coming into self-awareness. Nevertheless, with its ability to look back at the past with a particular bias and moral vision of the world, the memoir becomes a powerful vehicle for someone like Tijerina who leaps out of *Mi lucha por la tierra*'s pages fully formed and keen to the task of reordering history. And although the past is motivated by a representation of history that is "sometimes an argument, always a personal interpretation,"[34] the subjective intentionality does not preclude a careful, documented, and strategic substantiation of historical events. The past, as reconfronted and reappraised in the memoir, is not, however, necessarily a false one.

It is tantalizing to learn that the memoir is the predominant form of self-account chosen by Mexican writers. Employing Billson's criteria, Richard Woods notes that 60 percent (201) of 332 Mexican texts he examined fall squarely in the memoir category.[35] For instance, José Vasconcelos' monumental *Ulises Criollo*, considered the example of the Mexican autobiographical form *par excellence*, is in Woods' estimation much closer in character and to the task of the memoir. According to Woods, three out of the four volumes of Vasconcelos' autobiography deploy the vantage point of the memoir as "a vehicle for personal invective against enemies and for racial and cultural ideas, center[ing] on the external world," a description that also precisely describes Tijerina's text. Why the memoir form is so prevalent in Mexican texts, Woods concludes, is because "a formidable obstacle arrests the flourishing of autobiography—the Mexican character." As a group, he contends, there is a common feature in Mexican self-disclosing texts that "suggests a respect for family and privacy and a tendency to idealize childhood or a glossing over of family life and then a brusque leap into the public scene."[36] Woods's assessment of "the Mexican character" aside, applying the criteria and conclusions proposed by Billson and Woods about the memoir genre to even the most casual reading of *Mi lucha por la tierra* confirms its place as perhaps the premier example of the Mexican American/Chicano/a memoir.

In the delineation between the formal paradigm of the autobiography and the memoir, the standard genealogy of the autobiography in the West is traced back to the *Confessions* of Augustine. The need for reconciling the self and divinity in Augustine's text becomes the cause for the journey through life's stages and eventual return/conversion back to God. Augustine's central question for the autobiographical genre is "How can the self know itself?" This quest by humanity separated from God is the origin of the autobiographical impulse for writers in the west for 1,500 years afterward. Unfortunately, critics of the genre tend to downplay the presence of God in Augustine's text and the essentially religious meanings behind the actions of conversion and confession.[37] From a modern, western perspective, Augustine's search for knowledge of God and self are collapsed into an utterly singular drive for a self divorced from its submission to God in the life of faith. God having been removed as the object or agent of the search for self, the *Confessions* moves beyond mere conversion narrative, making God in the image of man and consequently opening the door to individual, autonomous human being/becoming. Even the recuperation of God as the agent of transformation eventually succumbs to the triumph of self. For example, in Robert Elbaz's masterful analysis of autobiography in the West, he concludes that "the anthropomorphism and personalisation of God open the door to a definition of man as a relatively independent agent capable of rational decision. God is responsible for every individual in his uniqueness, and watches his every act from above. The achievement of confession itself requires a process of interiorisation, the emergence of the awareness of self."[38] But is it always necessary to expel God after achieving self-awareness?

Thomas Couser's description of the "prophetic mode" in American autobiography and memoir helps us understand Tijerina's text. This view of autobiography retains the narrator's relationship to the sacred, which in turn infuses the text with authority. Speaking from this secure location, the narrator is free to expound, even preach to the reader and argue that the past is contained within a larger sacred history.[39] Interpreted through these considerations, it is clear that Tijerina's text conforms in some measure to American literary types while at the same time standing squarely in the Mexican memoir tradition. In addition, Tijerina's "prophetic mode" is given form through the fundamentalist jeremiad of his earlier writing.[40] *Mi lucha por la tierra*'s overlapping genres and prophetic quality is expressed, for example, in his announcement of judgment against the United States (or other corporate bodies) and the threat of apocalypse. Such rhetoric reveals an exaggerated, almost swaggering prophetic voice that is reinforced through a confident memoir subjectivity.

> My advice for the people is to seek out and demand leaders that are sons of the land, wise in the laws and values of the land, powerful in the knowledge of the land. In the end, ideologies and politics are superfluous. And especially in our times, when politics and politicians have become perverted to the point that there are no solutions. Already the people have lost faith in their political representatives and in a matter of days they will be vomited out.
>
> Like rebellious children, we must return to the land, as was written by wise ancient ones. And already we are seeing people returned to their ancient inheritances. The false and vain power of the White House has chosen to ignore our rights and pretends that it does not have to pay us any attention, supposing that only one crazy person accuses the United States of having stolen the land of our fathers: for this they committed Reies Tijerina to the Springfield, Missouri prison; for being crazy. But the crazy and psychotic one is in the White House.
>
> The time has ended for Anglosaxon lies. The entire world at last has overtaken the Anglo. Ever since the White House returned the land back to the inhabitants of Taos Pueblo, New Mexico, in October 1970, the people have demonstrated more faith in their property rights.[41]

Repeating precisely the formulas of his 1950s sermons, Tijerina returns to the preacher's strategy of his first career. Historic events and dates are offered as proof of the invisible God of Justice working on behalf of the people. But here it is not Tijerina's Pentecostal God of the Old Testament, rather God as Judge revealed in the legal protections of international law set in place by ancient Spanish law and the Treaty of Guadalupe Hidalgo.

Reminiscent of his sermon "The Provokers of Judgment," Tijerina writes himself into the narrative as the chosen target of evil forces, criticized and punished for his revelations and indictments. In the prophetic memoir he is granted the privilege of knowing that the failures and successes of his life have all been part of a larger scheme of divine justice. Although both his collection of sermons and the memoir emerge out of the same religious impulse, the memoir form allows him to interpret history as proof of God's unfolding justice and confidently write himself into the center of the drama. In *Mi lucha por la tierra* Tijerina combines the arsenals of his earlier texts: Scripture, legal secular authority, and divine revelation in his substantiation of history for the reader. Documents, correspondence, specific dates for media coverage, book titles, and diary entries are all inserted into the text substantiating his voice and anchoring his text to real events and people.

This manipulation of objective documentation in the memoir, particularly by political and public figures, is not unusual and in fact contributes to the narrator's role as a type of historian. This accumulated background material, Billson argues, establishes the narrator "as a repository of fact, a tireless investigator and sorter, a sober and impartial judge—a man in short, of authority, who is entitled not only to present the facts as he has established them but to comment on them, to tell the reader what to think and even to suggest what he should do." As a kind of historian the memoir's narrator, however, fails the task precisely because the "memoir-writer's self discipline and investigative methodology rarely conform to the rigorous standards expected in modern historiography" despite claims or assumptions of having done so.[42] Thus the genre's highly subjective representation of memory is, ironically, enhanced in the accumulation and presentation of documentary evidences. The authority of such proof, of course, is mediated by the particularity and quirkiness of the narrative voice. Thus, in the above quote, Tijerina offers as evidence the "wisdom of the wise ancient ones" and the 1970 return of Blue Lake to the Taos people, condensing into that example a long legal battle over indigenous sovereignty and self-determination. Veiled in the statement "many people returned to their ancient inheritances" is Tijerina's appeal to fulfilled Biblical prophecy concerning the restoration of Israel, a theme he later imports into his racialized concept of the Spanish American as Christian-Israelite.

Tijerina's text fails if it is compared against the demands of the auto-biographical genre and classic Chicano texts like Galarza's *Barrio Boy* or Rodríguez's *Hunger of Memory*. It lacks a developing subject who reaches out into the world of family, racism, labor, education, and politics (concerns prevalent in Chicano autobiographies). The "secretary" quality of *Mi lucha por la tierra* (in the replication of other documents and genres inside the text) and the visible hand of God destabilize the narrative. Tijerina's prophetic memoir is pulled between the world of human beings (letters, journal entries, newspaper citations, etc.) and the fundamentalist, yet mystical relationship between narrator and divinity, features not expected or usual, or even welcome in Chicana/o autobiography.

Producing the Text

The creation of *Mi lucha por la tierra* reveals Tijerina's ritualistic attitude toward the act of writing. There are, in addition, features of the text that will continue to prevent access for most readers. Nabokov reports that Tijerina transcribed his memories "in three months of marathon hand-writing that began with a ritualized thirty-day fast." Tijerina, however, indicates that he planned to complete the manuscript on his fiftieth birthday, 21 September 1976, and that he began writing on the New Year's Day previous.[43] Noting that he had reached his "Jubilee" year, he reached back into the Hebrew scriptures and initiated his memoirs as part of the Jubilee emancipation of Mexican American consciousness, dedicating his work to "Justo Juez de Jueces" (the Just Judge of Judges)."[44] The Jubilee Year, defined as "seven sabbaths of years—seven times, seven years—so that the seven sabbaths of years amount to a period of forty-nine years," was a time for the emancipation of slaves, returning land to former owners, and a year without sowing or reaping (Lev. 25: 8–54). Tijerina chose to write his memoir during his Jubilee year because it coincided with the themes of emancipation and the return of land. The idea for his book had been with him as early as his Alianza years, but he reports that "I knew I had to be tested more, and had to learn more, I had to mature." It was during his terrifying twenty-one month prison hospital ordeal when he realized it was imperative he write something for fear of losing his life. "While I was in prison, there were three attempts on my life," he recounted in an interview, "and that kind of encouraged me to speed up. I could be killed at any time and I would write nothing." Fearing physical harm and that his life and the motivation behind his work would be misunderstood or that "[s]omebody else would be writing for me, or interpreting my life . . ." he had always intended to tell his own version of his tumultuous life and so determine how history would remember him.[45]

The decision to commit his memories to writing was also influenced by Jaime Casillas's 1975 Spanish-language commercial film *Chicano*, a fictionalized version of Tijerina's life. During Tijerina's consultation with Casillas in Mexico in the last months of 1975, he presented then Mexican President Luís Echeverría with an appeal for Mexican assistance on behalf of Mexican Americans. It was at this time the president of Mexico asked Tijerina to write his memoir.[46] An offer by the prestigious Mexican publishing house Fondo de Cultura Económica to work with the manuscript and his association with Mexican scholar Jorge Bustamante sealed his decision. There had been at least one previous offer by an English language publisher for Tijerina's story, but he was uneasy and unwilling to reveal the details of his life in English.[47] His hesitation was partly due to a lack of confidence about writing a sustained narrative in the English language, but more so, an English version he felt would have made his accusations and naming of names accessible to his enemies. Writing his narrative in Spanish, "would keep a great number of my persecutors . . . off guard. They wouldn't know for sure exactly . . . I mean in Spanish— maybe one or two read Spanish, but not all. So that was a help, too. See, I would advance the information of the organized terror against my life and my family and the land grants to my people first, you know, [before] giving it to the opposition." Writing in Spanish was a strategic move designed to forestall his Anglo detractors: "See, I wanted that all the time.

I wanted my people to learn first. So if I was killed by the opposition, at least my people had plenty of knowledge, information."[48]

The practical motivations behind *Mi lucha por la tierra* are consistent with Tijerina's view of himself. Recall how he establishes himself as the protagonist in the struggle between good and evil in the account of Ira de Alá's birth. In the memoir dark conspiratorial forces consistently work to undermine the beleaguered remnant of righteous and persecuted defenders of justice. In the narrative the most difficult features that readers must overcome are Tijerina's constant repetition of accusations, continuous reminders of harm done to himself and his family, and the sermonizing quality of his insistence that Mexican Americans defend their rights and know their historical privilege. This haranguing effect, responsible for the criticism that the text is discursive, however, is a deliberate strategy. Tijerina's homiletic training and experience from his days as a Pentecostal evangelist are put to good use here. That is, Tijerina's seemingly endless denunciations against his foes and his constant chastising are practical preachers' devices meant to reach a subaltern Mexican American readership. Learning through his Alianza work that "I had to repeat like a father, a mother to a child . . . so that it would stay in their mind," Tijerina "developed that habit" of repeating his claims and main points:

> So by the time I wrote, I had developed that habit already. You know, more than ten years working with my people. I had to, I think . . . no, from '56, '66, '76—that's twenty years! And so, I was writing a very simple story for the Spanish speaking people of Texas, New Mexico, California . . . I was all the time and the same time trying to deliver to them not only their property rights, you know, but also their cultural rights. And that's why I had to tolerate and kept on, because I knew that they were going to read this book. And if you notice, it's close to 550 pages. It's a big book.[49]

His publisher told him that the four-volume handwritten manuscript was too repetitious. Tijerina argued that his text was aimed at a particular audience but accepted the inevitability of the editor's blue pencil. Likening his work to those of other teachers who struggled under similar misunderstandings, he observes that "Mohammed, and Jesus, and Moses, and others, they had the same thing. They had to repeat and repeat. They had to tackle, confront that problem."[50]

The published Spanish-language text is divided into seven chapters, covering the twenty years of his "struggle with the White House." The first chapter begins with the year 1956 where he recounts the circumstances around the Valle de Paz experiment. Except for the last chapter ("La CIA"), the narrative is arranged chronologically and details the year-to-year events and conflicts between Tijerina, the Alianza, and treacherous government bodies and officials. The core of the memoir—taking up more than half of the text—"Mi Vida de Fugitivo" (My Life Underground), covers Tijerina's most politically active years from 1957–1970. Chapters "1974," "1975," and "1976" replicate entries from Tijerina's copious journals that he has kept on a daily basis since the late 1950s.[51]

The chapter divisions and subdivisions in *Mi lucha por la tierra* were imposed by the publisher and do not always coincide with the divisions in Tijerina's original manuscript. Unfortunately, the heavy-handed editing of the original four-volume manuscript resulted in a published version markedly different from Tijerina's handwritten version. A comparison of the opening paragraphs shows, for example, the standardization of Tijerina's colloquial Spanish, the omission of adjectives, and even the omission of persons involved in the Valle de Paz effort. The editorial decision to translate the vernacular "Chicano" Spanish into a universal Castilian changed the narrator's voice, giving it a pompous quality. Yet, Tijerina's distinct, if moralistic, voice does manage to leak through the hundreds of changes. Unfortunately, the changes disguise the urgency and oral quality of Tijerina's intention.[52]

The summarizing chapter, "La CIA," departs from the previous journal entry style chapters. It constitutes Tijerina's reflection on the meaning and purpose of the memoir itself. He ends the narrative with a glimmer of hope in the electoral defeat of his old nemesis, Senator Joseph Montoya, in 1976. Here in this final chapter he summarizes the epic conflict between his people ("Mi pueblo") and the nefarious United States government represented by the covert and sinister Central Intelligence Agency. The chapter is a full circle return to the worldview of his earliest Pentecostal days. Now, within the context of national politics, Tijerina takes up the prophetic gestures of *¿Hallará Fe en la Tierra . . . ?*, exhorting, encouraging, and warning his people in a Spartan, moralistic tone:

> The heads of this nation do not know honor; this is the truth. Naturally, man feels proud and strives to demonstrate the honor of his word and his deeds, but the Anglosaxon of my time has completely lost any sense of decency.
>
> I am frightened that a large part of my brothers are mentally products of the Anglo. Although they call themselves, "Chicanos," "raza," etc., they continue to be a product of the oppressor. Their speech, sexual habits, behavior, and drugs point to their being Anglo products.
>
> If we want to redeem our heritage and our property, we first have to save ourselves from the Anglosaxon influence; we have to save ourselves from the oppressor.
>
> In the last debate, Jimmy Carter accused [Gerald] Ford of not having cared to speak with Alexander Solzhenitsyn, the Russian. As if this Russian was more important than the 15 million Indo-Hispanos in the American Southwest.[53]

Tijerina's sober conclusion, that "the salvation of my people depends on the ruin and destruction of the Anglosaxon government" leads him out of his memoir. In turn, his future work would take up his racialized theological speculations on the ultimate meanings of Latino peoplehood. He would also return to the apocalypticism planted back in the 1950s and nurtured here in the dark and claustrophobic indictments of the United States.

The Religious Impulse of the Memoir

The memoir opens, as we have already seen in Chapter Four, with the interiorization of Old Testament texts in Tijerina's narration of the Valle de Paz community. Tijerina borrowed the most well-known incidences from the books of Genesis and Exodus and discovered that his life replicated the patterns fixed in these sacred narratives. After the disastrous end to the Valle de Paz experiment, Tijerina releases the text from its Biblical framework at the same time he moves into secular politics. As the narrative moves into the details of his underground life, the land grant resistance and the continuing personal struggle with his critics, he maintains his confidence that the "Just Judge" and the protecting "angels" from his superdream will prevail. In addition, Tijerina's practice of preferring the sacred numbers three, seven, and forty in the text to precise measurements of time (seven days, forty days, three years, etc.) indicates that his sense of history operates at a different level of accounting. The cumulative effect of employing sacred numbers prevents the narrative from becoming a plodding chronology of dates. But more importantly, use of these numbers serves to sacralize the past and, in that sense, remind the reader that unseen forces control the outcomes of human affairs.[54]

It is the combination of Tijerina's resolute faith that justice will ultimately win out, preached by an imposing narrator, however, that cripples *Mi lucha por la tierra*. The drama that unfolds in the life of the autobiographical subject is by definition absent in the memoir. In his text the foregone conclusion that good triumphs over evil forecloses the reader's interest in the emplotment of Tijerina's struggle. It is not so much that the text fails to keep its autobiographical contract with the reader to deliver a life struggling to make its way in the world. Rather, *Mi lucha por la tierra* operates from a different impulse. It borrows Biblical narratives as its models and takes seriously its task of documenting the struggle and eventual triumph of the true man of God. Tijerina comes to his writing having already reconciled his differences with the divine, and so must use the memoir form. In addition, the ritualistic production of the text reveals that *Mi lucha por la tierra* is intended for those readers open to the truths beneath and beyond the ink and paper. The drama in the text comes not from the human actors, but from guessing when and how the hand of God will intercede. It is this religious quality of *Mi lucha por la tierra* that renders it problematic as Chicano autobiography (or history); not so much because of the content, but because of the relationship between the narrator and the God that controls the text. In this sense Tijerina's memoir is similar to hagiography. Michel de Certeau observes that "while [auto]biography aims to posit an evolution [of the narrator] . . . hagiography postulates that everything is given at the very beginning with a 'calling,' and 'election.'"[55]

Other Chicano texts that could be read as religious narratives include Richard Rodríguez's *Hunger of Memory* and Gloria Anzaldúa's *Borderlands/La*

Frontera. Rodríguez's bereavement over his estrangement from Catholicism, as he confesses in his chapter, "Credo," turns around his intellectual isolation from family and Church. Mourning the loss of mystery in the post-Vatican II liturgy and accepting his self-imposed isolation, Rodríguez realizes that he has become "like a Protestant Christian." His text like Tijerina's is focused on the individual standing before God. But unlike Tijerina, Rodríguez finds no consolation in community or in the presence of God in secular institutions. Caught up in the aesthetics of religion, Rodríguez confuses emotion for faith and is forced to retreat behind his loneliness when the Church of his childhood undergoes radical transformation and democratization.

Anzaldúa, on the other hand, consciously rebels against the smothering, patriarchal Catholicism of her childhood, choosing instead an individual New Age, post-Christian eclecticism. Writing her narrative to undermine the edifice of patriarchal Chicano culture, Anzaldúa ranges across writing genres, raiding and employing their tools (the personal voice, the nuance of the poetic form, the academic footnote) to dismantle and rebuild her spiritualized mestiza consciousness. Her narrative, oddly similar to Tijerina's in its collection and arrangement of diverse texts and documents, however, refuses to submit to the authority of any texts other than her own. Yet, for as far as *Borderlands/La Frontera* is from *Mi lucha por la tierra*, there is overlap in the magical realist quality to both and a shared understanding of the self in submission to the sacred. Rodríguez's mortal sin is the lack of faith in anything but himself. Anzaldúa on the other hand, writes to discover who or what grounds her being, her text enlivened by her wrestling with the terrifying goddess/*orisha*, Coatlicue.

All three texts, *Mi lucha por la tierra*, *Hunger of Memory*, and *Borderlands/La Frontera*, originate as "outsider" texts in Chicano literature. They all share a concern with religion but only the latter two have found their way into the Chicano canon. For despite their heterodox positions, Rodríguez and Anzaldúa free themselves from the Roman Catholic institution and move off in directions that are of interest to critics and other readers. Tijerina's text originates from and moves in different directions: from Christian fundamentalism and toward embracing the ancient Church. It is this return and submission to the institution of the Church that adds to the anathema of *Mi lucha por la tierra*.[56]

Reading *Mi lucha por la tierra* without an understanding of its religious impulse is to not read it at all. Ignoring ubiquitous formulaic "god-speak" phrases like, "You must have faith in the Great Just Judge of all the earth," or, ". . . the Just Judge of all the earth tried and punished my enemies," is tempting, but to do so violates the construction of the text as sacred artifact and sacred history. It is clear from the way Tijerina reads and how he ritualized the writing of the text that he intended his four volumes (the original handwritten manuscript) to be the first part of an unfolding divine master narrative.[57] A sympathetic approach to *Mi lucha por la tierra* means accepting the coextensive whole of history and sacred history, that is, between the affairs of humanity and the imposition of Heaven's intentions. Not so unlike the suspension of judgment required in reading autobiographical texts where fact and fiction collide, there is a need in Tijerina's memoir to distance and postpone verisimilitude in the supposed gap between history and sacred history, especially where the pull is toward the sacred.[58] Unfortunately, and ironically, the release of the abridged English translation in 2000 only adds to the obscuring of the sacred in Tijerina's memoir, as much of the religious content has been omitted.[59]

6   *Apocalipsis* / REVELATION

A New Science

IN HIS INTRODUCTION TO TIJERINA'S MEMOIR JORGE BUSTAMANTE warns the reader. *Mi lucha por la tierra,* the Mexican sociologist cautions, "will upset those who cannot manage to leave behind the epistemological framework where the validity of statements about experience is judged apart from positivist verifiability."[1] Explaining to the reader that Tijerina's "magical thinking" is a result of an "oppressive world and life," Bustamante reduces Tijerina's worldview to a product of macrosocial forces. In effect these preliminary comments defuse the impact of Tijerina's narrative strategy. As a measure of his "magical thinking," however, Tijerina's memoir should not be so easily dismissed or explained away as merely a compensatory reaction to viewing the world from the bottom of the socioeconomic ladder. It is better, and I think more the case, that Tijerina's extraordinary life is an example of a singular self drawn inexorably toward divine knowledge and illumination. Tijerina, who asked Bustamante to write the introduction, now regards it as too long and academic for his purposes.[2]

We have seen in previous chapters how events in Tijerina's life, remarkable in and of themselves, are invested by him with larger, more profound meanings. Almost always these extraordinary moments are viewed from a Pentecostal worldview of struggle between God and evil, but framed within a Mexican popular religious universe of divine visitations, penitential action, and ritual. Unlike the Biblesque fundamentalism of his 1950s sermons, *Mi lucha por la tierra* reveals the erosion of a strict fundamentalist training in favor of a hybrid combination of literalist reading with the fluid overlapping of sacred and profane worlds. Viewed through Tijerina's 1956 calling by his divine visitors to be the "secretary" of events around him, the magical realist episodes in his life and their retelling are premised upon the logic and proof of an inevitable and unfolding divine justice in the world.

Recall that in the memoir's opening account of his daughter's birth Tijerina not only set into motion the conflict between good and evil, but he accepts as normative the terrible reality of this combat that literally unwinds before him. In my interview where he confirmed that his daughter's birth had been threatened by a snake, he rather casually remarked:

> Yes, yeah, you know, we found that rattlesnake coiled, on top of our heads. He was there inside our dugout house. . . . Well, we saw it. That's why I called my daughter, Ira de Alá [Wrath of God]. . . . And the rattlesnake, it was the symbol of Satan, the symbol of the devil, of the evil, criminal element that was following us. And I would have it all the time. And I think that rattlesnake—I have dreamed, you know, every time I dream about enemies, I dream them as a rattlesnake. Oh I have had many dreams about rattlesnakes! . . . but they never bite me.[3]

It is, however, unlikely that at the time of his daughter's birth Tijerina glossed the snake's presence as the "criminal element" that so preoccupies his memoir written twenty years later. Nevertheless, it is precisely his close relationship to texts as keys for patterning and unlocking the meanings behind events both near and far from his own life (here the Genesis account of creation) that gives substance to the magical realist mind in *Mi lucha por la tierra*. This magical realism, or more aptly in his case, "magical literalism," connects him to Latin America more than it does to North America. Beyond the memoir it comes as no surprise that Tijerina's ideas are still met with puzzlement and incredulity by even his most sympathetic supporters.

Peter Nabokov's final encounter with Tijerina in his widely read book no doubt provided evidence for later charges that Tijerina had lost his mind. At the end of his book Nabokov could only conclude that Tijerina was simply "unfathomable." He wrote "the impulses of saviour and social bandit had converged in him through the land grant cause, yet that still said next to nothing about the source of his drive." Nabokov confessed, "I never plumbed this source, but I think I caught a glimpse of his interior wheel coming full circle, and if I still did not understand him, I believe I saw him begin to repeat that psychological process that was his mystery."[4] In the last chapter we saw how Nabokov's last conversation with Tijerina revealed "a new universal fourth dimensional language" that confused the journalist. Up to that point Nabokov had spent over a year researching and following Tijerina's every public move, yet Tijerina still remained "unfathomable" to him. What Nabokov did not know was that Tijerina had kept secret his rich nocturnal life of dreams and revelations for political reasons. It is clear, however, that Tijerina's "new science" was given substance late in the summer of 1969.

Although none of his other biographers mentions the jail revelation/vision in 1969, Tijerina described his experience in a speech at the University of Texas, months after his 1971 release from prison. According to the journalist who covered the event, Tijerina described it this way:

"I felt as if I were going 66,000 miles per hour around the sun and felt in my heart and mind a new awareness and consciousness with my feelings being stimulated from the space and reality beyond this planet. My mind was in space and watching the planet and the sun."

It was through his detached observations that he saw that there are discrepancies between justice in theory and justice as it is actually carried out.

"Written law doesn't mean justice," he said; "laws on the books are to the real spirit of the law as to what sex as an end to itself is true to love."[5]

If Tijerina did indeed have a "fourth-dimensional language" revealed to him, he never makes explicit reference to it after 1969. And no one else seems to have known about it. In any case, it is certain that prior to his frightening ordeal in the Springfield, Missouri, federal prison hospital, Tijerina was given a glimpse of his later work. In the 1980s, for instance, as he began linking the New Mexican land grant struggle to Palestinian efforts for sovereignty, Tijerina began to speak in the language of global justice and reconciliation that he had seen in his jail revelation.

The 1969 moon landing sparked a new revelation. This new vision provided Tijerina with an important clue to the mysteries of Biblical interpretation, and specifically, the consequences of Jesus's resurrection and ascension. If human beings were physically able to travel through space and land on the moon, then Biblical accounts about Jesus's ascensions could be factually true. The reality of space travel not only confirmed his literalist belief in the resurrection, but also verified his 1956 superdream visitation of three "interplanetary messengers" and their flying vehicle. No longer limited to deciphering the symbols and metaphors in his life and in the world, science and human ingenuity had validated the common-sense realism basic to evangelical Biblical interpretation.[6] But as a Mexican American, what was "common sense" or real to him did not preclude the revelatory power of dreams, visions, and omens. Tijerina writes that "the conquest of the moon served as a denominator or measure for . . . understand[ing] the principles of the Universe."

Ever since I was a child, I had felt the gravitational force of those cosmic values that pulled me to them. Despite my great interest it always ended, surrounded by doubts, caused by great obstacles between me and the Great Universe.

Once the trip to the moon had become a physical reality, all of my thoughts and interests in the Universe were revived. Now things were different. Now I had in my hands and within my reach a new measure which I applied day and night to revolutionize all of my opinions about our planet, life in its various dimensions, the Universe and nuclear structure, and the relationship between our material life and other forms of life in the Grand Universe.

While the conquest of the moon meant different things to different people, for me it meant a new way of thinking. Which is to say, I experienced a miraculous explosion that totally revolutionized my way of thinking and understanding of things. I had to transform all of my rationalizations and examine life in light of a new discernment.

The same spirit and force that had helped me in understanding these things, so important to me, helped me to understand the meaning of the truth of each thing. My work consisted, then, in discovering my truth, to know the truth within me.

This new orientation confirmed my feelings about the struggle for my people's rights. There was no conflict between my struggle for the land and this new concept on life and the values I now held.[7]

In this summation of his conceptual breakthrough, Tijerina is careful to write about it in nontheological language. In an interview situation where he was encouraged to reveal his religious influences, however, he is emphatic about how this "revolutionized" way of thinking had to be consistent with Biblical teachings. "For days and days and days [after the moon landing] I couldn't get myself to eat or sleep," he recalled. "It was just thinking, thinking so deep, so much; and the Bible itself became a new source. I had to interpret my own knowledge that I had on the Bible . . . I began to find the interplanetary footprints in the life of Christ." Recounting the postresurrection episodes between the risen Jesus and his followers, Tijerina pondered the mystery that Jesus would not allow Mary to touch him ("Do not hold onto me, for I have not yet returned to the father . . ." [John 20:17]), but that he encouraged Thomas to feel his wounds ("Put your finger here. . . . Reach out your hand and put it into my side . . ." [John 20:26]).

Those questions and those events were deeply, deeply [laughter] in my mind and I couldn't let go. I was like crazy! [Searching] throughout the prophets and the Apocalipsis [Book of Revelation] and mostly examining the life, the footsteps, the language [of Christ]. And I did find that Jesus said, . . . "I'm from above, you're from here. I'm not of this earth!" [John 18:36] So he was! Except that they thought he was just using symbolic terminology. But I think there were cases where—that Jesus slipped!—and spoke as an interplanetary being and not as an ordinary [human] being. So, what happened between Maria Magdalene and Tomás? "Maria, don't touch me; Thomas, come and touch me." What happened between those two persons and in the meantime?

You see! You see! Well, that's what the moon conquest impacted on me. That's what it did. And I'm just giving you a sample.[8]

These startling realizations that Tijerina reached in a New Mexican jail locate the genesis of Tijerina's shift from the single issue land grant effort to more universal, epic concerns prior to his federal prison hospital incarceration. And while activists might prefer him the victim of covert medical procedures as an explanation for the shift in his politics, he had already changed directions in his thinking before his harrowing ordeal in Springfield.

In his 1969 open letter from the New Mexico State Penitentiary, Tijerina seemed jubilant at having suffered for "the rights of my blood brothers to their property, their culture, and their inheritance."[9] Encouraged by his supporters and the publicity given to the land grant cause, Tijerina was prepared to endure his imprisonment. He had provoked his enemies into desperation and seemed confident that his suffering would exonerate him from charges he was defrauding his supporters. Although imprisoned, he could count on having regular contact with his family and supporters, but only if he was in New Mexico jails. A celebrity among the Chicano prisoners and jail attendants, his confinement would be burdensome but tolerable. The optimism expressed in his letter, however, came to an abrupt end when he was transferred to the medical facility at the Springfield federal prison. The gripping details of his "exile to the land of the insane" (referring ambiguously to both inmates and doctors) represents a climax of sorts in the memoir. In Springfield the cumulative experiences of harassment by government officials, visionary experiences, and an increasing suspicion of conspiracy directed against him coalesced into novel but troubling apocalyptic thoughts about the true nature of Latin Americans and the end of history.

"Into a dark world . . ."

Tijerina spent nearly two years imprisoned in the psychiatric ward of the United States Medical Center for Federal Prisoners in Springfield, Missouri.

The precise reason why he was sent there is still unclear, but the punishment was out of proportion to the crimes for which he had been found guilty: helping his wife burn a U.S. Forest Service sign and assaulting a Forest Ranger. The Federal Bureau of Prisons inmate records show his offense as "Injuring/Destroying Government Property."[10] Interpreting this exile as a strategy to keep him apart from his supporters and wife, he endured months of solitary confinement in the Texas La Tuna federal facility before his transfer to the Federal Medical Prison Facility. Again, there is confusion over the reason for his extended incarceration there. Predictably, his memoir indicates a conspiracy by the sentencing judge. Patty Newman reports that his chronic throat condition required surgery and that he was removed to Springfield for that reason. Quoting a terse response she received from the government to her request for information, she was informed that "outside medical consultants ha[d] been brought in and the determination is that he is medically sound."[11] At the time, the secrecy around why Tijerina had been moved hundreds of miles away from his family and supporters incubated rumors in activist circles that Tijerina was being treated for cancer or even that prison officials had "injected" cancer into him.

Later folklore about his incarceration and subsequent dramatic shift in his politics held that he had been an unwilling subject of lobotomization. Others suggested that the government had secretly plied him with mind-altering drugs as a way to contain his activism. His transfer to Springfield and the subsequent rumors about his abuse were no doubt helped along by his New Mexico State Penitentiary letter where he made it a point to describe his health as "excellent." He noted that his doctor, "Robert Castillo, of Albuquerque, is always advising me to take care of my throat by not talking so much." He also reiterates in the memoir that Castillo's visit found him in "in perfect health, except for my throat which had always bothered me."[12]

Justification for what can only be illegal involuntary commitment to the Springfield Medical Facility remains buried in federal prison records. At the time of his sentencing and confinement it was routine for prisoners to be transferred to mental health facilities without any prior professional psychological testing or evaluation. And in fact, there is no record in the prison bureau's inmate records about institutional commitment.[13]

Transfer between federal prisons, like the Texas La Tuna facility and the medical facility in Missouri was at the discretion of prison officials and viewed as a simple administrative matter.[14] Tijerina told me that he was sent to Springfield as an excuse to remove him from his hapless wife and "destroy his mind":

> I was asking for medication [for] my throat. Medication that can be found in Albuquerque, anywhere, see. They didn't have to send me to Springfield, Missouri. No. But they were using any excuse to say, "Well, Reies wants treatment, you know, medical treatment. We'll send him to Springfield, Missouri! That's a hospital." So, that was really the charge, and that was the excuse they used to send me . . . a thousand miles away from my wife. And, but, see, while they were trying to destroy my mind and my courage, my dreams . . . I think they hurt themselves, because I went into a dark world, see, [a world] that they use to intimidate, to break down the spirit of the leaders and dissenters.[15]

Tijerina's claim that he was afraid of losing his mind in the Springfield facility was not unreasonable. Scarcely a year previous to his imprisonment, the United States Court of Appeals had acknowledged the likelihood that a wrongfully committed prisoner might in fact become mentally ill in that setting.[16] And while he was being held at Springfield, a study on mental illness labeling was confirming the worst suspicions about the arbitrariness of psychiatric diagnosis. Planting his researchers in mental hospitals, psychologist David Rosenhan discovered that clinical workers were unable to discern insane patients from "sane" graduate students.[17] Far away from his family and culture Tijerina was in more danger than he could have known. According to psychological studies of Chicano prisoners, not only are diagnostic instruments biased against them, but disproportionate numbers of incarcerated Mexican Americans score in the psychotic range of personality tests.[18] Even had Tijerina undergone psychiatric examination prior to his transfer, his strong literalist religious life and his idiosyncratic worldview would have proven liabilities in an "objective" scientific diagnosis.

Initially he was confined with the most dangerously ill patients. Eventually he was moved in with the moderately ill prisoners. "Day and night, all I heard and saw were mentally ill prisoners," he records. "To survive it was necessary to listen to them, to pretend that I believed them and that I was one of them. I had to see the psychiatrists, take the medicines they gave me, otherwise they would put me in 'the hole' and I didn't want to have a bad record." He later told Nabokov that he was held "like a Soviet dissident" by the federal government.[19] Tijerina claims to have secretly arranged to view his prison files as a way to avoid conflict with his doctors and script out his behavior. Years later he learned that Springfield psychiatrists had labeled him "incorrigible, unable to be rehabilitated, schizophrenic, and that he believed himself to be a god."[20]

Tijerina was trapped in the routines and disciplines of the asylum. His fellow prisoners would tell him about seeing their bodily organs hanging and throbbing from the ceiling or claim persuasively that the president of the United States had come to visit them there in the hospital. Convinced that a prolonged stay in the prison hospital had unalterably changed the minds of prisoners, Tijerina decided to write his wife every day "to sustain my spirit."[21] Over time he managed to forge friendships and learned to survive from long-term patients. He even gained the sympathy of at least one of his psychiatrists whom he claims warned him of potential enemies. "Little by little I began to prepare to resist and avoid falling into the trap that my enemies were preparing for me. I began to study the best books on psychiatry that the older prisoners recommended. Although I had to keep them hidden, because if the Anglo psychiatrists found out, they would have locked me up just like they had many others, alleging that they were put away for their own good."[22]

Erving Goffman's landmark study on life in American asylums is useful here for understanding Tijerina's ordeal and his reactions to his confinement. Goffman's examination of how inmates work the system to exploit "a whole routine of official activity for private ends" accurately describes Tijerina's strategic friendships and his subversion and reapplication of psychiatric illness labeling.[23] In Tijerina's case, he "worked" the system on behalf of his community, making his incarceration that of all Spanish-speaking peoples at the hands of Anglos. Much of Goffman's sobering portrayal of inmate "mortification" in institutional life could apply to Tijerina's experience; except in his case, incarceration in the

Springfield Medical Facility was not based upon a psychiatric diagnosis of mental disorder, and so his "mortification" was doubly frightening.

In addition to the numbing regimes of institutional life and the continuous fear of becoming like his fellow inmates, there were three attempts on his life. Forced to accept the treatments prescribed for him, Tijerina was given an overdose of medications that left him temporarily paralyzed on the floor, alone and struggling to call out for help. Later he was placed in a cell with a violent right-wing extremist whom he feared would kill him. And, in a bizarre plot, Tijerina claims to have been transferred to the cell of a Mafia kingpin and warned not to eat the breakfast the next morning. The mafioso, apparently, was to be the target of a breakfast poisoning, but Tijerina would be an unintended victim.[24]

"Who is a Psychopath?"

Turning to the study of psychiatry during the long months of his imprisonment, Tijerina called upon his Pentecostal exegetical skills, honed in his political work, to unlock the meanings of psychiatry and save himself from insanity. "Psychiatry was being used by my enemies who wanted to destroy my mind," he remembers.

> I had to keep them from doing so. While in this asylum prison hospital this would be my struggle. I would gain a thorough knowledge of psychiatry so that the government psychiatrists could not have me declared psychopathic. What is Psychiatry? Is it a science? When and how did it arise? How is it used? Who uses it? What is correct interpretation? Who is a psychopath? I had to find answers to these questions. I had to—I was surrounded by psychotics and psychiatrists. The environment of my prison was full of the prisoners' agony.[25]

Tijerina turned the tables on his doctors. Piecing together his reading with observations of interactions between other prisoners and their psychiatrists, he learned the methods of diagnosis from group and individual therapy sessions. By so doing, he "discovered a new psychiatry." Originally he had intended to learn just enough to save himself. What he discovered led him to trace and uncover the clinical case history of the United States. In prison Tijerina discovered Freud and used the tools of psychoanalysis, as he understood them, to diagnose the illness of the Anglo mentality. "If the history of the individual reveals, according to psychiatrists, the reason for behavior, then the history of a race should reveal the reasons for its behavior," he reasoned.[26] In the quiet hours between the prison hospital routines of therapy, medication, and tedium, Tijerina channeled his anger and suspicion into his psycho-genealogical reconstruction of the white race. Blurring the distinctions between world history, sacred Christian history, and the clinical language of deviant psychology, he revealed the origins of Anglo psychopathology in the self-inflicted loss of legal/sacred inheritance at the infancy of the white race.[27] Tijerina says that he "began to study the history of the Anglo-Saxon race to discover whether my suspicions were well founded or not. . . . In my study I discovered that just as differences exist between individuals, so too one race from another."[28]

In his reconstruction of the Anglo clinical case history, the origins of psychopathology begin with the 1494 Treaty of Tordesillas. The Tordesillas Treaty, drawn up by Pope Alexander VI, had divided global conquest between Spain and Portugal, allowing Spain to monopolize (except for Brazil) exploration and settlement in the Western Hemisphere.[29] Because the Roman Church was the sole religious and political authority at the time in Europe, Tijerina argued that the Treaty of Tordesillas authorized Spain's claim to the Americas despite England's presence and eventual conquest of North America. So, Tijerina deduced, "The Anglo as a race is psychopathic . . . whose complex began when it suffered disinheritance" as a result of papal favoritism toward Spain and Portugal. "Thus began its mental condition. And over the years, the complex deteriorated to the point that they [the Anglo] rejected their own [Catholic] authority, their own [Catholic] faith and religion in order to grab the inheritance that by their own law belonged to Spain and Portugal." In an interview with Andrés Guerrero a decade after he had first diagnosed the Anglo mentality, Tijerina reiterated that as a result of Tordesillas, the Anglos

were left out of America, they didn't like the game, they created new rules; they dropped out of the [Catholic] Church and created a new Church [of England] to legalize their . . . crossing the Atlantic. But, according to the real international law and the Church—the true Church—they crossed the Atlantic illegally. And, they dropped out and created a new government; [a Protestant] Christian, religious government to create rights [for themselves] in America. But [in fact] they have none![30]

In his memoir account of this European competition for legitimate religious and legal claim to the New World, Tijerina understood England's psychopathology in the rejection of the Catholic Church's temporal authority:

> And so, the Anglo (ANGELS) lost at his own game and didn't like it. Fortune and blessing fell upon Spain and Portugal. Later, when it was too late, like Esau, Jacob's brother, he wanted to repent but to no avail. In his state of rage and envy, he mounted a protest in the name of religion, in order to deny the value and authority of the Treaty of Tordesillas. One crime led to another, and [England] saw fit to legalize pirates on the high seas. When he got what through law and divine decree did not belong to him, he invited all those nations who would choose to join him. In 480 years, the complex and psychopathy has worsened.[31]

In the original manuscript, Tijerina penned the Spanish word "ANGELES" in the text to explain the term "Anglo" through folk etymology. As far back as 1968 Tijerina had connected the terms although at the time the association was a rhetorical one.

> The Anglo . . . had many nicknames 2000 years ago. "Anglo" is one of the nicknames that Julius Caesar gave them when they found them in the caves of Britannia. He called them . . . "angeles" because they had blue eyes and blond hair. It was really a nickname, and "angeles" means angels and Anglo means "angeles." So really the Anglos chose that nickname [as] the best [one]. It is too bad that they are behaving [badly], and want the whole world to treat them as angels, when in fact it was nothing but a joke; a nickname.[32]

Although it is obvious he was drawing on the similarity between the words "Anglo" and "angel," the connection nevertheless stuck with him and became an etymological proof for his clinical diagnosis. In *Mi lucha por la tierra*, his fear of the Anglo-Saxon mentality would find its full expression in his enemies: the CIA, the FBI, and the White House.[33] A decade after his release from Springfield, Tijerina dropped his invective against the Anglo and transferred blame onto Jews for masterminding the Spanish American dispossession in the New World. In the new formulation Jews were responsible for prodding the English into challenging Spain's true heritage and divine right in the Americas.

> So, the non-Christian Jews, who refused to accept Christ as the Messiah . . . were driven out of Spain. And later [they] moved into Europe, England—and Benjamin Disraeli was a descendent of one of the Jews . . . that were driven out of Spain, . . . he built and created the blueprint for England and the United States' taking over of the world; ruling the world.[34]

Later, Tijerina would come across a 1665 law passed by the English Parliament extending protection to Jews in North America, thus proving to him that Jews were responsible for the English ascendancy over the Spanish in the Americas.[35] But what would prompt a Jewish conspiracy against Spain and her colonies? In 1980 Tijerina introduced an elaborate genealogy revealing that Spanish descendants in the New World were of Semitic origin. Responding to Andrés Guerrero's interview question regarding the meaning of the Biblical Exodus story for Chicanos, Tijerina responded in his typically digressive fashion:

> Well Andrés, my educational background and experience is based on the history of the Israelites and the Hebrew people. And the Exodus theme for me is very relevant; because I feel that we are the descendants of the Tribe of Joseph, son of Jacob, our forefather was sold by Judah, his brother, and Dan, his other brother. And we are going through a 400 year period that Israel was in Egypt; very similar . . . the liberation that we need and that we're fighting for is more than a liberation of our minds, or liberation of

our culture, or a liberation of our spirit. It's a liberation of—ignorance of our lost memory; our lost history. . . . [W]e lost track and we lost contact with our lineage.

According to Tijerina's historical revision, Jews were determined to cheat their brothers, the Spanish "Israelites" out of their birthright.

Because "Israel" is our name . . . the Jewish state built in Palestine should be called the state of Judah! And not the state of Israel. . . . We feel that we have a greater right to the name, "Israel," because of the Covenant; . . . we have been obedient to both Covenants. The non-Christian Jew was allegedly obedient to the Old Testament—to the Old Covenant. But he has not been obedient to the New Covenant. The Old and New Covenants are both Covenants of the Hebrew/Israelite people.[36]

Grafting the Christian doctrine of the new covenant onto this racialized reading of Jewish history, he had only to read Spanish-descent peoples back into Biblical prophecy to legitimize his genealogy. The following year, in a publicly broadcast interview for New Mexican public television, Tijerina detailed his position.

I have dedicated twenty-six years of my life to the roots of our property rights. That led me to the roots of our lineage, of our blood. Then I consulted the rabbis, the Jews here and in Mexico. And I began to research into the roots—not the legal roots of property, but the legal roots of our blood! And with the help of Jews and rabbis I uncovered the fact that all the Martinezes, Garcias, Valdezes, Tijerinas, Fernandezes . . . all these Spanish surnames . . . are Israelites: direct descendants of Israelite families. So we are Israelites, not by religion, like the Jews who are Jews by religion; we are Israelites by blood—not by religion. There's a great big difference.[37]

By the end of the 1980s Tijerina had completed the transfer of his analysis of Anglo psychopathology he had first formulated in 1971 onto

Jews. Coming out of the 1960s, Tijerina's quarrel with Anglos over the legal rights of deeded Spanish land grants had been superseded by a grander vision unfolding from his prison illuminations. Holding fast to new visions of the future rooted in Israelite genealogy, Tijerina came to believe that Spanish-speakers were an ancient Biblical people, but that Jews had stolen their Israelite blood birthright.

By 1987 Tijerina had completed his journey toward an unconventional, but unmistakable anti-Semitism. That year Tijerina charged Jews with wanting to create "a political means to disarm humanity" and revisited themes from his previous work. In Mexico City he charged:

> I understand them, because [as a race] they are a [mentally ill] patient; schizophrenia arises out of terror and suffering. In two thousand years of suffering the Jews have developed a mental disorder which might be labeled neurosis, psychopathy, schizophrenia. And this is why I contend that the world needs to treat this patient with care; otherwise, the state of Israel already owns 200 atomic bombs. As an Israeli leader explained it to me: "So that Russia and the United States cannot negotiate our independence, for love of peace in the Middle East, we have separate arms."[38]

It is possible but I think unlikely that Tijerina harbored anti-Semitic ideas earlier than the late 1970s. In 1967 Tijerina had caused an uproar when he remarked to an audience at St. John's College, Santa Fe, that Thomas B. Catron, the leader of the notorious land grabbing "Santa Fe Ring" had been a Jew. "It takes a well-developed race to do what they did to the Spanish people," he is reported to have said.[39] Peter Nabokov, however, concluded that the unfortunate (and apparently false) charge that Catron was Jewish was intended only to point out "that if the long span of Jewish culture could produce such legal and financial abilities, then [Tijerina's] equally ancient 'New Breed' could show forth as effectively."[40]

Prior to his incarceration, Tijerina had already embellished the idea that Mexicans were a "cosmic" race. His preferred term for Mexican descent people, "New Breed," was meant to indicate the novelty of a race at the intersection of Iberian and Native American lineages. What others call the process of *mestizaje* (mixed race heritage) or the birth of a *raza cósmica* (cosmic race) is an old idea among Mexican philosophers and nationalists. Its origin as a concept idealizes the birth of the Mexican out of the union between the Spanish conquistador, Hernan Cortés, and his Mayan translator/concubine, Malintzin (La Malinche).[41] Proving that Mexican Americans were a New Breed birthed in sixteenth-century Spanish legal documents, Tijerina proclaimed the New Breed "born October 19, 1514, by Law Two, Title 1 of Book 6 of *The Laws of the Indies* by decree of Ferdinand V." This "birthdate" Philip II reaffirmed in 1556, when he legalized marriage between Spaniards and native peoples.[42] The term "Mexican," Tijerina argued, was an inaccurate term that described nationality, a "political description of one born in Mexico" of any number of races. Similarly, the description "Spanish-American" was incorrect, implying as he saw it, a mixture of Spanish and Anglo.[43]

A month after his St. John's College comment, Tijerina delivered a rousing speech where he observed that "God had—in his divine wisdom—established *The Laws of the Indies* to govern the common lands, the land grants, the New Breed and the destiny of this hemisphere, this continent."[44] Making it clear that he saw the New Breed as distinct from the Jewish people, he compared the ages of the Anglo, the Jewish, and the Spanish American races to indicate the relative infancy of the Hispano New Breed:

> The Anglo is two thousand, five hundred years old; that's equivalent of a young man of twenty-five years old. The Jew is from five to six thousand years old, so that makes him an old man of sixty years old, worth plenty of intelligence accumulated. But the Spanish American—the New Breed—is only four years and some days and months old. So we just have hit the stage, the time when we now have found ourselves. We now know that this continent has bre[d]; brewed a New Breed; a new people.[45]

Later in his speech he linked the Jewish struggle for sovereignty in Palestine with the Spanish American land grant struggle and again made a clear distinction between Jews and Spanish Americans:

> We don't blame the Jews when they came to the help and rescue of Israel, June the fifth, when the Tierra Amarilla event also happened,

the same day. The Jews got together and gathered two hundred million dollars. . . . Their nation is here, their citizenship is here but besides that they got together and helped their brothers over there. What's wrong with that? Nothing. That's unity. That's protection. That's [the] law of nature. That is all we're doing, ladies and gentlemen; just like the Jew. We're learning from the Jew. We have an obligation, constitutional obligation, divine obligation to see for our brother, to see for our rights.[46]

Finally, perhaps in response to criticism leveled against him for his remark at St. John's College, Tijerina invoked American aid to Israel as an example of how legal authority and the "pressure of justice" would eventually lead to positive results.

We are expecting [help], just like all the Americans of the United States helped the Jews in the year 1947. Remember the Jew, for two thousand years he had been roaming the world, out of his country and those land grants given to them by Moses and Joshua had been possessed by the Arabs for two thousand years. But here we got together, we united and helped the Jew, and now he has the land. After two thousand years his land grants were returned to him. Why? Because he had title to that land. Now you understand that it's not something rare that we are preaching the land grants, invoking them, proclaiming, protesting them, demanding. Now you know why. This is the area of justice and claims. The Indian is doing it. The black man is doing it in his own way. . . . Now there are more than thirty-four all-African, nationalist independent nations. Why? Did they use atom bombs to secure their independence? No, ladies and gentlemen. The pressure of justice.[47]

After his release from prison in 1971, Tijerina continued to link the isolated history of the northern New Mexican "Spanish American" with the sacred history of Israel. "We are in an exceptional place, in a unique geographical area," he pointed out in 1973. Annexing the local land grant struggle to Israel's sacred geography, he noted New Mexico's liminal position between larger, potentially assimilating powers, "like Israel is in the Middle East between Europe and Asia. So we are between North and South America."[48]

The Christian-Israelite Hypothesis

Tijerina's speculations on race led him to a final synthesis, the Christian-Israelite hypothesis. His search for the origins of race difference had helped him explain the loss of the Spanish land grants. Now the pieces of his lifelong interests and research fell into place as he read the Bible alongside Spanish and Jewish history. Tijerina had only to link the authority vested in those texts with the Mexican idea of a "cosmic" race to reach the next step in his race thinking. The identification of the Mexican "New Breed" as the "chosen" people, however, was not forged until sometime in the late 1970s, between his penning of the memoir and the fully articulated genealogy in Guerrero's 1980 interview.[49] By the 1980s, Tijerina no longer found the term "New Breed" useful. He moved beyond the more popular "Indo-Hispano" formula and was defending the "Christian-Israelite" concept. Tijerina now argued that the descendants of Iberian New World colonists, by virtue of their legal status as Catholics and their hidden Hebraic genealogy, were rightfully coming into their divine inheritance. As the descendants of the northern kingdom of Israel that had been scattered into the world during their Assyrian exile in 735/734 BCE (I Chron. 5:26, II Kings 17:6), Christian-Israelites had been discovered living everywhere Spanish was spoken. As Roman Catholics they were also subjects of the most longstanding and divinely sanctioned authority on the earth.

Tijerina also moved beyond observing and commenting on the similarities between the Jewish return to Israel and the Indo-Hispano struggle for deeded land. Returning to the most authoritative text he knew, Tijerina searched the Old Testament for clues linking Israel with the Spanish-speaking peoples in the Americas. Earlier he had appealed to Isaiah 13:14 to explain the prophetic fulfillment of Israel's return to Palestine: "Like a hunted gazelle, like sheep without a shepherd, each will return to his own people, each will flee to his native land." There he also read the eventual victory for the New Mexican Hispanos. Tijerina also favored Ezekiel 37:19–22, which accounted for the split between the two

Hebrew kingdoms and promised the future reunion of the southern kingdom of Judah and the lost Israelite tribes of the North.[50] The visions of the prophet Zechariah that had provided the narrative structure for Tijerina's superdream in 1956, he now turned to for its prophecy regarding the return of the House of David to Jerusalem (Zech. 12).

Tijerina's transition from his early sectarian religiosity to land grant politics and then back again into religious vision explains how the Christian-Israelite hypothesis evolved. His quest for historical and legal precedent meant that he was always working the jurisprudence angle in his quest for spiritual and temporal authority. Through an elaborate finessing of Sephardic Jewish history read through Old Testament prophecy, Tijerina could claim that Iberian Catholics in the Americas were bound by the covenant made between Yahweh and Israel. And as Catholics, they were simultaneously subject to the authority of apostolic succession granted by Christ to Peter. The twin events of Columbus's trip to the New World and the expulsion of Jews from Spain in 1492, both made possible through the authorizing power of Spain's Catholic monarchs, were more than coincidence. Indeed, they revealed a larger scheme hidden in the Bible. Through his land grant work and his genealogical digging, Tijerina had been prepared as the vessel for rediscovering such hidden truths.

Ironically, this turn to a Christian-Israelite identity meant that it was no longer possible to sustain a Native American lineage. In earlier decades this shared blood heritage had proven crucial to the Chicano claims to indigenous land rights. Even as Chicanos were rediscovering the richness of their indigenous legacy (real or imagined), Tijerina veered off in the opposite direction. He adopted an idiosyncratic (and unpopular) celebration of the Spaniard as heroic Christian conquistador. Living for so many years among the New Mexican Hispanos, he came to accept their self-image of pure Castilian ethnicity. As putative descendants of the first sixteenth-century Spanish colonists to the northern frontiers of New Spain, Hispano New Mexicans retained distinctive linguistic and cultural practices Tijerina found useful in his politics. He had coined the terms "New Breed" and "Indo-Hispano" in recognition of the mixed-blood heritage. But when he claimed the Bible's promises made to the nation of Israel for the Christian-Israelites, there was no longer room for

Canaanites, the people who had first occupied the sacred homeland. "[Y]ou have to be careful because by *La Raza*, you can also mean the new breed of Spanish and the Indian," he remarked to Guerrero, "but I do not think so."

> I don't think that's *La Raza*. I think *La Raza* is the one that absorbed the other one. When the Spaniards came here, they gave their name to the Indian. The Indian did not absorb the Spaniard. Now, *La Raza*, the children of Joseph, left Palestine and went to Spain. There they did the same thing they did here. They absorbed the tribes of Spain. They imposed their thought, mentality, spirituality, their doctrine, and their religion on their tribes. They did this because the Hebrews, the Israelite religion, believed faith and monumental history were stronger and more acceptable than what the tribes had in the Iberian Peninsula. So when *La Raza* came here, they repeated it. They give. They absorb. Intermarrying with the Indian only shows that *La Raza* was flexible and had a mission and was not racist. We have Law II, Title I, Book VI of *The Laws of the Indies*, given, I think, on October 19, 1514. In that year, 1514, that law was issued to *La Raza* to legalize marriage between Spanish and Indian.[51]

Unwittingly, Tijerina had adopted the ideological conquest Mexico's Indian-blood Mexican philosopher José Vasconcelos had pushed in his formulation of the Mexican people as the "cosmic race." Vasconcelos had argued in the 1920s that the melting of races in the Americas would lead to a new era of improved humanity. Close reading of his argument reveals that Vasconcelos assumed that indigenous blood and cultures would give way to the improvements inherent in the superior Iberian race. The Christian-Israelite concept required Tijerina to de-emphasize indigenous bloodlines even though he considered the mestizo "the last extension of the House of Israel."[52] Like so many others in history laying claim to the privilege of Israelite descent, Tijerina's theory eventually hardened into an exclusionary racialization of insider status. Had he adopted previous theories about Native Americans as the Lost Tribes that others had promoted before him, he could have kept the mestizo ideal intact. But Tijerina was too closely tied to the epic grandeur and language of the Spanish Catholic texts to accept anyone else's formulas.[53]

In 1961 Tijerina had returned to the Roman Catholic Church, an act he explained at the time as a political move designed to confirm his stand with the Catholic Hispano community. "Because my people expect it," he explained to Richard Gardner. "They are like children about such matters. That might seem sort of lowdown to you, but to my people it means they can trust me more when they know I have a concrete interest in the land grant cause."[54] Only a few years earlier the idea of embracing the very institution that he had been trained to despise would have been unthinkable. Tijerina's casual explanation for his change of heart we now know masked a deeper set of race and religion issues. Rather than accept the interpretation that he returned to Roman Catholicism as political expediency or religious conviction, I suspect he was already testing a prophetic intuition about divine birthrights and genealogy but lacked documentary evidences and revelatory knowledge. Abruptly leaving behind his Protestant fundamentalism could only have appeared as calculated to his detractors. His reconciliation with Catholicism did not alter his Pentecostal commonsense realist way of reading or his deep suspicion of institutions. Rather, his return to Catholicism was a calculated political/theological move. It provided the weight and gravity of the Roman Catholic legal tradition he needed for his argument. The Roman Church he explained, embodies

the most powerful, the longest authority on earth, which is almost 2000 years [old]. We don't know of any kingdom, of any power that has lasted and survived all kinds of ideologies. Ideologies have come and gone, and the Church absorbed them [all]. . . . It was the truth, the law, the roots, the Christian sovereignty that brought me . . . to the understanding of the Old and New Covenants. And that's why I returned to Catholicism. Because I discovered the difference between the representatives of the Church and the power, the authority of the Church. It's established by Christ.

There's no excuse to deny . . . the authority of the Church. The corruption of the [Church] leaders is no excuse for us to tear it down and build another Christian authority. Just like a political nation will tolerate criticism of its leaders; but it will not tolerate the creation of another government within the government. No, no country in the world will tolerate that! The same thing with the Kingdom of Christ, with the Church of Christ. We have the right to criticize the corrupted leaders, but we have no right to create a new government, a new church, a new covenant. We have no right.[55]

More proof of his speculations about Jews and Israelites came from a most unlikely source. In 1979 Tijerina obtained his massive FBI file (running over five thousand pages) through the Freedom of Information Act. The number and frequency of agent surnames he assumed were Jewish attached to reports about his activities shocked him. Connecting the Jewish names with the harassment of his efforts as far back as the late 1950s, he adopted a facile and unfortunate Jewish conspiracy theory coincident with his intuitions about the genealogy of Latin Americans. The historical picture was now complete. Jews had stolen the Hispanic Israelite birthright and had actively conspired to prevent him from uncovering the truth.

The Christian-Israelite concept for Tijerina thus overcame all other identities for Spanish Americans. As he dug deeper into both the English and Spanish sources, he found the Lost Tribes in the movement of Israel into their Diaspora as they jumped from Biblical texts into medieval Spanish history and were then swept into the New World during the long colonization of the Americas. He had also uncovered a conspiracy of international Jewry against the Spanish American/Christian-Israelite and against him in particular.

But would the Lost Tribes ever return to their homeland as prophesied? The homeland issue has not been a central one in the many "rediscoveries" of the Lost Tribes throughout history so much as answering the question, "Who and where are they now?"[56] In the United States today, the Christian Identity movement promotes the thesis that the Lost Tribes made their way from their Assyrian captivity northward into the British Isles, hence the folk etymology applied by Identity Christians that the word "British" derives from the Hebrew, *B'rit-ish*, or "covenant [*b'rith*] people [*ish*]."[57] Celebrating the success and domination of English-speaking peoples in the world, this "British/Anglo-Israelist" mythology provides the basis for racist varieties of fundamentalist Christianity and branches of the American militia and Patriot movements.[58] Identity Christians see themselves as heirs to both the Old Covenant under Mosaic Law and the New Covenant under the resurrection of Jesus Christ. Their goal is not only to assert a racialized religious superiority, but also to protect white Christian America (as an extension of Anglo-Israelite divine right) against the illegal U.S. government and the inferiority of darker races. Identity Christianity claiming an Israelite genealogy permits a segment of the movement to engage in anti-Jewish conspiracy campaigns. This is done by arguing that Jews have usurped Israel's inheritance and diluted the purity of sacred bloodlines in the Diaspora.

Tijerina's Christian-Israelite concept is similarly constructed around folk etymologies and an idiosyncratic interpretation of western history. However, unlike Identity Christianity that requires the journey of the Lost Tribes into northern Europe to substantiate its racist theology, Tijerina's version locates the Lost Tribes in Spain. For Tijerina, the first Christian-Israelites are "conversos," Spanish Jews forced to convert to Catholicism. "You have to see the Hebrew people in three stages," he explained to Guerrero. "Their stage in Palestine, their stage in Spain, and their ultimate stage in America."

> As they grew, as we grew—not they but us as we grew—as a people, in Palestine, then Spain was given to us. We created Spain! The glory of Spain was created by Israel: the converted Israelites—Christian Israelites. As we grew and multiplied in Spain, then we were given, according to the blessing of Jacob and promise of God to Jacob's sons, Manassas and Ephraim. We were given a greater land, America. Which [was] called by Christopher Columbus—who was a converted Christian-Israelite himself—the "holy land." America was called [the] "Holy Land" . . . by Columbus; Cristóbal Colón.[59]

At the time of his interview with Guerrero, Tijerina had adopted part of the Anglo-Israelist mythology about the identity of the Lost Tribe, Dan, as the Scandinavian and Anglo descendants of the Vikings (i.e., *Den*mark).[60] Tijerina's launching point for vigorously tracing the journeys and destinations of the Lost Tribes came after his discovery of Enrique Flórez's eighteenth-century Iberian Church history, *España Sagrada*.

Included in this voluminous compendium are lists of Jewish family surnames, including common Mexican surnames ending in "-es" and "ez" (Martínez, González, Rodríguez, Torres, etc.).[61] Convinced that his genealogical reconstructions were leading him to the origins of Spanish-speakers in the New World, Tijerina took what was useful from Anglo-Israelist themes, rejected any nonscriptural ideas, and checked his findings against the multivolume *Encyclopedia of Judaism*.[62]

Tijerina's rediscovery of his lost Israelite identity meant, of course, that he had to contend with the charge that he was racist and anti-Semitic. Viewed alongside the Anglo-Israelist and Christian Identity movements, it was a foregone conclusion to his critics that he had crossed into dangerous and regrettable ideological territory. However, unlike the Anglo-Israelist anti-Semitism that cast Jews as reprobate or even a separate species of humanity, Tijerina remains faithful to the Biblical prophecies that Israel and Judah will be reunited. He interprets the split between Christian-Israelites and Jews as an ancient feud between estranged brothers. Much of the confusion about the Christian-Israelite idea by those who interviewed him in the 1980s can be attributed to their assumption that "Jews" and "Israelites" referred to the same people. Tijerina's anti-Semitism is spun out of what he perceives as the deceit promoted by Jews in their adoption of the name "Israel" and their claim to Palestine. "We [Christian-Israelites] are very much concerned with Jews engulfing the world in problems under the name of our forefathers . . . Israelites," he explained in a public interview in 1982:

3,726 years, the House of Judah and the House of Israel have been separated. Completely! The Jews have never mentioned, as a political name, Israel, until 1948. Before that, it was Judah. Judah is their nation . . . from one individual, named Judah, to the tribe of Judah, to the kingdom of Judah, to the nation of the Jews, and now, the religion of the Jews.

Interviewer: And in effect, you're saying the Jews have misappropriated the title, the name, "Israelite" . . . to their political cause because it is a blood issue?

Tijerina: Of course! Because Israel is blood. Jacob was Israel, and he gave legal rights to Joseph, Ephraim, and Manassas, to use the name Israel. And it was agreed upon, and the kingdom of the south, which was the kingdom of Judah always recognized [that fact]. Even in the census, the census of Israel was separated from the census of Judah. And, we are concerned because under the name of Israel, which the prophets—four major prophets—said in the Bible that in the last days, the House of Judah and the House of Israel are coming together. That's my dream. We will, but we need our brothers, who are divided in four groups: Orthodox Jews, Reform Jews, Zionists, and agnostics. It's hard to talk to them because you don't know to whom you are talking. But we are hoping and dreaming that we merge.

Interviewer: Are you saying in effect the problems that you perceive in the world today, especially as affects your people . . .

Tijerina: It's a family fight.

Interviewer: . . . is a family fight?

Tijerina: It was a family fight [that began] in Spain.[63]

It is important to repeat here that Tijerina's version of the Lost Tribes rediscovered is different from Christian Identity Anglo-Israelism in the United States. Although he kept a version of Anglo-Israelist myth about the Lost Tribes moving into northern and western Europe, Tijerina traced the remnants of Ephraim and Manassas into the Iberian Peninsula where they "absorbed" the indigenous Celtic tribes. For Anglo Christian Identity theorists, the tribes of Ephraim and Manassas are identified as England (Ephraim) and English-speaking America (Manassas). These are the two tribes who inherit Jacob's blessing as described in Genesis 48. James Aho, who examined Christian Identity in the American Northwest, notes that at least one theorist interpreted Spain as the accursed Simeon (Genesis 49: 5–7), whose alleged violence and ruthlessness is accomplished through Spain's cruel treatment of her conquered peoples.[64] Tijerina's reading of Genesis 48, however, locates Manassas and Ephraim in Spain, rerouting their Diaspora and claiming Jacob's blessing for the descendants of Sephardic Jews wherever Spain planted her colonies. Where Anglo-American Identity Christianity relies upon extra-Biblical speculation to support racist and anti-Semitic principles,[65] Tijerina is careful to substantiate his claims through scripture and through "legitimate" historical sources insofar as he is able to access texts, scholars, archives, and libraries. To the charge that he is anti-Semitic, he has only to point to his Israelite identity as proof that he could never be seen in the same racist light as white Identity Christians.

The similarities between Tijerina's Christian-Israelite hypothesis and the broad themes of contemporary Christian Identity are, nevertheless, too similar to be coincidental. In his broad search for materials to support his speculations, Tijerina could not have avoided the vigorous dissemination of white supremacist literature throughout the mountain and western states.[66] White supremacist arguments against blacks, Jews, Arabs, Asians, and Latinos, however, are directly opposed to the Christian-Israelite hypothesis that preserves the prophesied future reunion of Israel with Judah. Logically, Christian-Israelites include Spanish descendants of any racial amalgamation or absorption (Filipino, Chamorro, Afro-Caribbean, etc.), as well as Palestinians in the category of "chosen people."[67]

From the perspective of Identity Christianity, Tijerina's scheme would also be unacceptable in his rejection of an *Anglo*-Israelist first principle. That is, the belief that the truly blessed tribes of Manassas and Ephraim course through the pure bloodlines of Nordic and Celtic peoples in northern Europe. For Tijerina, the givenness of mestizaje as primordial to Mexican identity and the reality of race mixture throughout Latin America must be preserved in Christian-Israelite identity. And in this he violates and denies the medieval Spanish Catholic theory of *limpieza de sangre*, or purity of lineage. This technical problem, biological purity versus the forging of a *tertium quid* out of two races, Tijerina overcomes by subordinating biological race to the future, spiritualized peoplehood promised in the Bible. Through a joint appeal to Hebraic sacred tribal genealogy and the divine authority of Christian apostolic succession, Tijerina is able to put the facts of history on his side and claim a felicitous convergence of sacred genealogies in medieval Spain.

Once he revealed the sacred origins of Latin Americans, Tijerina returned to his 1950s premillennialism. It was, of course, inevitable that Christian-Israelites would play a crucial role in the final drama between good and evil. Now he scrutinized the ancient scriptures for clues as to how the Just Judge would render his last verdict on humanity. The power of his early Pentecostal indoctrination now reasserted its influence in his prophecy that the atom bomb would be the instrument of God's retribution. Reanimating the urgency of nuclear threat in his 1950s sermons, Tijerina prophesied that nuclear holocaust would be the "cleansing" agent for humanity. In his new scheme Tijerina blamed the renegade Anglo and the Jewish races for having built the atomic bomb. The Anglo, he had argued throughout the 1960s, had degenerated mentally and morally after rejecting the Catholic Church. Jews, he added, had rejected their messiah and lost their divine and blood lineage rights. Surely they would reap God's anger. Tijerina told a *Rio Grande Sun* reporter in 1987 that he had had "a glimpse of the coming retribution and destruction through a vivid dream." "It was horrible," he said,

> "I saw everything like a movie." In it, he saw scientists in a panic over a strayed nuclear missile. Three waves of bombardment followed. . . . According to Tijerina, Mexico, which he called the "ark," and New Mexico, by proximity, will be spared nuclear disaster because of wind currents and other natural phenomena.
>
> After the nuclear purge, he said, "We're going to go back to the drawing board—humanity's drawing board. People are going to go back to the municipal system. They will not be fooled by politicians."
>
> Tijerina said he believed that after the disaster a "nuclear trial" presided over by the people would occur. "It will be raw justice," he predicted. "The judicial system has terrified the world; judges will disappear overnight." . . .
>
> Tijerina said the most important work still facing him is to create and preserve a record for the coming era. "I am making it a high priority in my life to see that my beliefs, my leadership, my teachings, survive the atomic holocaust bath and ritual." . . .
>
> Meanwhile, Tijerina suggested that his hardest days of struggle are in the past. "I don't have feelings that I should push," he said. "I have done the hard part—I've paid the price."[68]

Behind the sensationalism of the reporter's highlights and despite his Roman Catholic affiliation, Tijerina still retains his Pentecostal premillennialism. Moreover, he still believes in the charge given to him by the three angelic beings in 1956 that he serve as observer and recorder. In June 1997,

Tijerina was reported to have predicted a nuclear "detonation between the East and West" for 17 October 1997.[69] The information had come to him in a dream. At the time he was still living only a short distance from the Los Alamos National Laboratories, where the fact of nuclear weapons is a continual reminder of his earlier prophecies about the last days. The continuing theme of nuclear holocaust as judgment and purification in his most recent writing and dreaming is, frankly, understandable.

Apocalypse

In its original meaning the term "apocalypse" translates as "unveiling" or "revelation." Popular use of the term, however, brings to mind images of doomsday, of Armageddon, massive global destruction, or the total annihilation of humanity. For Tijerina, apocalypse refers to the continuing unveiling of divine purpose in his life. Revelation through scripture, legal texts, dreams, visions, and the patterns of his unfolding life is an expected and welcome aspect of his unwavering faith in a sober God of justice. Operating with the full expectation that Biblical prophecy about Israel will be accomplished, Tijerina is convinced he has unveiled a divine genealogy. What is left to be revealed now is how exactly Christian-Israelites and Jews will find reconciliation.

Tijerina's prison revelations opened him up to a world of new discoveries. His vision of a "new science" directed his attention to issues of universal importance he could only have learned after his research and struggles on behalf of the Spanish land grant heirs. He spent years poring over microfilmed documents and sitting for hours on end scanning fragile manuscripts for legal prooftexts that would return the land to the Hispano. His dreams and illuminations, however, led him to uncover the Hispano's genealogical origins in the landscapes of the Old Testament. The angels in his superdream charged him with a responsibility he spent the next decade trying to understand and fulfill. In the prison revelations he was given the interpretive tools to pursue his charge. These tools, in combination with his "revelations" about psychiatric diagnosis, led in turn to a re-reading of medieval Spanish texts and the rediscovery of Spain's sacred genealogy.

If in fact there was a descent into madness as some have suggested, it did not occur inside his head. Rather, it was all around him in the disciplined regimes of the prison hospital where, through sheer determination and strategic use of his charismatic abilities, he reversed and usurped what Foucault called the "thaumaturgical virtues" of the psychiatrist in his healing role. Tijerina identified the methods of clinical diagnosis in psychoanalytic practice, applied the magical powers of the psychiatrist to the Anglo, and found that race in unresolved conflict with the Catholic Holy Father.[70] In his examination of Anglo psychopathology, Tijerina diagnosed the Anglo race's insanity in their conquest of North America. They had tried to silence him by imprisoning him but had failed.[71] His final victory over his enemies, however, had already been determined and was already working its way onto the world stage. The revelation that he was doubly chosen, as an Israelite and a Roman Catholic, meant he had only to watch for the final, saving apocalypse of God's justice.

 EPILOGUE

A Continuing Vision

WHAT DO WE MAKE OF TIJERINA'S UNCONVENTIONAL LIFE? Throughout this book, I have tried to avoid the imposition of academic theory that might draw attention away from Tijerina's own voice and point of view. That being said, it is naive to believe that it is possible (or even desirable) to escape personal and ideological shadings in this particular project. I began this book with the suggestion that the terrain of Tijerina's life shares similarity with features common in American religion and political life. Tijerina's charismatic leadership in both religious innovation and racial politics has translated into a robust life that mirrors the tumultuous worlds of those arenas. He spent over three decades in the public eye and so there is no lack of opinion about who he is. The sources are tendentious, and many claims made here are certainly subject to future revision.

The standard interpretations of Tijerina's life, apart from the Chicano nationalist one, are social-scientific cookies cut from the theories of cultural change, revitalization, or nativistic movements. Because he is interpreted through the Alianza, Tijerina has been viewed by Peter Nabokov, Frances Swadesh, Nancie González, and others as a type of primitive rebel or secular prophet. Such an interpretation of the rugged, self-made frontier visionary is invariably poised against dominant American culture, the juggernaut of modernity, or the crushing weight of race/class poverty and deprivation.[1] Seen this way, there is a tendency to lionize, or in this case, "tigerize" the leader of an ethnic grassroots movement locked in a battle against elites and institutions. Tijerina's lifelong struggle against evil (real or perceived) lends to the drama of his life a built-in sympathy or even a scholarly paternalism. The result is a kind of accidental hagiography because scholars have focused on Tijerina's "type" at the expense of listening carefully to the singular voice in his writing. What is lacking in the work of these scholars is a serious acknowledgment of the interior religious motor that has animated Tijerina. These scholars do, nevertheless, find that employing the vocabulary of religious movements helps them make sense of the less tangible features of Tijerina's political leadership. Thus González speaks of the "supernatural elements" and the "esoteric doctrines" of the Alianza. Swadesh wrestles with trying to fit the Alianza into A. F. C. Wallace's template of religiously motivated "revitalization movements," and Nabokov speaks of the messianism of the primitive rebel.[2] These interpretations of Tijerina are useful insofar as they show him in relationship to the Alianza. Yet there remains in these interpretations an unresolved tension between a desire to know Tijerina as an enigmatic individual and as the leader in the New Mexico land grant effort in the larger chaos of the late 1960s. I think Nabokov sensed this tension when he observed:

> But some of Tijerina's archetypal characteristics were anachronistic in the second half of the twentieth century. They even conflicted with each other. The fundamentalist and the social bandit clashed over the specific use of violence. The millenarian and the reformer argued over the kind of future to plan for. The revolutionist and the messiah could not get together over the contradictions between long-range and short-range goals.[3]

The other, Chicano revisionist interpretation of Tijerina is also unsatisfactory. I have argued that Chicano history has not illuminated Tijerina's life so much as it has exposed the continuing function of traditional male leadership in cultural nationalist discourse. The installation of a specific, useful image of Tijerina in the 1960s pantheon of movimiento leadership not only circumscribed his career within the 1960s, but it also literally erased him from the textbooks and consciousness of Chicanos into the present day. Like the social scientific interpretations, the standard Chicano studies view of Tijerina is the one linked to the Alianza. But unlike the social science views, the hagiography in Chicano history is anything but accidental.

How then can we begin to understand Tijerina apart from, prior to, and after the Alianza? I suggest three themes: religion, race, and texts. First, we can only begin to make sense of the whole Tijerina by taking seriously the religious nature of Tijerina's thinking and actions in relationship to his Mexican American identity. This quality of mind, combining the theological with the identity politics around race, we detect at work behind his attempts to understand his life in relation to his God and to his community. For it is in the intersection of his evangelical Christian worldview with his struggles as a Mexican American where his religious and political innovations are fashioned. For Tijerina the world around him continues to unfold as a religious enterprise. This we see in his earliest dreams of walking hand in hand with Jesus, his experience as a child of death and resurrection, and the comforting and moral lessons recalled so fondly at his mother's knee. Even during his most political years, we now know through interviews and his memoir that he continued to receive illumination from divine sources and went about his work expecting an outcome of divine justice and retribution.[4]

But life for Tijerina is also inescapably marked by race difference. As a Mexican American Tijerina is continually reminded of his outsider status in American culture. Even during his happiest months hidden away at Valle de Paz, race politics managed to intrude into his utopia as it locked him into the real world of secondary labor markets and the transnational labor exchange with bracero laborers and other minorities. When he realized that theology was no longer capable of subsuming race difference, Tijerina turned to the promises Mexican identity held in the documents of the Spanish land grants. Eventually, the documents themselves became sacred texts, combining religion and race in the Christian-Israelite hypothesis.

Finally, understanding Tijerina's obsession with texts is necessary for making sense of how he orders and understands his life. We have to appreciate the way he reads and writes, appropriates, and then deploys the tropes and gestures of texts. His Bible Institute education taught him that power could be unleashed from the written word, and that texts meant what they said. Thus his land grant arguments derive not so much from the strength or support of the Alianza, or even the mesmerizing power of his charisma, but from the simple enactment of his reading in the United States Constitution that he is guaranteed certain unalienable rights as an American citizen. In a similar and scandalous way his intertextual reading of Old Testament prophecy about the "Chosen" people alongside the history of Spanish Jewry and their presence in the Americas is evidence of a strategy meant to reanimate and create these texts anew. This kind of innovative revision, or what Carlo Ginzburg called "conjectural knowledge," relies not on the rigors of scientific, verifiable experimentation or cumulative quantitative knowledge, but on the "mute forms of knowledge in the sense that their precepts do not lend themselves to being either formalized or spoken. . . . In knowledge of this type imponderable elements come into play: instinct, insight, or intuition."[5] For Tijerina, such conjectural knowledge is supported and shaped by his literalist evangelical worldview and the Mexican Catholic universe of the miraculous.

For Tijerina the sense of a text is not limited to academic interest or theological speculation. For him, as for the unlucky peasant Menocchio and other "pre-moderns," as Steven Justice describes them, texts do not just mean or exist, but they *happen*.[6] That is, for Tijerina the dream narratives of the Hebrew prophet Zechariah, the moldering parchment of the San Joaquín del Cañon del Río de Chama land grant, Article X of the Treaty of Guadalupe Hidalgo, Book 6, Title 1, Law 2 of *The Laws of the Indies, Las Siete Partidas*, the United States Constitution, the Bill of Rights, *The Jewish Encyclopedia*, and even textbooks on psychiatric diagnosis, all occur as mandates, as texts that require embodied action and moral behavior. These texts collide, interact, and are rearticulated in Tijerina's life precisely through instinct, insight, intuition, and divine illumination. It is this maelstrom of voices, histories, and ideologies through which Tijerina forges the past and peers into the future. Such idiosyncratic "conjectural" formulations, some of them troubling and dark, are nevertheless proof of the immeasurable power of religious faith working itself out in the world.

The unique and eccentric quality of Tijerina's arguments and actions confirms what Leonard Primiano points out is the insufficiency of received academic templates regarding "folk" or "popular" religion. Throughout the book I have studiously avoided these terms in favor of Primiano's adoption of the term "vernacular."[7] For Primiano, "vernacular" religion describes and allows for the particularities and singularity of individual or group constructions of belief as they see and live them out. Unlike the concepts "popular," or "folk," or "low" religions, vernacular religions are released from a comparison with "official," "institutional," or "high" religions and can account for the widest display of human interactions with the sacred even as they might occur under the watchful and suspicious eye of institutions. Primiano's fresh view of the multiplicity of religious forms and relationships permits Reies Tijerina to stand on his own in the landscape of American religion without having to be supported by arguments over why, how, and where he "fits." In another way Primiano's concept, spun out of Henry Glassie's work on vernacular architecture, is ideal for thinking about Tijerina and especially how he conceived and constructed the Valle de Paz community. Forming his subterranean home out of earth, car parts, sheets of discarded metal, flagstones, wire, metal poles, and wooden planks, the symmetry between Tijerina's religious ideas and his physical life would never again be so perfect.

In my interviews with Tijerina at his home in the City-State of San Joaquín, I asked him about his revelatory experiences, suspecting and fearing that he was claiming to hear or see God. His response to this issue not only dispelled rumors about his state of mind but also confirmed that, like many of us, he continues to struggle with the limitations of human ability to know the will of heaven.

> When I hear these preachers on the TV on Sunday morning. . . .
> You know, that they say it was so easy [to reach God]. You know,
> that they say, "I talked to God," "God told me this; God told me
> that"! And so repetitiously, you know: "He told me." That, "I saw
> him," "God told me," and "God talked to me." I say, "Wait a
> minute! What have they done?" I suffered a lot! I think that I've
> been to hell and back many times and don't I get to see . . . [laugh-
> ter]!? Don't I get to hear his voice?

So, I mean, I have my own *sentimientos* [sorrows, grief] because I say, "Well, I have never seen him! I have never heard him!" I mean, he intends to put me through life without seeing him? Without hearing him?

Pausing just long enough to catch his breath, King Tiger took comfort in the words from the book that continues to speak to him: "Of course . . . he did say, 'Blessed are those who do not see and yet believe!' "

NOTES

Introduction

1. Robert Tice, *The Rhetoric of La Raza* (Kingsville: Texas A & I University/M.A.Y.O., 1971), 22.

2. See for example the image chosen for the cover story on the thirtieth anniversary of the Tierra Amarilla courthouse raid in the Albuquerque *Weekly Alibi*, June 1997.

3. Reies López Tijerina, *Mi lucha por la tierra* (Mexico D.F.: Fondo de Cultura Económica, 1978). An abridged English translation of Tijerina's memoir is titled *They Called Me "King Tiger": My Struggle for the Land and Our Rights*, José Angel Gutiérrez, ed. and trans. (Houston: Arte Público Press, 2000).

4. Rudy V. Busto, "Like a Mighty Rushing Wind: The Religious Impulse in the Life and Writing of Reies López Tijerina," (PhD diss., University of California at Berkeley, 1991). Norma Alarcón, "Conjugating Subjects: The Heteroglossia of Essence and Resistance," in *An Other Tongue*, Alfred Arteaga, ed. (Durham, N.C.: Duke University Press, 1994), 125–38.

5. For example, see Gastón Espinosa, "'El Azteca': Francisco Olazábal and Latino Pentecostal Charisma, Power and Faith Healing in the Borderlands," *Journal of the American Academy of Religion* 67:3 (1999), 597–616.

6. I am speaking specifically about Chicano studies and, to a similar degree, Asian American studies. For reasons of history and political struggle, religion's centrality for African Americans and Native Americans has long been acknowledged in scholarship. The larger point I am making here has to do with the general flavor and development of academic ethnic studies.

7. I am borrowing Robert Blauner's distinction between "ethnic immigrants" and "colonized minorities" who differ historically in their voluntary/involuntary incorporation into the United States, relative success and ease in the labor market, and their ability to maintain cultural forms (*Racial Oppression in America*, [New York: Harper & Row, 1972]).

8. Bert Corona and Mario Garcia, *Memories of Chicano History: The Life and Narrative of Bert Corona* (Berkeley: University of California Press, 1994), 343.

9. "Chicano Leader Speaks at UNM. Tijerina Donates Rare Land Grant Archive Information to Center for Southwest Research," *New Mexico Daily Lobo* (University of New Mexico), 20 October 1999.

Chapter One

1. "Web of Death: 'The Next Level,'" *Newsweek*, 7 April 1997, 26–43, 46–47.
2. "Shutting Down a Siege: In Texas, an Armed Standoff Comes to a Sudden End," *Newsweek*, 12 May 1997, 46.
3. Carlo Ginzburg, *The Cheese and the Worms: The Cosmos of a Sixteenth-Century Miller*, John and Anne Tedeschi, trans. (Baltimore: Johns Hopkins University Press, 1980).
4. Ginzburg, *The Cheese and the Worms*, 51, 5–6.
5. Steven Justice, *Writing and Rebellion: England in 1381* (Berkeley: University of California Press, 1994).
6. Orlando Espín, "Popular Catholicism among Latinos," in *Hispanic Catholic Culture in the U.S.: Issues and Concerns*, Jay Dolan and Allan Figueroa Deck, eds. (Notre Dame, Ind.: University of Notre Dame Press, 1994), 308–59.
7. Michael Jenkinson, *Tijerina: Land Grant Conflict in New Mexico* (Albuquerque: Paisano Press, 1968); Peter Nabokov, *Tijerina and the Courthouse Raid* (Albuquerque: University of New Mexico Press, 1969); Richard Gardner, *Grito!: Reies Tijerina and the New Mexico Land Grant War of 1967* (Indianapolis: Bobbs-Merrill Company, 1970); Patricia Bell Blawis, *Tijerina and the Land Grants: Mexican Americans in Struggle for Their Heritage* (New York: International Publishers, 1971).
8. Jenkinson, *Tijerina: Land Grant Conflict in New Mexico*, 23.
9. See Maurilio Vigil's massive dissertation, "Ethnic Organizations among the Mexican Americans of New Mexico: A Political Perspective" (PhD diss., New Mexico Highlands University, 1974) for a good example of how extensively Gardner and Nabokov are used.
10. Few Chicano histories, for example, deal with the Brown Beret occupation of Catalina Island off the California coast in September of 1972. Richard Griswold del Castillo sees this event as a "relatively minor incident" in comparison with Tijerina's takeover of the Echo Canyon Amphitheater in 1966 (*The Treaty of Guadalupe Hidalgo: A Legacy of Conflict* [Norman: University of Oklahoma Press, 1990], 144).
11. Gardner, *Grito!*, 39. Italics in original text.
12. Gardner, *Grito!*, 259.
13. Gardner explains that he had returned to New Mexico where he had spent his childhood to write another book. Writing his book on Tijerina was more or less accidental (*Grito!*, 8–9).
14. Nabokov, *Tijerina and the Courthouse Raid*, 137–39. Nabokov allowed himself to be blindfolded and led at gunpoint to Tijerina's hiding place in order to interview him.
15. Reies Tijerina, *Mi lucha por la tierra* (Mexico, D.F.: Fondo de Cultura Económica, 1978), 159.
16. Peter Nabokov's notes, various interviews, and collected documents are housed in the Zimmerman Library, Special Collections, University of New Mexico, designated as Archive #93, Peter Nabokov Papers. Items are cited as Nabokov Papers, followed by Box, folder, item, and page number where appropriate.
17. Nabokov, *Tijerina and the Courthouse Raid*, 280–81.
18. Jenkinson, *Tijerina: Land Grant Conflict in New Mexico*, 25.

19. She sets the tone of her approach early on in her preface: "This book follows the career of Tijerina up to the present time, a man who met racial oppression from his earliest childhood as a migrant farm worker. We shall observe the ways he found of fighting it and leading others in the fight, first in the isolation of his own national group, then gradually in the recognition that a common front of all hurt by racism, including the "good Anglos," is what must bring the monster down (*Tijerina and the Land Grants*, 10).

20. Blawis, *Tijerina and the Land Grants*, 34, 36.

21. Tijerina, *Mi lucha por la tierra*, 302, 325. He also adds at the end of the memoir that the Nabokov and Gardner biographies "hurt the cause and made my life more difficult" (*Mi lucha por la tierra*, 326).

22. Carlos Muñoz, Jr., interview with Reies López Tijerina, Albuquerque, New Mexico, 3 August 1975.

23. Griswold del Castillo, *The Treaty of Guadalupe Hidalgo*, 132. In his study of the nineteenth-century secretive "White Caps" (*las Gorras Blancas*) land grant resistance movement, Robert Larson credits the Chicano Movement with raising the issues about land grant resistance. The White Caps, he concludes, "provided an example of resistance that would not be duplicated until Reies Tijerina's Alianza movement of the 1960s." "The White Caps of New Mexico: A Study of Ethnic Militancy in the Southwest," *Pacific Historical Review* 44:2 (May 1975), 171–85. See Nancie L. González's assessment of the Alianza's impact in *The Spanish-Americans of New Mexico: A Heritage of Pride*, 2nd ed. (Albuquerque: University of New Mexico Press, 1969), 180–86.

24. Gilbert White, Koch, Kelly, and McCarthy, and the New Mexico State Planning Office, *Land Title Study* (Santa Fe: New Mexico State Planning Office, 1971). In 1971 Tijerina charged the State of New Mexico and the Federal Government Four Corners Commission, co-sponsors of the study, with attempting to suppress the Study claiming that the "land grant part of the report completely backs up and supports the position of myself and of the Alianza Federál de Pueblos Libres over the past decade . . ." Reies López Tijerina, "Statement," December 2, 1971 (Nabokov Papers Box 1, Folder 30, Item 24).

25. Matt S. Meier and Feliciano Rivera, *The Chicanos: A History of Mexican Americans* (New York: Hill and Wang, 1972); Rodolfo Acuña, *Occupied America: The Chicano's Struggle Toward Liberation* (San Francisco: Canfield Press, 1972).

26. Alejandro Morales, "Expanding the Meaning of Chicano Cinema: Yo Soy Chicano, Raíces de Sangre, Seguín," *Bilingual Review/Revista Bilingüe* 10:2–3 (May–December 1983), 121–37.

27. *CHICANO! The History of the Mexican American Civil Rights Movement* [film], Hector Galán, Series Producer (Los Angeles: National Latino Communications Group—Galán Productions, 1996).

28. Ignácio Garcia, *United We Win: The Rise and Fall of La Raza Unida Party* (Tucson: University of Arizona Press, 1989). See Gutiérrez's thoughts on the movement in John C. Hammerback, Richard J. Jensen, and José Angel Gutiérrez, *A War of Words: Chicano Protest in the 1960s and 1970s* (Westport, Conn.: Greenwood Press, 1985), 121–62.

29. See the collected essays on various idealizations of the Aztlán utopia in *Aztlán: Essays on the Chicano Homeland*, Rudolfo A. Anaya and Francisco Lomelí, eds. (Albuquerque: University of New Mexico Press, 1989).

30. Alex Saragoza, "The Significance of Recent Chicano-Related Historical Writings: An Appraisal," *Ethnic Affairs* 1 (Fall 1987), 25–62; Carlos E. Cortés, "New Chicano Historiography," in *Borderlands Sourcebook: A Guide to the Literature on Northern Mexico and the American Southwest*, Ellwyn R. Stoddard, et al., eds. (Norman: University of Oklahoma Press, 1983), 61.

31. Tomás Almaguér, "Ideological Distortions in Recent Chicano Historiography: The Internal Colonial Model and Chicano Historical Interpretation," *Aztlán* 18:1 (Spring 1987), 7–28.

32. Saragoza, "The Significance of Recent Chicano-Related Historical Writings," 28–29. Saragoza explains that Acuña's use of the term "Hispanic" in the third edition added a new texture to *Occupied America*. Previous editions had been guilty of "flattening out" the diversity within Chicano histories and experiences.

33. Rodolfo Acuña, *Occupied America: A History of Chicanos*, 3rd ed. (New York: Harper & Row, 1988), 450.

34. Rodolfo Acuña, *Occupied America: A History of Chicanos*, 4th ed. (New York: Longman, 2000).

35. Alex Saragoza explains the "them versus us" in Chicano history as the product of convergence of the civil rights movement and the emergence of social history's concern for non-elite subjects: "This tendency influenced a generation of scholars, including most students of the Chicano past at the time. Thus, the intellectual roots of Chicano history were nourished by the profession's enthusiasm for labor, urban, family, and related historical fields that fell under the rubric of social history. Furthermore, the orientation of the practitioners of the new social history tended to be revisionist, critical of previous treatments of minorities, workers, and women. This view within the profession facilitated (if not spurred) the emergence of Chicano history and its intrinsic disapproval of an assimilationist perspective on ethnic/race relations in American history. As a result, the beginnings of Chicano history were by and large implicitly nationalist in origin" ("Recent Chicano Historiography: An Interpretive Essay," *Aztlán* 19:1 [1988–1990], 8–9).

36. Alex Saragoza, "Recent Chicano Historiography," 39.

37. Carlos Muñoz, Jr., *Youth, Identity, Power: The Chicano Movement* (London: Verso, 1989), 7–8.

38. The efforts by racial minorities in the United States were linked to various liberation efforts in the Third World by Internal Colonial theorists. See Blauner, *Racial Oppression in America*, especially his chapter, "Immigrant and Colonized Minorities"; Acuña, *Occupied America*, 1st ed. (1972), 77.

39. Acuña, *Occupied America*, 3rd ed., 338.

40. Acuña, *Occupied America*, 3rd ed., 449.

41. Acuña, *Occupied America: A History of Chicanos*, 2nd ed. (New York: Harper & Row, 1981), 364; Acuña, *Occupied America*, 3rd ed., 341, 449. The original version, however, without the benefit of hindsight, pointed out that Tijerina was becoming fatalistic prior to his imprisonment. This judgment allowed the reader to draw her own conclusion as to the reasons for Tijerina's dramatic shift to conciliatory politics after his release. The folklore that continued to circulate even into the 1990s about a forced lobotomy and mind-altering drugs in the prison hospital make clear the intention of Acuña's vagueness.

42. Acuña, *Occupied America*, 4th ed., 370–71.

43. Juan Gómez Quiñones, *Chicano Politics: Reality and Promise, 1940–1990* (Albuquerque: University of New Mexico Press, 1990), 118.

44. Gómez Quiñones, *Chicano Politics*, 118.

45. Saragoza, "Recent Chicano Historiography," 52. See also John R. Chávez, *The Lost Land: The Chicano Image of the Southwest* (Albuquerque: University of New Mexico Press, 1984), 138–41, for another standard retelling of Tijerina's activism.

46. *CHICANO! The History of the Mexican American Civil Rights Movement* (Episode 1, "Quest for a Homeland"); Francisco A. Rosales, *CHICANO! The History of the Mexican American Civil Rights Movement* (Houston: Arte Público Press, 1996).

47. Rosales, *CHICANO!*, 167, 170.
48. Rosales, *CHICANO!*, 169. To his credit, Rosales's portrayal does connect Tijerina's activism to earlier Hispano agrarian resistance and hints at the devastation of his federal imprisonment as "no other major Chicano Movement leader spent as much time incarcerated; and while many were harassed by the police, it was not to the same degree."
49. Tijerina seems to have escaped the disappointment by some Chicano activists in the 1980s who felt that the other Horsemen had "sold out." Editorials in the Chicano paper, *La Prensa* (San Diego) said of Corky Gonzáles: "Not nice of Corky Gonzáles to come and preach revolution to local Chicanos . . . and then jet out to Colorado. Corky, latest middle age revolutionary who made one million selling property in Colorado. Come on Corky, it's tough to swallow from a successful capitalist" (27 April 1984, 4); of Gutiérrez: "Union carried an interesting hate-raza letter dredging up name of José Angel Gutiérrez. . . . If Union wanted to strike fear in Anglo community, forget it. Angel Gutiérrez, is currently completing his PhD work at U. of Texas. After that, he will be heading for Oregon to run for State Rep. Gosh, how American can you be?" (3 August 1984, 3); of Chávez: "In his heyday, Chávez commanded the undying loyalty of the Mexican American residents of the great Southwest. Success however led to an arrogance of power which caused an exodus of top loyalists. Retreating into isolation, Chávez surrounded himself with Unionists, mostly white, who used Chávez and the Farm Workers Union for narrow limited focused concerns. The major over-riding issues of the movement were ignored or forgotten. In the process, Chávez lost touch with the 4 million Chicanos of California." (27 January 1984, 4).
50. Acuña, *Occupied America*, 3rd ed., 340.

Chapter Two

1. An indication of the irregularities in even the most simple biographical facts in Tijerina's life is his birth date, given variously as 1932 (Blawis; Tice), 1926, or 1927 (Jenkinson). 1926 is the correct date and is corroborated by Nabokov (1969), Gardner, Grayson, and Tijerina (1968), and the U.S. Department of Justice (1997). Right wing columnist, Alan Stang, accused Tijerina of manufacturing a birth certificate in 1956 ("Terror Grows: 'War on Poverty' Supports Castroite Terrorists," *American Opinion* 11:3 [March 1968], 3–4). His brothers are Margarito, Anselmo, Ramón, and Cristóbal. His two sisters, who are absent in his biographies, are Josefina, and Maria. See Mario Barrera, *Race and Class in the Southwest: A Theory of Racial Inequality* (Notre Dame, Ind.: University of Notre Dame Press, 1979), 77–83, for the structural location of Mexican labor in the 1920s. Paul Taylor discusses the relationship between Mexican and black agricultural labor and details how cotton growers rationalized the exploitation of racially ethnic labor ("Mexicans North of the Rio Grande," *Survey Graphic* 19:2 [May 1931], reprinted in Paul Taylor, *On the Ground in the Thirties* [Salt Lake City: Peregrine Smith Books, 1983], 1–16). See David Montejano's chapter on "Segregation, 1920–1930" for details on the increasingly rigid racial hierarchy and the impoverishment of Mexican labor in Texas during this time period (*Anglos and Mexicans in the Making of Texas, 1836–1986* [Austin: University of Texas Press, 1987]).
2. Reies López Tijerina, *Mi lucha por la tierra* (Mexico, D.F.: Fondo de Cultura Económica, 1978), 381.
3. Richard Gardner, *Grito!: Reies Tijerina and the New Mexico Land Grant War of 1967* (Indianapolis: Bobbs-Merrill Company, 1970), 32–33; Clark Knowlton, "Tijerina: Hero of the Militants," *The Texas Observer* 61:6 (28 March 1969), 1. Tijerina says little about his father, Antonio, whom he portrays as a meek and defeated man.

4. Author's field notes, Coyote, New Mexico, April 1990.

5. Nabokov Papers, Box II, folder 22, Item 16, 4; A. B. Collado, "Reies Tijerina: ¿Héroe o Malhechor?" *El Hispano* 2:8 (8 August 1967). For an "objective" but sobering overview of migrant worker conditions see also Selden C. Menefree, *Mexican Migratory Workers of South Texas* (Washington, D.C.: Federal Works Agency, WPA, 1941).

6. Nabokov Papers, Box II, folder 22, Item 18, 5.

7. A. B. Collado, "Reies Tijerina: ¿Héroe o Malhechor?" *El Hispano* 2:9 (15 August 1967). For background on Mexican American labor in Michigan during the 1940s, see Jane B. Haney, "Migration, Settlement Pattern, and Social Organization: A Midwest Mexican-American Case Study" (PhD diss., Michigan State University, 1978), 89–97; Harvey M. Choldin and Grafton D. Trout, "Mexican Americans in Transition: Migration and Employment in Michigan Cities" (East Lansing: Department of Sociology, Michigan State University/U.S. Department of Labor, Rural Manpower Center, 1969), 173–87; and Dennis Nodin Valdés, *El Pueblo Mexicano en Detroit y Michigan: A Social History* (Detroit: Wayne State University Press, 1982), 45–78. A government study of Texas-Mexican migrant workers noted that many Texans spent the winters in Texas and in the spring the two major routes north were from San Antonio to either Greeley, Colorado, or Saginaw, Michigan, the latter being the route followed by the Tijerinas (*Texas-Mexicans in Sugar Beets, Vegetables and Fruits: A Report on Improved Relations between Migratory Farm Workers and Agricultural Employers in North Central and Great Plains States, 1943–1947* [Washington, D.C.: U.S. Department of Agriculture, Extension [Service] Farm Labor Program, 1948], 3).

8. Nabokov Papers, Box II, folder 22, Item 18, 5.

9. Victor de Leon, *The Silent Pentecostals: A Biographical History of the Pentecostal Movement among the Hispanics in the Twentieth Century* (Taylors, S.C.: Faith Printing, Co., 1979), 68–90.

10. Author's interview with Reies Tijerina, Coyote, New Mexico, April 1990.

11. "Bible Institutes, Colleges, Universities," s.v., *Dictionary of Pentecostal and Charismatic Movements*, Stanley M. Burgess and Gary B. McGee, eds. (Grand Rapids, Mich.: Regency Reference Library, 1988), 62.

12. "Bible Institutes," 62.

13. Nabokov Papers, Box II, Folder 22, Item 16, 5.

14. Nabokov Papers, Box II, Folder 22, Item 16, 6 shows him in Mexico (1949), New York (1952), Los Angeles (1952). My field interview (1990) records him pastoring churches in Saginaw and Pontiac, Michigan; Victoria and Eden, Texas. Other locations include Chama, New Mexico (1950) and New York City (1953). Tijerina's collection of sermons includes cities and dates for Melvin, Michigan (Illinois?) (9 May 1953), San Antonio, Texas (3 August 1953), New York City (27 November 1953), Austin, Texas (22 February 1953), Victoria, Texas (12 March 1954), El Monte, California (15 April and 22 November 1954), and Carlsbad, California (30 June 1954). Tijerina's memoir notes that he and his followers were in Fruita, Colorado in the summer of 1955.

15. Matthew 19:21, Mark 10:21, Luke 12:33, 18:22, I John 3:17.

16. Gardner, *Grito!*, 39.

17. Gardner, *Grito!*, 39. Nabokov puts this event between 1957 and 1960 (*Tijerina and the Courthouse Raid* [Albuquerque: University of New Mexico Press, 1969], 203–4), Gardner locates it in 1946. However, the conclusions Tijerina reaches are consonant with those reached in his sermon, "El Sabio Perdido" (Lost Wisdom) which he wrote in the spring of 1954 in El Monte. This date is also closer to his shift from an itinerant preacher to leader of his own sect in 1955.

18. Gardner, *Grito!*, 38–39.

19. Author's Tijerina interview, 1990.

20. Gardner, *Grito!*, 44.

21. Jesse Miranda, personal communication, 1 September 2000.

22. Nabokov, *Tijerina and the Courthouse Raid*, 210; Gardner, *Grito!*, 43–44.

23. Gardner, *Grito!*, 256.

24. Michael Jenkinson, *Tijerina: Land Grant Conflict in New Mexico* (Albuquerque: Paisano Press, 1968), 21.

25. Reies López Tijerina, *¿Hallará Fe en la Tierra . . . ?* (n.p, 1954?), inside cover.

26. Gardner, *Grito!*, 46–47; Nabokov, *Tijerina and the Courthouse Raid*, 202–3. A reproduction of Tijerina's alleged FBI record in Alan Stang's jingoist editorial lists his Arizona arrest record as "grand theft" 19 March 1957, and 5 April 1957; and "aiding a prisoner to escape," 7 July 1957 ("Terror Grows," 7). A similar list appears in the "Tijerina Dossier— O.E.O.," Nabokov Papers, Box II, Folder 48, Item 1–5, 3.

27. Robert J. Rosenbaum and Robert W. Larson, "Mexicano Resistance to the Expropriation of Grant Lands in New Mexico," in *Land, Water, and Culture: New Perspectives on Hispanic Land Grants*, Charles L. Briggs and John R. Van Ness, eds. (Albuquerque: University of New Mexico Press, 1987), 299, 306. See also Gardner, *Grito!*, 66–84.

28. Tijerina, *Mi lucha por la tierra*, 46; Gardner, *Grito!*, 77–78.

29. Tijerina indicates that he was first introduced to the idea of land rights by Kenzy Savage, the director of the Instituto Biblico Latino Americano: "He was the first witness, the first . . . person with authority that pointed out the fact that the claims, the people's rights, the people's claims were right and they had their rights and the land had been taken away from them" (Author's field notes, 1990).

30. Gardner, *Grito!*, 79.

31. Mario Gill, *Nuestros buenos vecinos*, 5th ed. (Mexico City: Editorial Azteca, 1959), 87. My translation.

32. Richard Griswold del Castillo notes that as recently as 1984, the United States has avoided any discussion of the Treaty, although it has acknowledged the intent of the Treaty's protection of Mexican American land grant rights (*The Treaty of Guadalupe Hidalgo: A Legacy of Conflict* [Norman: University of Oklahoma Press, 1990], 106). The *Voz de Aztlán* newspaper (Albuquerque) reported in 2001 that "that the U.S. Government Accounting Office . . . released an Exposure Draft of a report that will review land grants that were issued by Spain and later by the Republic of Mexico. . . . In this report, the first in a series, the U.S. government agreed to (1) define the concept of community land grants and (2) identify the types of community land grants in New Mexico that meet the definition. Subsequently, the government will describe the procedures established to implement the treaty, identify concerns about how the treaty was implemented, and what alternatives may be available to address these concerns" ("United States Government to Review New Mexico Land Grants Under the Treaty of Guadalupe-Hidalgo" [January 31, 2001]).

33. Tijerina, *Mi lucha por la tierra*, 44–45.

34. Patty Newman, *¡Do it up Brown!* (San Diego: Viewpoint Books, 1971), 24–25; Knowlton, "Tijerina: Hero of the Militants," 2. Tijerina's possible association with Mexican secessionist factions when he was in Mexico is supported by his connection to Mario Gill (aka Carlos Velasco Gil), the author of a book on synarchism written for the partisan Comité de la Revolución in the 1940s.

35. Nabokov, *Tijerina and the Courthouse Raid*, 203.

36. Ernest S. Stapleton, Jr., "The History of Baptist Missions in New Mexico, 1849–1866," (MA thesis, University of New Mexico, 1954), 212–37; Tijerina, *Mi lucha por la tierra*, 58–59. William DeBuys explains that "Strong in numbers and united in outlook in the late nineteenth century, a number of local Penitente chapters began to dabble in politics. Predictably, their participation in public issues, although never entirely explicit, provoked angry condemnations from Anglo and Anglicized Hispanos. The reluctance of the Brothers to discuss their internal affairs publicly only added to the general fear that the Penitentes obediently submitted to the control of one demagogue after another. Their unseemly political character, as perceived by the rest of the country, was probably a significant factor in the delay of New Mexican statehood until 1912" (*Enchantment and Exploitation: The Life and Hard Times of a New Mexican Mountain Range* [Albuquerque: University of New Mexico Press, 1985], 129–30. For a responsible and sympathetic background on the Penitentes see Fray Angélico Chávez, "The Penitentes of New Mexico," *New Mexico Historical Review* 29 (1954), 635–46; Marta Weigle, *Brothers of Light, Brothers of Blood: The Penitentes of the Southwest* (Albuquerque: University of New Mexico Press, 1967). Rosenbaum and Larson note that the Penitentes are popularly acknowledged as closely tied to land grant struggles, although hard evidence [documentation] is lacking ("Mexicano Resistance to the Expropriation of Grant Lands in New Mexico," 306). Tijerina is much more forthright about these connections (*Mi lucha por la tierra*, 58–59).

37. Thomas Weaver, "Social Structure, Change and Conflict in a New Mexican Village" (PhD diss., University of California at Berkeley, 1965), 27–28, 132–33; de Leon, *The Silent Pentecostals*, 121–122.

38. Nancie L. González, *The Spanish-Americans of New Mexico: A Heritage of Pride* (Albuquerque: University of New Mexico Press, 1969), 99; Frankie McCarty, *Land Grant Problems in New Mexico* (Albuquerque: Albuquerque Journal, 1969), 16; Tijerina, *Mi lucha por la tierra*, 58; Joseph L. Love, "La Raza: Mexican Americans in Rebellion," *TRANS-action* (February 1969), reprinted in *Pain and Promise: The Chicanos Today*, Edward Simmens, ed. (New York: Mentor/New American Library, 1972), 279.

39. Tijerina, *Mi lucha por la tierra*, 60.

40. Tijerina, *Mi lucha por la tierra*, 68–70, 73–74, 201–2. Newman is similarly reluctant to implicate Tijerina in this pre-Alianza activism (*¡Do it up Brown!*, 26).

41. He notes that the family was unable to receive general assistance aid for fear that his fugitive status would be revealed. Because he was limited in his ability to work, he writes that Maria was "the only way out" of the family's economic hardship (*Mi lucha por la tierra*, 78).

42. He notes that he used a wig he had bought in Mexico and that with women's clothing he had "many times escaped ambushes" by officials (*Mi lucha por la tierra*, 76).

43. "Is New York Sitting on a 'Powder Keg'?" *U.S. News and World Report*, 3 August 1959, 48–51.

44. Tijerina, *Mi lucha por la tierra*, 80.

45. Note the themes in Elijah Muhammad's 1959 Nation of Islams Saviour's Day convention address and the details of the Nation's race-based theology in Claude A. Clegg III, *An Original Man: The Life and Times of Elijah Muhammad* (New York: St. Martin's Press, 1997), 41–731, 117–23. See also E. U. Essien-Udom, *Black Nationalism: A Search for an Identity in America* (Chicago: University of Chicago Press, 1962), 283–85; and Elijah Muhammad, *Message to the Blackman in America* (Philadelphia: Hakim's Publications, 1965), 222–24. Barton Lee Ingraham recognized the similarities between the Nation of Islam's Yakub myth and Tijerina's interpretation of the mestizo trope as early as 1966 in "Reies López Tijerina and the Spanish Americans of New Mexico: A Study in Cultural

Conflict," (MA Thesis, University of California at Berkeley, 1968), 99, fn 45. Lieu reports that in 1987 Tijerina acknowledged that Elijah Muhammad had discussed the idea of "nuclear rebirth" with him during these conversations; an idea that Tijerina develops in the late 1980s ("The Courthouse Raid: Twenty Years Later," *Rio Grande Sun* [28 May 1987]). Claude Clegg, III, does not recall any mention of Tijerina's visit to Muhammad in his research, but confirmed that he was in the habit of receiving visitors graciously (personal communication 17 August 1997).

46. See Frances L. Swadesh's useful analysis of Tijerina's efforts in Mexico based upon Mexican newspaper accounts in "The Alianza Movement of New Mexico," in *Minorities and Politics*, H. J. Tobias and C. E. Woodhouse, eds. (Albuquerque: University of New Mexico Press, 1969), 53–84.

47. "Minorities: Crusade Against Gringos," *Newsweek*, 3 January 1966, 17.

48. Nabokov, *Tijerina and the Courthouse Raid*, 211.

49. The radio show ran through September, 1966. The television program continued until New Year's Eve, 1967. Tijerina, *Mi lucha por la tierra*, 114–15.

50. He recounts the humiliating event in *Mi lucha por la tierra*, 108–10.

51. Knowlton, "Tijerina: Hero of the Militants," 3. For an overview of land use issues in Rio Arriba County, see Alvar W. Carlson, *The Spanish-American Homeland: Four Centuries in New Mexico's Río Arriba* (Baltimore: Johns Hopkins University Press, 1990), 111–26.

52. Tijerina, *Mi lucha por la tierra*, 113, 116–17.

53. Frances L. Swadesh, "The Alianza Movement: Catalyst for Social Change in New Mexico," in *Spanish-Speaking People in the United States, Proceedings of the 1968 Annual Spring Meeting of the American Ethnological Society*, June Helm, ed., (Seattle and London: American Ethnological Society/University of Washington, 1969), 168.

54. John Thomas Vance, *The Background of Hispanic-American Law: Legal Sources and Juridical Literature of Spain* (New York: Central Book Company, 1943), 93–107.

55. Tijerina, *Mi lucha por la tierra*, 122; Gardner, *Grito!*, 142–53.

56. Vance, *Background of Hispanic-American Law*, 100–102.

57. Tijerina, *Mi lucha por la tierra*, 122. See Vance, *Background of Hispanic-American Law*, 121ff; and S. Lyman Tyler, ed. and comp., *Spanish Laws Concerning Discoveries, Pacifications, and Settlements among the Indians*, Occasional Papers 17 (Salt Lake City: American West Center, University of Utah, 1980).

58. Tijerina, *Mi lucha por la tierra*, 125; Gardner, *Grito!*, 122.

59. "Land Grant Officials State Their Claim," *New Mexican* [Española], 10 November 1966; Blawis, *Tijerina and the Land Grants: Mexican Americans in Struggle for Their Heritage* (New York: International Publishers, 1971), 27–31; Malcolm Ebright, "New Mexican Land Grants: The Legal Background," in *Land, Water, and Culture: New Perspectives on Hispanic Land Grants*, Charles L. Briggs and John R. Van Ness, eds. (Albuquerque: University of New Mexico Press, 1987), 41–50; Clark S. Knowlton, "Violence in New Mexico: A Sociological Perspective," *California Law Review* 58 (1970), 1064–68. There were two attempts to occupy the Echo Amphitheater. The first attempt was on October 15, but there were no reporters or government officials there to witness it or challenge the group.

60. Jim Neal, "Analysis: Alianza Chalked Up Another Win," *The New Mexican* [Santa Fe], 27 October 1966; Tijerina, *Mi lucha por la tierra*, 126ff; Nabokov, *Tijerina and the Courthouse Raid*, 51–54; Gardner, *Grito!*, 127–32; Patricia Bell Blawis, *Tijerina and the Land Grants*, 56–66. Tijerina told the court later that he had chosen the amphitheater because "it was a public place, and it was in good position, where tourists would go by, and easy for reporters to approach" (*United States v. Tijerina*, 407 F.2d 349 [1969] at 352fn4).

61. Tijerina, *Mi lucha por la tierra*, 134–41. Victor Westphall notes that the Court of Private Land Claims was biased toward government retention of disputed lands. Despite the Alianza's claim that the San Joaquín grant covered almost 500,000 acres, the Court of Private Land Claims recognized only a narrow strip of 1,422 acres (Victor Westphall, *Mercedes Reales: Hispanic Land Grants of the Upper Rio Grande Region* [Albuquerque: University of New Mexico Press, 1983], 251, 257). See also McCarty, *Land Grant Problems in New Mexico*, 7–10.

62. "200 Alianza Members Parade at Statehouse," *Santa Fe New Mexican*, 18 April 1967; Gardner, *Grito!*, 142.

63. Clark S. Knowlton, "Reies López Tijerina and the Alianza: Some Considerations," paper presented at the Rural Sociological Society Annual Meeting, College Station, Texas, 24 August 1984, 14–16.

64. Tijerina, *Mi lucha por la tierra*, 150.

65. Tijerina, *Mi lucha por la tierra*, 146–55; Nabokov, *Tijerina and the Courthouse Raid*, 75–92; Gardner, *Grito!*, 1–7; Blawis, *Tijerina and the Land Grants*, 80–89. The summary of events by Knowlton ("Reies López Tijerina and the Alianza") is particularly useful, as is the brief account in Barton Lee Ingraham, "Reies López Tijerina and the Spanish Americans of New Mexico," 1–4. Larry Calloway's first person account appeared in "The American Revolution of 1967," *Argosy* (2 February 1968), 121–23.

66. Clark S. Knowlton, "Violence in New Mexico," 1082; "New Mexico Band Eludes Pursuers: 550 Guardsmen and Police Hunt land-Dispute Rebels," *El Grito del Norte*, 7 June 1967. See the eyewitness accounts by Alianza members in Rubén Darío Sálaz's "Asuntos Nuevo Mexicanos" column in *El Hispano*, 2:11 (29 August 1967), 2; 2:12 (5 September 1967), 2.

67. Poor People's Campaign of New Mexico, "Press Release" n.d., Nabokov Papers, File #93, Box 1, Folder 30, Item 24. See also, Reies López Tijerina, "The People's Column: Tijerina Answers Back [letter to editor]," *Albuquerque Journal*, 1 May 1968, n.p.; Nabokov Papers, File #93, Box 1, Folder 30, Item 71), for Tijerina's defense of his position. See Frances L. Swadesh's assessment of the tension between Tijerina and the SCLC leadership at the Poor People's Campaign in "The Alianza Movement of New Mexico."

68. "Reies Meets with Panthers," *La Hormiga* [Oakland, Calif.] 1:2 (August 1968).

69. "Nuevo Partido Nomina Tijerina," *El Grito Del Norte*, 1:1 (24 August 1968), 1, 2; "Enters Governor's Race," *Albuquerque Journal*, 28 July 1968, E10; Maurilio Vigil notes that the Partido Constitucional del Pueblo was "the first modern effort to form a separate Mexican American party" preceding the more well known La Raza Unida Party's formation in Texas, 1970 ("Ethnic Organizations among the Mexican Americans of New Mexico: A Political Perspective [PhD diss., New Mexico Highlands University, 1974], 185). Reies López Tijerina, "Por Qué Me Decidí Correr?" *El Grito Del Norte*, 1: 1 (1968), 4.

70. Tijerina, *Mi lucha por la tierra*, 234–67; Nabokov, *Tijerina and the Courthouse Raid*, 257–67; Gardner, *Grito!*, 265–82; Clark Knowlton, "Reies López Tijerina and the Alianza Federál de Mercedes: Seekers after Justice," *Wisconsin Sociologist*, 22:4 (Fall 1985), 134; See also Carrol W. Cagle and Harry P. Stumpf, "The Trial of Reies López Tijerina," in *Political Trials*, Theodore L. Becker, ed. (Indianapolis: Bobbs-Merrill, Company, 1971), 183–203, for details of the trial. See also Bob Huber, "Verdict Strengthens Tijerina Movement," *The Denver Post*, 29 December 1968, reprinted by Alianza Federál de Pueblos Libres. For a hostile account of the trial see Alan Stang, "New Mexico: The Coming Guerrilla War," *American Opinion* 12:3 (March 1969), 49–62.

71. *The New Mexico Review and Legislative Journal*, 30 January 1969, 4.

72. "Episcopalian Fund Asked," *Albuquerque Journal*, 6 June 1969; "Southwest Episcopal Diocese To Withhold Mission Funds," *The Christian Century* 87:2 (14 January 1970), 38; Blawis, *Tijerina and the Land Grants*, 174–75; "Right Rev. Kinsolving Can't Go Along with the Episcopal Church," *The New Mexico Review and Legislative Report*, January 1970, 6–7; Nabokov, *Tijerina and the Courthouse Raid*, 278–79.

73. "Presbyterians, Alianza Spar for Rights to Ranch Lands," *Albuquerque Journal*, 2 June 1969, A1, 7; Blawis, *Tijerina and the Land Grants*, 172–74; Tijerina, *Mi lucha por la tierra*, 289–90. Nabokov adds that the Presbyterians eventually offered instead a $50,000 grant to aid Chicano development and that Tijerina refused to take it (*Tijerina and the Courthouse Raid*, 272–73). For background on the disposition of the Ghost Ranch property, see Paul Kutsche and John R. Van Ness, *Cañones: Values, Crisis, and Survival in a Northern New Mexico Village* (Salem, Wisc.: Sheffield Publishing Co., 1981), 205–7.

74. Nabokov, *Tijerina and the Courthouse Raid*, 269–70.

75. Blawis, *Tijerina and the Land Grants*, 168–69; "Aztlán! Porque?," Preliminary Draft, Alianza Federál de Pueblos Libres, 1969[?], typewritten copy, Vertical Files, Chicano Studies Library, University of California at Berkeley. In interviews meant for a wide audience, Tijerina has always been careful to point out that he does not promote ethnic separatism. Note his comments to Robert Laxalt, a reporter for *National Geographic*: "We don't want any more violence. All we want is a Congressional investigation of the whole land-grant problem. We want the land back so it can be divided up and put to productive use. Maybe that way we can get our people off welfare." ("New Mexico: The Golden Land," *National Geographic* 138:3 [September 1970], 326).

76. "[Tijerina] Says Wife Assaulted by State Troopers," *Albuquerque Journal*, 24 October 1971; "Norvell denies claim of Tijerina That His Wife Was Raped by State Policeman," *Albuquerque Journal*, 15 November 1971; "The Rape of La Raza," *Somos Aztlán* 2:1 (1972); "Reies López Tijerina Charges Failure to Arrest a State Policeman for an Alleged Sexual Assault on His 14-Year-Old Son," *Albuquerque Journal*, 12 April 1973; "Former State Police Officer Albert Vega Judged Competent to Stand Trial in Connection with a Charge of Sexual Assault on the 14-Year Old Son of R. L. Tijerina," *Albuquerque Journal*, 2 October 1973; Knowlton, "Reies López Tijerina and the Alianza: Some Considerations," 26. Tijerina, *Mi lucha por la tierra*, 382–86.

77. Knowlton, "Reies López Tijerina," 27. In his paper, Knowlton details how the *Albuquerque Journal* "devoted a whole editorial to me in which they requested me to stay out of New Mexico," 28.

78. Clark S. Knowlton, "Reies López Tijerina and the Alianza," 22.

79. Blawis, *Tijerina and the Land Grants*, 155; Tijerina, *Mi lucha por la tierra*, 200–204; Nabokov, *Tijerina and the Courthouse Raid*, 243.

80. Knowlton, "Reies López Tijerina and the Alianza," 26; Nabokov, *Tijerina and the Courthouse Raid*, 271.

81. Matt S. Meier, *Mexican American Biographies: A Historical Dictionary, 1836–1987* (Westport, Conn.: Greenwood Press, 1988), 220.

82. Newman, *¡Do it up Brown!*, 66.

83. "Raza Unida Conference: Unidos Ganaremos," *La Luz* 1:6 (October 1972), 12.

84. "First Chicano Congress for Land & Cultural Reform," *La Luz* 1:8 (December 1972), 12–14.

85. Reies López Tijerina, "Brotherhood Awareness Conference," Civic Auditorium, Albuquerque, New Mexico, 8 April 1972. Vertical File, Ethnic Studies File, "Land Grants," (Zimmerman Library, University of New Mexico, 1972), 1–2; Reies López Tijerina, "Brotherhood Awareness," *La Luz*, 2:4 (August 1973), 16.

86. *El Gallo*, December 1970, 1, quoted in Newman, *¡Do it up Brown!,* 67; "Torture of Tijerina," *El Grito del Norte* (8 October 1970). This conspiracy theory continues to be widespread among Chicano activists and circles. As recently as 1997 I was asked by a Chicano scholar in casual conversation about Tijerina's lobotomy.

87. *Albuquerque Journal,* 7 June 1977.

88. "Community Forum: Alianza Federál de Mercedes," *Seers* 5:20 (13 August 1976); "Reyes & the North: Eight Years Later," *Seers* (15–29 November 1975).

89. Peter Nabokov, "'Remembering Tierra Amarilla': Chicano Power in the Feudal West," *The Nation* (8 October 1977), 337–38; Donald Dale Jackson, "Around Los Ojos, Sheep and Land are Fighting Words," *Smithsonian* 22:1 (April 1991), 37–44, 46–47.

90. In the second courthouse raid trial he was convicted of false imprisonment of then Deputy Sheriff Pete Jaramillo, and assault with intent to kill or maim jailer Eulogio Salazar ("Tijerina Was Granted Apodaca Pardon in '78," *Albuquerque Journal,* 9 January 1979). See also "Forum: Reies López Tijerina Jailed," *La Luz* 3:9 (December 1974), 9.

91. Charles R. Garrett, II, "El Tigre Revisited," *Nuestro* 1:5 (August 1977), 17.

92. Rodolfo Acuña, *Occupied America: A History of Chicanos,* 3rd ed. (New York: Harper & Row, 1988), 356.

93. Rees Lloyd, "Behind the Mask of Middle-Class Decency: Inside the Albuquerque Journal," *The New Mexico Review and Legislative Journal* 2:2 (February 1970), 1–2, 20–24.

94. "Beating Death Indictments Not Returned," *Albuquerque Journal,* 29 August 1977; Jocelyn Lieu, "The Courthouse Raid: Twenty Years Later"; "Time Slams Door on Salazar Slay Probe," *Albuquerque Journal,* 3 January 1978.

95. Garrett, "El Tigre Revisited," 18; Nabokov, "'Remembering Tierra Amarilla,'" 340.

96. "Money to Replace Land: Texas Land Grant Heirs Give In," *El Diario de la Gente* 5:3 (15 March 1977).

97. Nicholas C. Chriss, "Spanish Americans Meet to Discuss Claim Against Mexico for Land Seized in 1800s," *Los Angeles Times,* 23 January 1978; "Noticias," *Nuestro* 2:3 (March 1978). The *Los Angeles Times* (18 February 1978) reported that "Tijerina and his followers charged [the claimants] $10 each for attending their own meeting and collected an estimated total of $20,000 to $30,000. He charged an additional $22 to process an individual set of records."

98. "Land Claimants Form a New Association," *San Antonio Express,* 5 February 1978.

99. "Anxiety Increases Among Hispanic Land Claimants," *Albuquerque Journal,* 10 March 1978; "Mexico Will Refuse to Pay Americans Who File Claims for Ceded Land," *Arizona Republic,* 24 February 1978; Nicholas C. Chriss, "Mexico Says It Won't Pay Land Claims of 1800s," *Los Angeles Times,* 18 February 1978. Griswold del Castillo reports that the Asociación de Reclamantes tried to regain title to their lands from the United States, but lost their lawsuit in 1984 (*The Treaty of Guadalupe Hidalgo,* 106); Rodolfo O. de la Garza, "Chicanos and U.S. Foreign Policy: The Future of Chicano-Mexicano Relations," *The Western Political Quarterly* 33:4 (December 1980), 576–78.

100. "Group Will Air Rights Abuses in Mexico," *El Paso Times,* 8 June 1978; Steve Peters, "Anti-American Feelings Explode," *El Paso Times,* 16 June 1978; Steve Peters, "Denouncement Of Anglos, Press Ignored By Mexican Newspapers," *El Paso Times,* 17 June 1978.

101. "Tijerina Notified: Old Land Grant Documents Found," *Albuquerque Journal,* 20 March 1979. Field interview, 1990.

102. Eugene Ward, "San Joaquín Grant Heirs Halt Loggers," *Albuquerque Journal,* 4 July 1979; "Mondragon, Tijerina Talk On Land Grant Logging," *Albuquerque Journal,* 11 July 1979; "Land Grant Heirs Told Case Needs Federal Attention," *Albuquerque Journal,* 20 July

1979; Author's Tijerina interview, 1990; deBuys, *Enchantment and Exploitation*, 277; "Conflict: 'This Land Is Our land,'" *Nuestro* 4:1 (March 1980), 46.

103. *Tierra y Libertad* 1:3 (May 1979); Griswold del Castillo, *The Treaty of Guadalupe Hidalgo*, 137–38.

104. *Tierra y Libertad* 2:6 (November 1980); "Tijerina Wins Children-School Battle," *Albuquerque Journal*, 28 November 1979.

105. Sylvia Rodríguez, "Land, Water, and Ethnic Identity in Taos," in *Land, Water, and Culture: New Perspectives on Hispanic Land Grants*, Charles L. Briggs and John R. Van Ness, eds. (Albuquerque: University of New Mexico Press, 1987), 373–74, 382.

106. Author's field notes, 1990.

107. Lieu, "The Courthouse Raid"; Mary Fei, "Coyote Gathering Marks Rio Arriba Courthouse Raid," *Albuquerque Journal*, 5 June 1987.

108. Matt S. Meier, "'King Tiger': Reies López Tijerina," *Journal of the West* 27:2 (April 1988), 66.

109. Centro de Enseñanza para Extranjeros, *Encuentro Chicano Mexico 1987: Memorias, Testimonios y Ponencias* (Mexico, D.F.: UNAM, 1988), 97–105.

110. John Christiansen, "A Real 'Milagro Beanfield War' in New Mexico," *San Francisco Chronicle*, 5 July 1988; John Christiansen, "Amador Flores's Beanfield War," *The Progressive* (October 1988); *Business Week*, 15 August 1988; *Unity/La Unidad* 11:13 (29 August 1988); "Occupied Mexico: Land Struggle in Tierra Amarilla," *Breakthrough Political Journal of Prairie Fire Organizing Committee* 13:1 (Spring 1989); Lucy R. Lippard and Chris Takagi, "Land or Death in Tierra Amarilla," *Guardian* (New York) 40:43 (17 August 1988).

111. John Nichols, *The Milagro Beanfield War* (New York: Random House, 1974); Dan Guerrero, "The Milagro Beanfield War," *Vista* 3:7 (6 March 1988), 18; John Nichols, "Reies López Tijerina, A Man Like the Northern Weather," *The New Mexico Review and Legislative Journal* 3:11 (November 1971), 12–13. See also John Christiansen, "A Real 'Milagro Beanfield War,'" *San Francisco Chronicle*, 5 July 1988. See Archuleta's criticism of Tijerina in "Amador's War," *Rio Grande Sun*, 6 September 1990. Tijerina's criticism of Archuleta's organization is recorded in Nabokov, "'Remembering Tierra Amarilla,'" 340.

112. Tuss Callanan, "Coyote: A Town Without Pity," *Chicago Tribune*, 12 April 1987, 9–11, 13–20, 27.

113. Lieu, "The Courthouse Raid"; Author's Tijerina interview, 1990.

114. Rees Lloyd, "'King Tiger'—Reies López Tijerina—Still Roars for Justice on 'Cinco de Junio' 2003. Is There a Welsh 'Tiger' for Justice?" Online: http://www.welshamerican.com/Rees/tiger.htm

Notes to Chapter Three

1. Reies López Tijerina, *¿Hallará Fe en la Tierra . . . ?* (n.p., 1954?), 84.

2. Nabokov Papers, Box 2, Folder 22, Item 16, 5.

3. A U.S. Department of Agriculture study of Texas-Mexican migrants in the Midwest noted the lack of access to Catholic services for them. This situation proved to be a boon for evangelical missionaries (*Texas-Mexicans in Sugar Beets, Vegetables and Fruits: A Report on Improved Relations between Migratory Farm Workers and Agricultural Employers in North Central and Great Plains States, 1943–1947* [Washington, D.C.: U.S. Department of Agriculture, Extension [Service] Farm Labor Program, 1948], 18).

4. Edwin Sylvest, "Hispanic American Protestantism in the United States," in *Fronteras: A History of the Latin American Church in the USA since 1519*, Moisés Sándoval, ed. (San Antonio: Mexican American Cultural Center, 1983), 290; Timothy Matovina, *Tejano*

Religion and Ethnicity: San Antonio, 1821–1860 (Austin: University of Texas Press, 1995), 14–16; Martha Remy, "Protestant Churches and Mexican-Americans in South Texas" (PhD diss., University of Texas at Austin, 1970); Juan Francisco Martinez, "Origins and Development of Protestantism among Latinos in the Southwest United States, 1836–1900" (PhD diss., Fuller Theological Seminary, 1996).

5. R. Douglas Brackenridge and Francisco O. Garcia-Treto, *Iglesia Presbiteriana: A History of Presbyterians and Mexican Americans in the Southwest* (San Antonio: Trinity University Press, 1974), 1–2; Martha Remy, "Protestant Churches," 100–113; Matovina, *Tejano Religion and Ethnicity*, 14–16, 39–41; Daisy L. Machado, *Of Borders and Margins: Hispanic Disciples in Texas, 1888–1945* (New York: Oxford University Press, 2003), 67f.

6. See the details of the separate Texas-Mexican Presbytery effort initiated in 1908 and dismantled in 1955 in Brackenridge and Garcia-Treto, *Iglesia Presbiteriana*, 87–125.

7. Brackenridge and Garcia-Treto, *Iglesia Presbiteriana*, 107–9, 161. The Presbyterian seminary curriculum consisted of Church History and Government, Bible, Systematic Theology, Religious Education, and Homiletics.

8. Remy, "Protestant Churches," 149–50.

9. Sylvest, "Hispanic American Protestantism," 303, 324–26; Remy, "Protestant Churches," 114–15. Matovina also quotes sources indicating that Anglo Protestant missionary work among Mexicans going into the second half of the nineteenth century in Texas resulted in very few converts (*Tejano Religion and Ethnicity*, 61, 80). See Machado, *Of Borders and Margins* for a similar disappointing record of evangelizing by the Disciples of Christ among Mexicans in Texas.

10. Remy, "Protestant Churches," 113.

11. See the excellent discussion of the *corrido*'s function in Américo Paredes, *"With His Pistol in His Hand": A Border Ballad and Its Hero* (Austin: University of Texas Press, 1958), and the elaboration of its use by Chicanos as resistance in Ramón Saldívar, *Chicano Narrative: The Dialectics of Difference* (Madison: University of Wisconsin Press, 1990), 26–42.

12. Bertha Blair, Anne O. Lively, and Glen W. Trimble, *Spanish Speaking Americans: Mexicans and Puerto Ricans in the United States* (New York: Home Missions Division, National Council of Churches, 1959), 142.

13. Ernest S. Stapleton, Jr., "The History of Baptist Missions in New Mexico, 1849–1866" (MA thesis, University of New Mexico, 1954), 4.

14. For details on Baptist efforts among Mexican Americans in Texas, and the Southwest in general, see Joshua Grijalva, "The History of Hispanic Southern Baptists," *Baptist History and Heritage* 18:3 (July 1983), 40–47; Albert McClellan, *The West is Big* (Atlanta: Home Missionary Board, Southern Baptist Convention, 1953), 58–68; Joshua Grijalva, *A History of Mexican Baptists in Texas, 1881–1981* (Dallas: Baptist General Convention, 1982); Edwin Atkinson, "Hispanic Baptists in Texas: A Glorious and Threatened History," *Apuntes* 17:2 (Summer 1997), 41–44.

15. Ferenc Szasz, *The Protestant Clergy in the Great Plains and Mountain West, 1865–1915* (Albuquerque: University of New Mexico Press, 1985), 139.

16. Remy notes that the Episcopal Church "has never had a separate structure for either the Negro or the Mexican-American. Its organization is unitary. The Presbyterian Church, U.S. (Southern) first had a unified structure, then a separate presbytery for Mexican-American work, but dissolved it in 1955. The United Methodist Church 'allows' the Rio Grande [Mexican American] Conference to maintain its present separate identity" ("Protestant Churches," 129).

17. Grijalva, "The History of Hispanic Southern Baptists," 41; "Spanish-Speaking People, Missions to," *s.v., Encyclopedia of Southern Baptists*, V. II (Nashville: Broadman Press, 1958), 1289. Remy reports that "Record of the first Mexican Baptist Church received into the San Antonio Association, which at the time included all of South Texas, was not made until 1888 . . ."("Protestant Churches," 170).

18. Grijalva, "The History of Hispanic Southern Baptists," 42–44. Sylvest records the generation of sixty-one Mexican American Southern Baptist congregations twenty years after one missionary's work in Los Angeles in 1949 ("Hispanic American Protestantism," 328). By the beginning of the 1940s the Southern Baptist missionary efforts were greatly expanded, particularly on the Pacific coast following a general population migration to the west and fewer debts incurred by the Home Mission Board arm of the Convention ("Home Mission Board," *s.v., Encyclopedia of Southern Baptists* [Nashville: Broadman Press, 1958], 645).

19. "Spanish-Speaking People, Missions to," 1289; Remy, "Protestant Churches," 172–73; McClellan, *The West is Big*, 66.

20. Treatments of Pentecostalism I find to be particularly useful include Donald W. Dayton, *Theological Roots of Pentecostalism* (Grand Rapids, Mich.: Francis Asbury Press/Zondervan, 1987); Guy P. Duffield and N. M. Van Cleave, *Foundations of Pentecostal Theology* (Los Angeles: L.I.F.E. Bible College, 1983); Robert Mapes Anderson, *Vision of the Disinherited: The Making of American Pentecostalism* (New York: Oxford University Press, 1979); Vinson Synan, *The Holiness-Pentecostal Movement in the United States* (Grand Rapids, Mich.: William B. Eerdmans Press, 1971); Walter J. Hollenweger, *The Pentecostals* (London: SCM Press, 1972); Margaret M. Poloma, *The Assemblies of God at the Crossroads: Charisma and Institutional Dilemmas* (Knoxville: University of Tennessee Press, 1989); Edith L. Blumhofer, *Restoring the Faith: The Assemblies of God, Pentecostalism and American Culture* (Urbana: University of Illinois Press, 1993); and Grant Wacker, *Heaven Below: Early Pentecostals and American Culture* (Cambridge: Harvard University Press, 2003).

21. Blumhofer, *Restoring the Faith*, 1–42; George Marsden, "By Primitivism Possessed: How Useful is the Concept 'Primitivism' for Understanding American Pentecostalism?" and, Grant Wacker, "Searching for Eden with a Satellite Dish: Primitivism, Pragmatism, and the Pentecostal Character," both in *The Primitive Church in the Modern World*, Richard T. Hughes, ed. (Urbana: University of Illinois Press, 1995), 34–46, 137–66.

22. Anderson, *Vision of the Disinherited*, 7.

23. Quoted in Dayton, *Theological Roots of Pentecostalism*, 10.

24. Anderson, *Vision of the Disinherited*, 69.

25. Poloma, *Assemblies of God at the Crossroads*, xv; Blumhofer reports that in 1990 the Assemblies boasted 2.2 million adherents in 11,353 churches in the United States, and 23 million members in "sister churches" worldwide (*Restoring the Faith*, 268–72).

26. Robert Lee Maril, *Poorest of Americans: The Mexican Americans of the Lower Rio Grande Valley of Texas* (Notre Dame, Ind.: University of Notre Dame Press, 1989), 35.

27. David Gutiérrez, *Walls and Mirrors: Mexican Americans, Mexican Immigrants, and the Politics of Ethnicity* (Berkeley: University of California Press, 1995), 56–68.

28. B. A. Hodges, *A History of the Mexican Mission Work Conducted by the Presbyterian Church in the United States of America, in the Synod of Texas* (Waxahachie: The Woman's Synodical of Texas, 1931), 12.

29. Vernon Monroe McCombs, *From Over the Border: A Study of the Mexicans in the United States* (New York: Council of Women for Home Missions and Missionary Education Movement [Methodist Episcopal Church], 1925), 128–30.

30. Pedro Jaramillo, or "Don Pedrito," arrived in south Texas from Mexico in 1880 and is reported to have cured hundreds of people before his death in 1903. He is still regarded as a "saint" by many Mexican Catholics (Ruth Dodson, "The Life of Don Pedro Jaramillo: Benefactor of Humanity," *Perspectives in Mexican American Studies* 1 [1988], 69–74). Niño Fidencio (1898–1938), another famous Mexican *curandero*, has achieved the status of popular saint and cult figure beyond the border. His spirit is said to still heal through other curanderos who act as his media (Kay F. Turner, "'Because of This Photography': The Making of a Mexican Folk Saint," in *Niño Fidencio: A Heart Thrown Open*, Dore Gardner, ed. [Santa Fe: Museum of New Mexico Press, 1992], 120–34).

31. Whitney R. Cross, *The Burned-Over District: The Social and Intellectual History of Enthusiastic Religion in Western New York, 1800–1850* (Ithaca, N.Y.: Cornell University Press, 1950). My suspicion is that research would indicate that the entire border region from Texas to the California coast was *quemada*, easily accounting for the Azusa Street revivals in California and various communitarian experiments along the border. Eldon Ernst has made the case for California as a "burned-over" territory in "The Emergence of California in American Religious Historiography," *Religion and American Culture* 11:1 (Winter 2001), 31–52.

32. Matovina, *Tejano Religion and Ethnicity*, 83–93.

33. Guadalupe San Miguel, Jr., *"Let All of Them Take Heed": Mexican Americans and the Campaign for Educational Equality in Texas, 1910–1981* (Austin: University of Texas Press, 1987), 13–18.

34. Remy, "Protestant Churches," 131.

35. Blumhofer reports that members of the Apostolic Faith Movement under Charles Fox Parham held a camp meeting in Houston, August, 1906 (*Restoring the Faith*, 81–82).

36. Anderson, *Vision of the Disinherited*, 126.

37. Victor de Leon, *The Silent Pentecostals: A Biographical History of the Pentecostal Movement among the Hispanics in the Twentieth Century* (Taylors, S.C.: Faith Printing Co., 1979), 45, 52.

38. The history of Latino Pentecostalism remains a male narrative. Except for a few recognized exceptions like Romanita Valenzuela's leadership in the Latino Apostolic Assemblies, women's contributions in the early movement remain obscure. See Daniel Ramírez, "Hispanic Pentecostals: History and Mission. Response to Dr. Esdras Betancourt," paper presented to the Society for Pentecostal Studies Conference, Guadalajara, Mexico, 5 November 1993; and "Borderlands Praxis: The Immigrant Experience in Latino Pentecostal Churches," *Journal of the American Academy of Religion* 67:3 (1999), 573–96.

39. de Leon, *Silent Pentecostals*, 29. See also Gastón Espinosa, "'El Azteca': Francisco Olazábal and Latino Pentecostal Charisma, Power and Faith Healing in the Borderlands," *Journal of the American Academy of Religion*, 67:3 (1999), 597–616.

40. Espinosa, "El Azteca,"; Ramírez, "Borderlands Praxis"; Arlene M. Sánchez Walsh, *Latino Pentecostal Identity: Evangelical Faith, Self, and Society* (New York: Columbia University Press, 2003).

41. See Clifton L. Holland, *The Religious Dimension in Hispanic Los Angeles: A Protestant Case Study* (Pasadena, Calif.: William Carey Library, 1974) for a description of Mexican American Pentecostal growth in Los Angeles; also Miguel Guillén details the early success of Latino Pentecostal missionary work in Texas, the Midwest, and New York in his *La Historia del Concilio Latino Americano de Iglesias Cristianas* (Brownsville, Tex.: Latin American Council of Christian Churches, 1982).

42. Henry C. Ball, "Short History of the Spanish Assemblies of God," unpublished manuscript, 1970, quoted in Holland, *The Religious Dimension in Hispanic Los Angeles*, 348.

43. See Richard L. Hough, "Religion and Pluralism among the Spanish-Speaking Groups of the Southwest," in *Politics and Society in the Southwest: Ethnicity and Chicano Pluralism*, Z. Anthony Kruszewski, Richard L. Hough, and Jacob Ornstein-Galicia, eds. (Boulder, Colo.: Westview Press, 1982), 178–89, for an historic overview of Mexican Americans in the Catholic Church and Protestantism. See Alberto Pulido, "Race Relations within the American Catholic Church: An Historical and Sociological Analysis of Mexican American Catholics" (PhD diss., University of Notre Dame, 1989), and Carmen Tafolla, "The Church in Texas," in *Fronteras*, Sándoval, ed., 183–94, for examples of strife between the American Catholic hierarchy and local Mexican American communities.

44. Hough, "Religion and Pluralism," 171.

45. Robert Orsi's description of turn of the century Italian American Catholicism is applicable here. Catholic faith the practice, centered around the home (the *domus*) and preserved by women is similar in many ways with features of Mexican Catholicism (*The Madonna of 115th Street: Faith and Community in Italian Harlem, 1880–1950* [New Haven, Conn.: Yale University Press, 1985]).

46. Gilbert R. Cadena, "Chicano Clergy and the Emergence of Liberation Theology," *Hispanic Journal of Behavioral Sciences* 11:2 (May 1989), 109.

47. Ricardo Ramírez, *Fiesta, Worship and Family* (San Antonio: Mexican American Cultural Center, 1980), 39–45.

48. This is not to foreclose the possibility that he might have joined the Nazarenes, Adventists, or even the Jehovah's Witness sects; "outsider" groups that were also actively recruiting Mexican Americans at the time.

49. John W. Storey, *Texas Baptist Leadership and Social Christianity, 1900–1980* (College Station: Texas A & M University Press, 1986), 114. Storey concludes that despite all of its efforts, "It was abundantly clear that Texas Baptists believed the gospel of Jesus was the solution to the nettlesome race problem. But it was equally clear they did not expect Christianization to advance the cause of racial inequality" (94).

50. "The Mexican Baptist Convention of Texas," *s.v.*, *Encyclopedia of Southern Baptists* (Nashville: Broadman Press, 1958); Arthur B. Rutledge, *Mission to America: A Century and a Quarter of Southern Baptist Home Missions* (Nashville: Broadman Press, 1969), 155–56.

51. Quote is from de Leon, *Silent Pentecostals*, 110, 197; Mario Hoover, "Origin and Structural Development of the Assemblies of God" (MA thesis, Southwest Missouri State College, 1968), 55; Holland, *The Religious Dimension*, 350. De Leon also reports that in 1926 Ball began classes for nine Mexican students in San Antonio (*Silent Pentecostals*, 68, 78).

52. de Leon, *Silent Pentecostals*, 82. Although Tijerina might have attended the Mexican Baptist Seminary run by the Southern Baptist's Foreign Mission Board in El Paso, the Baptists did not open their two specifically Mexican American seminaries until 1947 ("Spanish-Speaking People, Missions to," 1289).

53. Author's interview with Reies Tijerina, Coyote, New Mexico, April 1990.

54. H. Richard Niebuhr, *The Social Sources of Denominationalism* (New York: Henry Holt and Company, 1929), 19.

55. de Leon, *Silent Pentecostals*, 194.

56. David G. Gutiérrez, *Walls and Mirrors*, 39–68.

57. Thomas O'Dea and Renato Poblete, "Anomie and the 'Quest for Community': The Formation of Sects among the Puerto Ricans of New York," *American Catholic Sociological Review* 21 (Spring 1960), 18–36.

58. Mario Barrera, *Race and Class in the Southwest: A Theory of Racial Inequality* (Notre Dame, Ind.: University of Notre Dame Press, 1979); Walter R. Goldschmidt, "Class Denominationalism in Rural California Churches," *American Journal of Sociology* 49 (1944), 348–55.

59. O'Dea and Poblete, "Anomie and the 'Quest for Community.'"

60. David Montejano notes that mechanization in Texas throughout the thirties increased productivity despite a drop from 981,000 laborers in 1934 to 555,000 in 1949. The importation of Mexican *bracero* labor, coupled with higher wages and better working conditions in other states, forced many Texas Mexican Americans into cities or to move out of Texas altogether (*Anglos and Mexicans in the Making of Texas, 1836–1986* [Austin: University of Texas Press, 1987], 268, 272–74). See also Gutiérrez, *Walls and Mirrors*, 138–46.

61. President's Commission on Migratory Labor, *Migratory Labor in American Agriculture*, (1951), quoted in Blair, Lively, and Trimble, *Spanish Speaking Americans*, 39.

62. Savage himself had gone through the Instituto, was well disposed toward Mexicans, and served from 1943 to 1950 as director of the school (de Leon, *Silent Pentecostals*, 81).

63. Richard Gardner, *Grito!: Reies Tijerina and the New Mexico Land Grant War of 1967* (Indianapolis: Bobbs-Merrill Company, 1970), 39.

64. Author's Tijerina interview, 1990.

65. "Free Tijerina and Borunda," *Seer's Catalogue*, 1976, 11.

66. Clark Knowlton, "Violence in New Mexico: A Sociological Perspective," *California Law Review* 58 (1970), 1053–54; Tony Hillerman, "Quijote in Rio Arriba County," in *The Great Taos Bank Robbery* (Albuquerque: University of New Mexico Press, 1973), 111–33.

67. George Grayson, Jr., "Tijerina: The Evolution of a Primitive Rebel," *Commonweal* 86:17 (28 July 1967), 464–66.

68. Nabokov Papers, Box 2, Folder 22, Item 16, 5.

69. Author's copy has "Publicado en Abril de 1954" (Published in April of 1954) in Tijerina's distinctive handwriting inside the front cover.

70. Holland, *The Religious Dimension*, 351.

71. John Tebbel, *The Great Change, 1910–1980: A History of Book Publishing in the United States*, Vol. 4 (New York: R.R. Bowker, 1981), 591.

72. Ellipses in Spanish indicate either a sudden break in thought or an interruption.

73. Note the more juridical "justicia" in the Spanish Reina-De Valera translation (1602) where the King James reads "righteousness." It is critical to appreciate the differences between these traditionally authorized versions of the Bible.

74. Martin Dibelius, *From Tradition to Gospel* (New York: Charles Scribner's Sons, 1965), 17.

75. I have preserved the archaic, "biblesque" style of the Spanish in my translations here.

76. "Bible Institutes, Colleges, Universities," *s.v.*, *Dictionary of Pentecostal and Charismatic Movements*, Stanley M. Burgess and Gary B. McGee, eds. (Grand Rapids, Mich.: Regency Reference Library, 1988), 6. Tijerina recalls that *¿Hallará Fe en la Tierra . . . ?* "was the first marks of my ability in life and writing" (Author's field notes, Coyote, New Mexico, April 1990).

77. Dates and places include El Monte, California, April 15, November 22, 1954; Austin, Texas, February 22, 1954; New York City, November 27, 1953; Victoria, Texas, March 12, 1954; San Antonio, Texas, August 3, 1953; Melvin, Michigan, May 9, 1953; Carlsbad, California, June 30, 1954.

78. "La fe sin misericordia," *¿Hallará Fe en la Tierra . . . ?*, 56–57.

79. Tijerina confuses Zedekiah (the blinded king) with the next king in exile, Johoiachin, whom Jeremiah says "did continually eat bread" before the new Babylonian King, Evilmerodach (Jer. 52:31–34).

80. Claus Westermann, *Basic Forms of Prophetic Speech* (London: Lutterworth Press, 1967).

81. Westermann, *Basic Forms of Prophetic Speech*, 191.

82. "El Afán de los que Adoran," *¿Hallará Fe en la Tierra . . . ?*, 47. See Paul Boyer's discussion of how American religious leaders reacted to the atom bomb in *By Bomb's Early Light: American Thought and Culture at the Dawn of the Atomic Age* (New York: Pantheon Books, 1985), 270–72.

83. It is interesting that Francisco Olazábal, perhaps the most influential and famous Mexican American Pentecostal evangelist in the 1930s, also identified himself publicly as simply, "a Christian." See Espinosa, "El Azteca," 607.

84. "Palabras a la Ultima Generación," *¿Hallará Fe en la Tierra . . . ?*, 108.

85. According to Blumhofer, restorationism "sounded the call to Christian perfection and religious reform" and "advocated purifying religious forms and testing practices and beliefs against the New Testament." It "promoted assumptions of Christian unity and simplicity" and "reminded believers of their fundamental oneness in Christ." Restorationism was millennial and "nurtured anti-denominationalism" as a result of its combined millennialism, optimism about Christian unity, and perfectionism (*Restoring the Faith*, 12–15).

86. Michael Jenkinson, *Tijerina: Land Grant Conflict in New Mexico* (Albuquerque: Paisano Press, 1968), 21.

87. The sermon "The Conquered People" ("El Pueblo Vencido," 89) also condemns cutting hair, but nothing specifically about shaving. A montage of photographs in the KNME interview with Tijerina shows him standing with several older bearded men and a woman (*Tixerina: Through the Eyes of a Tiger: An Interview with Reies Tijerina* [with Harold Rhodes] [video] [Albuquerque: KNME-TV, University of New Mexico, 1982].) Gardner mentions that Tijerina's 1958 arrival in New Mexico found him heavily bearded in flowing white robes called "los barbudos" (the bearded ones) by the local communities (Gardner, *Grito!*, 30, 48). Tijerina remembers the local people around Chama, New Mexico, warning that "*Los Barbones aquí andan*" ("Here come the bearded ones") (Author's field notes). Daniel Ramírez suggests that this sect may have been a splinter group from the Apostolic ("Oneness") branch of Mexican Pentecostalism referred to as Aronistas (Aaronites), now known as the Luz del Mundo ("Light of the World") sect. (Personal Communication, 7 April 1995). Tijerina attempted to meet with a "very famous holy man" in Jalisco sometime in the late 1940s or early 1950s (Gardner, *Grito!*, 256), possibly Eusebio Joaquín González, ("Aaron") the founder of Luz del Mundo. Aaron founded the "La Hermosa Provincia" (The Beautiful Province) colony east of Guadalajara, Jalisco, in 1953 and may have inspired Tijerina's attempt to create a separate, isolated community in 1955.

88. Blumhofer, *Restoring the Faith*, 203–19; Tom Craig Darrand and Anson Shupe, *Metaphors of Social Control in a Pentecostal Sect* (New York: Edwin Mellen Press, 1983), 33–60.

89. Blumhofer, *Restoring the Faith*, 208ff.

90. Quoted in Blumhofer, *Restoring the Faith*, 207.

91. Darrand and Shupe, *Metaphors of Social Control*, 38.

92. "Latter Rain Movement," *s.v., Dictionary of Pentecostal and Charismatic Movements*, Stanley M. Burgess and Gary B. McGee, eds. (Grand Rapids, Mich.: Regency Reference Library, 1988), 532–34.

93. See Marsden, *Fundamentalism and American Culture: The Shaping of Twentieth-Century Evangelicalism, 1870–1925* (New York: Oxford University Press, 1980), 93–101, for details on the theological origins of this animosity, and Blumhofer, *Restoring the Faith*, 180–202.

94. Max Weber, *The Protestant Ethic and the Spirit of Capitalism*, Talcott Parsons, ed. (London: George Allen and Unwin, 1930 [1904–1905]), 175.

95. Unnamed informants quoted in Goldschmidt, "Class Denominationalism in Rural California Churches," 353.

96. de Leon, *Silent Pentecostals*, 192–93.

97. "La Imagen Perdida," *¿Hallará Fe en la Tierra . . . ?*, 2.

98. "La Justicia que no Pereces," *¿Hallará Fe en la Tierra . . . ?*, 73.

99. "¿Faltan Maestros?," *¿Hallará Fe en la Tierra . . . ?*, 74.

100. It is unclear why Tijerina's estrangement from the Assemblies of God did not result in an affiliation with the strongly Mexican Apostolic ("Oneness") branch of Pentecostalism or the Latin American Council of Christian Churches, a Mexican American schism of the Assemblies of God.

101. Author's field notes, 1990.

102. Nabokov Papers, Box 2, Folder 22, Item 8, 11.

103. Gardner reports a similar story Tijerina remembers from 1949 when an elderly Anglo man waited in a church to speak to him after everyone had left. Reies spent five hours listening to this man tell him stories about the victimization of Mexicans in Texas. The man reportedly told him that in order to redeem a "great big sin against God," he had to tell "the truth about his [Anglo] people." Tijerina reports, "Well, I was the minister and I had the influence of the Bible and the Pentecostal type of thinking, and for a while it did not bother me, all those things that he said, but I got rid of it, or I thought I got rid of it, and I went on preaching here and there and holding campaigns" (Gardner, *Grito!*, 43–44).

Chapter Four

1. Tijerina's title comes from Proverbs 19:25b: "y corrigiendo al entendido, entenderá ciencia" ("rebuke a discerning man, and he will gain knowledge" NIV). *¿Hallará Fe en la Tierra . . . ?*, (n.p., 1954?), 104–5.

2. Richard Gardner, *Grito!: Reies Tijerina and the New Mexico Land Grant War of 1967* (Indianapolis: Bobbs-Merrill Company, 1970), 44.

3. The published memoir lists seven men (and their families) who accompanied him. The original handwritten MS lists nine. Blawis records nineteen families; Gardner and Nabokov list seventeen families. The English translation of Tijerina's memoir repeats the error of the published Spanish edition.

4. Michael Jenkinson, *Tijerina: Land Grant Conflict in New Mexico* (Albuquerque: Paisano Press, 1968), 21.

5. Reies López Tijerina, *Mi lucha por la tierra* (Mexico, D.F.: Fondo de la Cultura Económica, 1978), 27. Translations are mine.

6. Gardner, *Grito!*, 45.

7. Tijerina, *Mi lucha por la tierra*, 28.

8. Tijerina, *Mi lucha por la tierra*, 28.

9. Author's interview with Reies Tijerina, Coyote, New Mexico, April 1990.

10. Author's Tijerina interview, 1990: "Three. All coming from above. Flying, flying. And they landed; just like a movie. They landed; and separate, but they became one . . . one cloud, one vehicle, and they were all three sitting . . . they had long dress, loose hair, no shoes . . . and all three spoke, you know, the same thing: "We have come to take you." "Where to?" "To an old, to a very old kingdom," that's what they said. At that time, Maria, my first wife, intervened and said, "Why? Why him?" They said, "We have traveled the world over

and found nobody. He's the only one that can do . . . that's why we're taking him." And they said one word in Spanish, "Secretaria" . . . that's when I went into the word, what does "secretaria" mean? It means screening, it means sorting, it means investigation, it means administration, it means government.

11. Author's Tijerina interview, 1990: But what about the dark forest? At that time there was no forest in Arizona (Valle de Paz). No forest in my life. . . . What about the fear? Terrifying fear in the dark, in the forest? It was not dark like night, no. It looked like when the sun is setting . . . you know, twilight.

12. Author's Tijerina interview, 1990: [The horses] were not dead! They were frozen. I mean, that could be the bones of Ezekiel 38, you know, dried bones. But that's not the same! Dried bones is the opposite of frozen meat; frozen entire animals or persons . . . I could see . . . something like one hundred feet from where I [stood] was the cemetery of frozen horses. I could see them all!

13. Tijerina, "Mi lucha por la tierra" original MS, vol. 1, 8–10.

14. Gardner, *Grito!*, 47.

15. Tijerina, *Mi lucha por la tierra*, 139–40.

16. Beyond the small circle of his followers Tijerina notes that he was later reluctant to tell members of the Alianza organization about the dream because he felt that he had to earn their trust before revealing such an extraordinary experience (*Mi lucha por la tierra*, 139–40).

17. David Carrasco is the first Latino scholar to take note of the hierophantic quality of Tijerina's dreaming in "A Perspective for a Study of Religious Dimensions in Chicano Experience: *Bless Me, Ultima* as a Religious Text," *Aztlán* 13 (1982), 201–2.

18. See Harry T. Hunt, *The Multiplicity of Dreams: Memory, Imagination, and Consciousness* (New Haven, Conn.: Yale University Press, 1989), 132–40. Big dream is a catch all term defined by Anthony Stevens as "powerful dreams, which anthropologists call 'culture pattern dreams' (Linton) or 'official dreams' (Malinowski) . . . considered by Jung to be archetypal expressions of the human collective unconscious, and, as he noted, they commonly coincide with a subjective and sometimes overpowering sense of awe, dread, fascination, and wonder, which Rudolf Otto described as *numinous*—the very essence of genuine religious experience" (*Private Myths: Dreams and Dreaming* [Cambridge: Harvard University Press, 1995], 12).

19. For example, his error in writing "*losa*" [gravestone], instead of "*cosa*" [thing] prior to introducing the cemetery into the dream narrative may be worth contemplating. In the MS, Volume I, 10: "*Al hallarme yo en este oscuro bosque, me rodeo un miedo horrible. Jamas habia yo sentido un terror tan extraño. Yo solo pensaba en aquella hora en una losa [sic]: como escapar o salir de aquel lugar. Corri muy fuerte buscando salida. Y luego al poco me enfrente con un cemeterio lleno de caballos*" ["Upon finding myself in this dark forest, I was surrounded by a horrible fear. Never had I felt such an extraordinary terror. I could only think at the time of a gravestone (*losa*): how to escape or leave from here (the dark forest). I ran fast looking for a way out. And before long I came across a cemetery full of horses."] The heavily edited published version lessens the urgency of this passage as indicated in the original manuscript by removing the personal pronoun (*yo*), and distances Tijerina from the action by substituting "*apoderarse de*" [possessed by] for the more frightening original "*rodear*" [surrounded], and "*toparse*" [stumble] for "*enfrente*" [confront]: "*Al hallarme yo en este oscuro bosque se apodero de mi en un miedo horrible. Jamas habia [yo] sentido un terror tan extraño. En aquella hora [yo] solo pensaba como escapar o salir de alli. Corri muy fuerte buscando salidas y al poco tiempo me tope con un cemeterio lleno de caballos*" (31).

20. See Betty Leddy, "La Llorona in Southern Arizona," *Perspectives in Mexican American Studies* 1 (1988), 9–16, for an overview of the La Llorona legend.
21. See Morton T. Kelsey's discussion of western Christianity's deep suspicion and fear of the power of dreams and modern Christianity's eventual dismissal of dreams as legitimate avenues of divine revelation or communication (*Dreams: The Dark Speech of the Spirit: A Christian Interpretation* [Garden City, N.Y.: Doubleday & Co., 1968], 164–83).
22. He goes on to state that "Generalizations made by other individuals in the community strongly suggest that [in my research sample] I did not accidentally stumble upon an unrepresentative cluster of 'haunted' individuals, but had among my circle of acquaintances a representative number of individuals who had experienced such phenomena." ("Voices, Visions and Strange Ideas: Hallucinations and Delusions in a Mexican-Origin Population [PhD diss., Northwestern University, 1974], 254, 257–58). See also Ari Kiev, *Curanderismo: Mexican-American Folk Psychiatry* (New York: Free Press, 1968) for a classic statement on the subject of visions and dreaming in Mexican American communities. Unfortunately most if not all of the research on visions and dreaming among Mexican Americans has occurred in the context of clinical research among the mentally disordered, dismissing or at best ignoring the complex nature of Mexican religious beliefs within American Protestant, civil religious culture.
23. Samuel Roll, Richard Hinton, and Michael Glazer, "Dreams of Death: Mexican-Americans vs. Anglo Americans," *Interamerican Journal of Psychology* 8:1–2 (1974), 111–15; C. Brooks Brenneis and Samuel Roll, "Ego Modalities in the Manifest Dreams of Male and Female Chicanos," *Psychiatry* 38 (May 1975), 172–85; Samuel Roll and C. Brooks Brenneis, "Chicano and Anglo Dreams of Death: A Replication," *Journal of Cross-Cultural Psychology* 6:3 (September 1975), 377–83; C. Brooks Brenneis and Samuel Roll, "Dream Patterns in Anglo and Chicano Young Adults," *Psychiatry* 39 (August 1976), 280–90; Samuel Roll, "Chicano Dreams: Investigations in Cross-Cultural Research," Southwest Hispanic Research Institute, Working Paper #107, University of New Mexico (Fall 1984); Connie M. Kane, Ronald R. and Pamela Mellen, and Italo Samano, "Differences in the Manifest Dream Content of Mexican, Mexican American, and Anglo American College Women: A Research Note," *Hispanic Journal of Behavioral Sciences* 15:1 (February 1993), 134–39.
24. Miguel Guillén, *La Historia del Concilio Latino Americano de Iglesias Cristianas* (Brownsville, Tex.: Latin American Council of Christian Churches, 1982); Anthony Quinn, *The Original Sin: A Self Portrait* (Boston: Little, Brown and Company, 1972), 118–19. Quinn recounts his involvement as a youth with Aimee Semple McPherson's Foursquare Gospel of Jesus Christ branch of Pentecostalism in the 1920s. Filtered through his adult memory and narrated to his therapist, Quinn revisits a recurrent dream about his ascent into heaven that began just prior to his Pentecostalism. Quinn admits that his musical experience in Pentecostalism and especially McPherson's stage presence as "the greatest actress of all times" greatly influenced his decision to become an actor (129). Another example is from Chile, recorded in Christian Lalive d'Epinay, *Haven of the Masses: A Study of the Pentecostal Movement in Chile*, Marjorie Sandle, trans. (New York: Friendship Press, 1969), 74–75.
25. Guillén, *La Historia del Concilio*, 179–85.
26. Guillén, *La Historia del Concilio*, 179–80. My translation.
27. Guillén, *La Historia del Concilio*, 185.
28. Orlando Espín argues that Latino Catholicism is conditioned by its popular quality and has its origins not in Roman Catholicism, but in pre-Tridentine "western Christianity in its Iberian form" ("Popular Catholicism among Latinos," in *Hispanic Catholic Culture in*

the *U.S.: Issues and Concerns*, Jay P. Dolan and Allan Figueroa Deck, eds. [Notre Dame, Ind.: University of Notre Dame Press, 1994], 315).

29. The close relationship between dream image formation and imposed linguistic narrative structure is discussed in Hunt, *The Multiplicity of Dreams*, 159ff.; and especially in the work of David Foulkes, *Dreaming: A Cognitive-Psychological Analysis* (Hillsdale, N.J.: Lawrence Erlbaum Associates, 1985), 18–49; and *A Grammar of Dreams* (New York: Basic Books, 1978), 10–18. This cognitive approach to dream formation and interpretation suggests that dreams function similarly to the mental actions of wakefulness (thinking and reading) rather than simply disorganized and random "perception." Although Foulkes does not address the influence of reading on dreaming, he does note that the cognitive processes are very similar. See also, G. E. Swanson's study "Trance and Possession: Studies of Charismatic Influence," *Review of Religious Research* 19 (1978), 253–78, for another interpretation of how religious states like possession and trance can include mundane activities like reading. My intuition here is that the affect of Latino evangelical reading of the Bible is similar to the vision/dream experiences of Latino Catholics.

30. Note the almost complete absence of dreaming and visions as part of the American Pentecostal *charisma* in major treatments such as Robert Mapes Anderson, *Vision of the Disinherited: The Making of American Pentecostalism*, (New York: Oxford University Press, 1979), 10–27; and Donald W. Dayton, *Theological Roots of Pentecostalism* (Grand Rapids, Mich.: Francis Asbury Press/Zondervan, 1987). In his study of glossolalia Morton T. Kelsey compares the ecstatic experience of speaking in tongues with dreams and visions, arguing for their common alternative state of consciousness (*Tongue Speaking: An Experiment in Spiritual Experience* [New York: Waymark Books, 1968], 211–17).

31. Tijerina, *Mi lucha por la tierra*, 85. Of course a more refined study of religious dreams and visions would take on a more social scientific approach and cast a larger net over available narratives. My point is to suggest contrasts between evangelical/Pentecostal visionary experiences and those of Roman Catholics based upon these two narratives. See the suggestive studies of glossolalia and the attendant differences between glossolalic Pentecostals and glossolalic charismatic Catholics summarized in H. Newton Malony and A. Adams Lovekin, *Glossolalia: Behavioral Science Perspectives on Speaking in Tongues* (New York: Oxford University Press, 1985). Benedict J. Mawn's conclusion that Catholic Pentecostals resolved a "transcendency deprivation" when they became charismatic may not apply to Mexican American Catholics who are culturally predisposed to hierophantic experiences ("Testing the Spirits: An Empirical Search for the Socio-Economic Situational Roots of the Catholic Pentecostal Religious Experience" [PhD diss., Boston University, 1975]). It is interesting to note that the Catholic Charismatic movement began with the influence of the Spanish origin *Cursillo* movement in the United States and the introduction of Teen Challenge Pentecostalism at the National Cursillo Convention in 1966 (Kevin and Dorothy Ranaghan, *Catholic Pentecostals* [New York: Paulist Press, 1969]).

32. Tijerina, *Mi lucha por la tierra*, 32.

33. Christopher Partridge, "Understanding UFO Religions and Abduction Spiritualities," in *UFO Religions*, Christopher Partridge, ed. (New York: Routledge, 2003), 13–14. In contrast, note the evolution of alien beings and their sinister interpretations in Jonathan Z. Smith, "Close Encounters of Diverse Kinds," in *Religion and Cultural Studies*, Susan L. Mizruchi, ed. (Princeton, N.J.: Princeton University Press, 2001), 3–8.

34. J. Allen Hynek, *The UFO Experience: A Scientific Inquiry* (New York: Galantine Books, 1974); Tijerina, *Mi lucha por la tierra*, 32; Author's Tijerina interview, 1990; C. D. B. Bryan, *Close Encounters of the Fourth Kind: A Reporter's Notebook on Alien Abduction, UFOs, and the Conference at M.I.T.* (New York: Penguin, 1995), 1–64 *passim*.

35. Whitley Strieber, *Transformation: The Breakthrough* (New York: Avon Books, 1989), 96, 134.

36. Yet another interpretation is that Tijerina is filtering shamanistic initiation and "journeying" through his fundamentalism. As a leader, community "healer" and preacher of God's word (i.e., a medium), Tijerina's charismatic power may be the result of his extensive dream/vision life common among shamans. See the collected classic statements defining shamanism in the *Reader in Comparative Religion: An Anthropological Approach*, 2nd ed., William A. Lessa, and Evon Z. Vogt, eds. (New York: Harper & Row, 1965), 451–86.

37. See the interesting connections between Christianity and UFO culture in John A. Saliba, "Religious Dimensions of UFO Phenomena," in *The Gods Have Landed: New Religions from Other Worlds*, James R. Lewis, ed. (Albany, N.Y.: SUNY Press, 1995), 31–41.

38. Tijerina, *Mi lucha por la tierra*, 29.

39. Tijerina, *Mi lucha por la tierra*, 33.

40. Tijerina, *Mi lucha por la tierra*, 35–36.

41. It is unclear to which Supreme Court case he is referring. The Amish case, *Wisconsin v. Yoder* (406 U.S. 205 [1972]) was still a decade away. He may be conflating the issue of taxation exemption for Quakers and Mennonites with the education issued in his reconstructed memory.

42. Tijerina, *Mi lucha por la tierra*, 37.

43. Tijerina, *Mi lucha por la tierra*, 38.

44. Sometime later in the spring or early summer, Tijerina, his brother Margarito, and Zebedeo Martinez returned to Valle de Paz to work in nearby agriculture and send money back to the families in New Mexico. Trouble with the local sheriff over charges of stolen property landed them in jail for ninety days. Tijerina and Martinez served their time, but Margarito was held for violating his parole in Indiana. What happened next is unclear, but according to Nabokov, "a jailbreak involving a smuggled hacksaw was attempted in the Pinal County jail in early July. Reies was accused of being at the wheel of the getaway car after the alleged scheme to free his brother failed, and he was released on $1,000 bond." Tijerina's version is different. On the day of his hearing, Tijerina walked out of the courthouse during a recess and never came back. This was the beginning of his life as a fugitive (Nabokov, *Tijerina and the Courthouse Raid* [Albuquerque: University of New Mexico Press, 1969], 202–3; Tijerina, *Mi lucha por la tierra*, 41–42).

45. See Mario Barrera, *Race and Class in the Southwest: A Theory of Racial Inequality* (Notre Dame, Ind.: University of Notre Dame Press, 1979), 113–49; Rodolfo Acuña, *Occupied America: A History of Chicanos*, 3rd ed. (New York: Harper & Row, 1988), 251–306.

46. James E. Officer, "Sodalities and Systemic Linkage: The Joining Habits of Urban Mexican Americans" (PhD diss., University of Arizona, 1964), 86–92.

47. Bradford Luckingham, *Minorities in Phoenix: A Profile of Mexican American, Chinese American, and African American Communities, 1860–1992* (Tucson: University of Arizona Press, 1994), 48–49.

48. Employment Security Commission of Arizona, "Pinal County Agricultural Employment Study, September 1956-August 1957" (Phoenix: Arizona State Employment Office, 1957), 3; Pinal County Development Board, "Pinal County Arizona: An Industrial and Commercial Summary" (Florence, Ariz.: Pinal County Development Board, 1957), 8. D.W. Meinig points out that irrigation developments between 1911 and 1940 in Arizona had a

considerable impact upon the economic and social geography, creating by 1940 "an almost continuous broad arc of highly developed irrigation lands from Eloy and Coolidge on the south and east, to Peoria and Buckeye on the north and west" (*Southwest: Three Peoples in Geographical Change, 1600–1970* [New York, Oxford University Press, 1971], 71).

49. "Pinal County Agricultural Employment Study," 5–6.

50. Acuña, *Occupied America* (3rd ed.), 265.

51. Tijerina, *Mi lucha por la tierra*, 41.

52. Raymond Johnson Flores, "The Socio-Economic Status Trends of the Mexican People Residing in Arizona" (MA thesis, Arizona State College, 1951), 17.

53. Acuña, *Occupied America* (3rd ed.), 267.

54. Officer, "Sodalities and Systemic Linkage"; David Gutiérrez, *Walls and Mirrors: Mexican Americans, Mexican Immigrants, and the Politics of Ethnicity* (Berkeley: University of California Press, 1995).

55. Max Weber defines charisma at one point as "an extraordinary quality of a person, regardless of whether this quality is actual, alleged, or presumed. 'Charismatic authority,' hence, shall refer to a rule over men, whether predominantly external or predominantly internal, to which the governed submit because of their belief in the extraordinary quality of the specific person" ("The Social Psychology of the World Religions," in *From Max Weber: Essays in Sociology*, H. H. Gerth and C. Wright Mills, trans. and eds. [New York: Oxford University Press, 1964], 295). This difference may be interpreted as one of emphasis between Weber and Durkheim on the origin of the charismatic personality. Whereas Weber was satisfied to acknowledge the visceral, numinous characteristic of charismatic individuals, Durkheim's emphasis on the collective saw the charismatic individual as the receptacle of communal experience. See Charles Lindholm, *Charisma* (Cambridge, U.K.: Basil Blackwell, 1990), 22–35.

56. The mechanisms of insulation and isolation are described by Bryan R. Wilson, "An Analysis of Sect Development," *Sociological Review* 24 (February 1959), 3–15.

57. Robert S. Fogarty, "Introduction: 'Paradise Planters,'" in *Dictionary of American Communal and Utopian History* (Westport, Conn.: Greenwood Press, 1980), xx.

58. Stephane Quoniam, "A Painter, Geographer of Arizona," *Environment and Planning D: Society and Space* 6 (1988), 6, 9.

59. Edward Soja, *Postmodern Geographies: The Reassertion of Space in Critical Social Theory* (London: Verso, 1989), 7.

60. Soleri's Arcosanti project would become dependent upon optimistic volunteers, the proceeds of tourist visits and the sale of expensive ceramics and wind chimes. Paolo Soleri, *The Bridge Between Matter and Spirit Is Matter Becoming Spirit: The Arcology of Paolo Soleri* (Garden City, N.Y.: Anchor/Doubleday & Cosanti Foundation, 1973); Arcosanti promotional brochure.

61. John Polk Allen, a metallurgist and graduate of the Harvard Business School, had come to Arizona after leaving his Synergia Ranch experimental colony outside Santa Fe, New Mexico. Sun-Space Ranch seems to have been the original name for what eventually became Biosphere2 (which has since changed direction and is no longer associated with Allen's original ideas). Allen's earlier endeavors at utopia are detailed in Laurence Vesey, *The Communal Experience: Anarchist and Mystical Counter-Cultures in America* (San Francisco: Harper & Row, 1973), 279–406.

62. Del Webb, Arizona's foremost developer and best known for his Sun City community, built the Poston internment facility. The Poston camp Webb considered his proudest achievement. He is quoted as saying, "I think the greatest thing our company ever did

was move the Japs out of California. We did it in 90 days back in the war" (quoted in John M. Findlay, *Magic Lands: Western Cityscapes and American Culture After 1940* [Berkeley: University of California Press, 1992], 177).

63. Michel Foucault defined heterotopias as spaces "capable of juxtaposing in a single space several spaces, several sights that are in themselves incompatible" ("Of Other Spaces," *Diacritics* 16, [1986], 25).

64. Nigel Thrift quoted in Allan Pred, *Lost Words, Lost Worlds: Modernity and the Language of Everyday Life in Late Nineteenth-Century Stockholm* (Cambridge: Cambridge University Press, 1990), 7–8, 246, 251 ftn 41. Pred's comment is about local vocabularies. I have extended its meaning here.

65. The property was eventually sold in 1963 to raise money for the Alianza headquarters in Albuquerque.

66. Dolores Hayden, *Seven American Utopias: The Architecture of Communitarian Socialism, 1790–1975* (Cambridge: The MIT Press, 1976), 323; Philip W. Porter and Fred E. Lukermann, "The Geography of Utopia," in *Geographies of the Mind: Essays in Historical Geosophy in Honor of John Kirtland Wright*, David Lowenthal and Martyn J. Bowden, eds. (New York: Oxford University Press, 1976), 197–223.

67. "Promotional Brochure," *Sunland Visitor Center*, 5:2 (Spring/Summer 1996), 4.

68. Carl Abbott, *The Metropolitan Frontier: Cities in the Modern American West* (Tucson: University of Arizona Press, 1993), 68. See also, David Jeffrey, "Arizona's Suburbs of the Sun," *National Geographic* 152:4 (October 1977), 487–517. Jeffrey's caption beneath a picture of Arizona City reads: "With lots for sale since 1959, the development called Arizona City— complete with tennis courts, pool, park, and lake, but far from employment centers—is now home to only about 1,300 of a projected 25,000 residents. Here in the 'golden corridor' between Phoenix and Tucson, other developments have failed totally. Some never delivered amenities; some were hurt by publicity on land fraud; and some had too little water. Like played-out mines, they have been abandoned to the desert" (504–5).

69. See the essays in James Duncan and David Ley, *Place/Culture/Representation* (New York: Routledge, 1993).

70. The Warranty Deed sold by Tijerina describes the property as "160 acres being the North West Quarter of Section 20, Township 7, South Range 7, East of the Gila and Salt River Base and Meridian, Pinal County, State of Arizona. "Warranty Deed," 9 June, 1964, Docket 388, Page 494, Pinal County Recorders Office, Florence, Arizona.

71. Edward W. Soja comments that "Every ambitious exercise in critical geographical description, in translating into words the encompassing and politicized spatiality of social life provokes . . . linguistic despair. What one sees when one looks at geographies is stubbornly simultaneous, but language dictates a sequential succession, a linear flow of sentential statements bound by that most spatial of earthly constraints, the impossibility of two objects (or words) occupying the same precise space (as on a page). All that we can do is re-collect and creatively juxtapose, experimenting with assertions and insertions of the spatial against the prevailing grain of time" (*Postmodern Geographies*, 2).

72. Michel de Certeau, "Reading as Poaching," in *The Practice of Everyday Life* (Berkeley: University of California Press, 1984), 176.

73. During Tijerina's visit to the Guadalajara archives in 1959 he would discover the theft of documents that Reavis had stolen in 1880 (Tijerina, *Mi lucha por la tierra*, 120). See also Rosanna Miller, "The Peralta Land Grant," *Western Association of Map Libraries* 22:2 (March 1991), 121–26.

74. Tijerina, *Mi lucha por la tierra*, 76.

Chapter Five

1. Juan Bruce-Novoa, "Canonical and Noncanonical Texts," *The Americas Review* 14:3–4 (Fall–Winter 1986), 122. See also Richard D. Woods, "The Chicano Novel: Silence after Publication," *Revista Chicano-Riqueña* 4:3 (Summer 1976), 42–47.

2. Luis Leal, "El paso y la huella: The Reconstruction of Chicano Cultural History," in *Estudios Chicanos and the Politics of Community*, Mary Romero and Cordelia Candelaria, eds. (Boulder, Colo.: National Association for Chicano Studies, 1989), 26.

3. See Rudy V. Busto, "Like a Mighty Rushing Wind: The Religious Impulse in the Life and Writing of Reies López Tijerina," (PhD diss., University of California at Berkeley, 1991) for the complete bibliography too long to list here.

4. See Busto, "Like a Mighty Rushing Wind"; For another type of absence see *Chicano Art: Resistance and Affirmation, 1965–1985*, Richard Griswold del Castillo, et al., eds. (Los Angeles: Wight Art Gallery, UCLA, 1991) which, despite its attempts to the contrary, finds little if any value in the Alianza's New Mexican land grant effort in terms of "exhibitable" markers for Chicano culture and resistance.

5. Graciela Phillips, "La Gesta de un Pueblo Entre Dos Mundos," *Comercio Exterior* 29:1 (Enero 1979), 113–16. Author's field notes, Coyote, New Mexico, April 1990.

6. Richard Griswold del Castillo, *The Treaty of Guadalupe Hidalgo: A Legacy of Conflict* (Norman: University of Oklahoma Press, 1990) quotes one sentence (135), and Matt S. Meier, "'King Tiger': Reies López Tijerina," *Journal of the West* 27:2 (April 1988), 60–68, used it sparingly for his overview of Tijerina's career. Texts that mention *Mi lucha por la tierra* include John Chávez, *The Lost Land: The Chicano Image of the Southwest* (Albuquerque: University of New Mexico Press, 1984); Mario Barrera, *Beyond Aztlán: Ethnic Autonomy in Comparative Perspective* (New York: Praeger Press, 1988); Andrés G. Guerrero, *A Chicano Theology* (Maryknoll, N.Y.: Orbis Press, 1987); Rodolfo O. de la Garza, "Chicanos and U.S. Foreign Policy: The Future of Chicano-Mexican Relations," *The Western Political Quarterly* 33:4 (December 1980), 571–82. The best use of *Mi lucha por la tierra* has been in Clark Knowlton's sociological advocacy scholarship. See Clark Knowlton, "Reies López Tijerina and the Alianza Federál de Mercedes: Seekers after Justice," *Wisconsin Sociologist* 22:4 (Fall 1985), 133–44.

7. John C. Hammerback, Richard J. Jensen, and José Angel Gutiérrez, *A War of Words: Chicano Protest in the 1960s and 1970s* (Westport, Conn.: Greenwood Press, 1985).

8. Hammerback, Jensen, and Gutiérrez, *A War of Words*, 176. Note that they misspell the publisher as "Fondo de la Cultura" and give the wrong publication date, suggesting that they did not have access to the text, or that they decided it was unnecessary to their analysis.

9. Tomás Almaguér, "Ideological Distortions in Recent Chicano Historiography: The Internal Colonial Model and Chicano Historical Interpretation," *Aztlán* 18:1 (Spring 1987): 7.

10. Francisco A. Rosales, *CHICANO! The History of the Mexican American Civil Rights Movement* (Houston: Arte Público Press, 1996). Note the careful and cautious use of interview materials with Tijerina here. I suspect that the interviewers for the documentary project (like other interviewers since the 1970s) were stunned at the conspiratorial and apocalyptic pronouncements in their meeting with him and so explains their dependence on interviews with other players from the 1960s land grant drama.

11. Observe that later the writings of John Rechy, previously regarded as a "gay" writer, were also pulled under the umbrella of Chicano literature. It is interesting that few if any critics discuss the problematic/alternative notions of religion or spirituality in either Anzaldúa or Rodríguez.

12. The legal issues raised by the Treaty of Guadalupe Hidalgo have yet to be addressed adequately by the United States government. See Malcolm Ebright, "New Mexican Land Grants: The Legal Background," in *Land, Water, and Culture: New Perspectives on Hispanic Land Grants*, Charles L. Briggs and John R. Van Ness, eds. (Albuquerque: University of New Mexico Press, 1987), 15–64.

13. Reies López Tijerina, *Mi lucha por la tierra* (Mexico, D.F.: Fondo de Cultura Económica, 1978), 34.

14. John Thomas Vance, *The Background of Hispanic-American Law: Legal Sources and Juridical Literature of Spain* (New York: Central Book Co., 1943), 133–38; Tomás Polanco Alcántara, *Las reales audencias in las provincias de Americanas de España* (Madrid: Editorial MAPFRE, 1992), 23–24.

15. The Mano Negra (Black Hand) is described as one of a number of secretive organizations expressing Hispano resistance through fence cutting, arson, robbery, and outright violence. Tijerina seems to be conflating them with the overlapping Gorras Blancas (White Caps), a turn of the century Hispano masked and mounted band best known for their fence cutting. See Robert J. Rosenbaum and Robert W. Larson, "Mexicano Resistance to the Expropriation of Grant Lands in New Mexico," in *Land, Water, and Culture: New Perspectives on Hispanic Land Grants*, Charles L. Briggs and John R. Van Ness, eds. (Albuquerque: University of New Mexico Press, 1987), 269–310.

16. Reies López Tijerina, "The Spanish Land Grant Question Examined" (Albuquerque: Alianza Federál de Mercedes Reales/Pueblos Libres, 1966), 18.

17. Tijerina, "The Spanish Land Grant Question Examined," 20.

18. Reies López Tijerina, "From Prison: Reies López Tijerina," in *The Chicanos: Mexican American Voices*, Ed Ludwig and James Santibañez, eds. (Baltimore: Penguin, 1971), 215–22. See his account of his various jail sentences in his memoir, *Mi lucha por la tierra*, 304–48 *passim*.

19. Tijerina, "From Prison," 215.

20. He cites Law 7, Title 20, Section 3.

21. He is referring to the possibility that District Attorney Alfonso Sánchez was asking for the death penalty for the courthouse raid violence (Handwritten letter from Reies Tijerina to Jose Madrid, Nabokov Papers, Box 1, Folder 16, Item 31, 1).

22. Reies López Tijerina, "Letter from the Santa Fe Jail, 15–17 August 1969," *El Grito del Norte*, 26 September 1969. An excerpt is reprinted in *A Documentary History of the Mexican Americans*, Wayne Moquín and Charles Van Doren, eds. (New York: Praeger, 1971), 484–87.

23. Peter Nabokov, *Tijerina and the Courthouse Raid* (Albuquerque: University of New Mexico Press, 1969), 264–65; Richard Gardner, *Grito!: Reies Tijerina and the New Mexico Land Grant War of 1967* (Indianapolis: Bobbs-Merrill Company, 1970), 281.

24. Nabokov, *Tijerina and the Courthouse Raid*, 280; second emphasis added. Neither Gardner nor Blawis include this information.

25. For examples of how these issues continue to trouble the genre of autobiography, see Robert Elbaz, *The Changing Nature of the Self: A Critical Study of the Autobiographical Discourse* (London: Croom Helm, 1988), 1; Thomas Couser, *American Autobiography: The Prophetic Mode* (Amherst: University of Massachusetts Press, 1979), 6; James Olney, *Autobiography: Essays Theoretical and Critical*, (Princeton, N.J.: Princeton University Press, 1980), 11–12; Roy Pascal, *Design and Truth in Autobiography* (Cambridge: Harvard University Press, 1960). See William C. Spengemann's discussion of definitions for the autobiography in his Bibliographic Essay in *The Forms of Autobiography: Episodes in the History of a Literary Genre* (New Haven, Conn.: Yale University Press, 1980), 183–89.

26. Olney, *Autobiography*, 5.

27. See Hector Calderón, "To Read Chicano Narrative: Commentary and Metacommentary," *Mester: Revista literária de los estudiantes graduados* 11:2 (May 1983), 3–14; Ramón Saldívar, "Ideologies of the Self: Chicano Autobiography," *Diacritics* (Fall 1985), 25–34; Antonio Márquez, "Richard Rodríguez's *Hunger of Memory* and the Poetics of Experience" *Arizona Quarterly* 40:2 (Summer 1984), 130–41; Genaro M. Padilla, "The Recovery of Chicano Nineteenth-Century Autobiography," *American Quarterly* 40:3 (September, 1988), 286–306; William Anthony Nericcio, "Autobiographies at 'La Frontera': The Quest for Mexican American Narratives," *The Americas Review* 16:3–4 (Fall-Winter 1988), 145–64; Alfredo Villanueva-Collado, "Growing Up Hispanic: Discourse and Ideology in *Hunger of Memory* and *Family Installments*," *The Americas Review* 16:3–4 (Fall-Winter 1988), 75–90.

28. Saldívar, "Ideologies of the Self," 32–33; Padilla, "Recovery of Chicano Nineteenth-Century Autobiography," 301–5.

29. Saldívar, "Ideologies of the Self," 30–33; Renato Rosaldo, "Changing Chicano Narratives," in *Culture and Truth: The Remaking of Social Analysis* (Boston: Beacon Press, 1989), 147–67.

30. I am not discussing the *testimonio* genre because it depends upon the conscious mediation of the historian/recorder/scholar between the subject and reader. See Rosaura Sánchez, "Testimonials as Dependent Production," in *Telling Identities: The Californio Testimonios* (Minneapolis: University of Minnesota Press, 1994), 1–15.

31. Marcus Billson, "The Memoir: New Perspectives on a Forgotten Genre," *Genre* 10:2 (Summer 1977), 261.

32. Richard Woods, "An Overview of Mexican Autobiography," *a/b Auto/Biography Studies* 3:4 (Summer 1988), 13, 15.

33. Billson, "The Memoir," 161.

34. Billson, "The Memoir," 126.

35. Woods, "An Overview of Mexican Autobiography," 13.

36. Woods, "An Overview of Mexican Autobiography," 21–22.

37. Note Spengemann's rather long argument against the grain of traditional critical commentary on the meaning of Augustine's phrase, "Cognoscam te, cognitor meus, cognoscam, sicut et cognitus sum," which he interprets to mean Augustine's final understanding of himself, thereby collapsing knowledge of God with knowledge of self (*The Forms of Autobiography*, 16–19).

38. Elbaz, *The Changing Nature of the Self*, 35. For a similar assessment of the *Confessions* as descriptive of autonomous selves in autobiography, see Geoffrey Galt Harpham, "Conversion and the Language of Autobiography," in Olney, *Studies of Autobiography*, 42–50.

39. See Anne Hunsaker Hawkins, *Archetypes of Conversion: The Autobiographies of Augustine, Bunyan, and Merton* (London and Toronto: Associated University Presses, 1985); and G. Thomas Couser, Introduction and Chapter 12 on the "prophetic" voice in autobiography in his *American Autobiography*; and Daniel B. Shea, *Spiritual Autobiography in Early America* (Princeton, N.J.: Princeton University Press, 1968).

40. Couser writes, "I have chosen to call prophetic autobiography a mode rather than a subgenre because it seems to me a way of writing autobiography that can adapt various conventional forms such as confession, memoir, and apology—and even other genres such as travel writing and journalism—to its own requirements and purposes" (*American Autobiography*, 5–9).

41. Tijerina, *Mi lucha por la tierra*, 417.

42. Billson, "The Memoir," 278.
43. Authors' interview with Reies Tijerina, Coyote, New Mexico, April, 1990. These dates are confirmed in the original manuscript. A note in the left margin reads: "*Principie a Escribir este libro el Dia Primero de Enero de 1976. Fué Publicado en Mexico por orden del Presidente de Mexico, Luis Echeverria Alvarez. Lo Terminé el 21 de Sept. 1976. El dia de mis cumple-años.*" ["Began to write this book the first day of January 1976. It was published in Mexico by order of the president of Mexico, Luís Echeverría Alvarez. I finished it the 21st of September 1976. The day of my birthday."] See also fn1, Chapter One in the English translation, Reies López Tijerina with José Angel Gutiérrez, ed. and trans., *They Called Me "King Tiger"*, xviii.
44. Peter Nabokov, "'Remembering Tierra Amarilla': Chicano Power in the Feudal West," *The Nation*, 8 October 1977, 340; Tijerina, *Mi lucha por la tierra*, 537.
45. Author's Tijerina interview, 1990.
46. Tijerina, *Mi lucha por la tierra*, 531–35.
47. McGraw-Hill contacted him in May, 1969. Tijerina, *Mi lucha por la tierra*, 288; Author's Tijerina interview, 1990.
48. Author's Tijerina interview, 1990.
49. Author's Tijerina interview, 1990. On various occasions during his most active speaking years, Tijerina would switch from English to Spanish as a way to speak "confidentially" to the Chicanos in his audiences. In his 1971 speech at Trinity University, he began his switch by saying to his audience in Spanish, "Brothers and sisters, I want to tell you a secret." ("Speech at Trinity University, San Antonio, 26 October 1971," *Magazín* 1:32 (December 1971), 67.
50. Author's Tijerina interview, 1990.
51. These handwritten journals are repositories of Tijerina's daily activities and his reflections on local and world events at the time. His disciplined and sustained record keeping, beyond *Mi lucha por la tierra*, represents an invaluable source documenting the last half of the twentieth century, and surveying the origins, rise, and decline of the Chicano Movement from his perspective. Their disposition after the arson fire that destroyed his home in 1993 is unknown.
52. Any comprehensive critical and close reading of the memoir will require access to the original manuscript, which may have been lost in a fire in November 1993. Purportedly, a photocopy of the entire manuscript was made in 1999 from copies in Mexico and is deposited in the University of New Mexico Zimmerman Library (Carolyn Gonzales, "Tijerina Archive Aids Research, Offers Insight," *Campus News* [University of New Mexico], 15 October 2001).
53. Tijerina, *Mi lucha por la tierra*, 562–63.
54. I am indebted to Claude Clegg III for confirming my suspicion that Tijerina was using these numbers to add religious significance to his text. Clegg pointed out that Tijerina's claim that Elijah Muhammad hosted him for seven days was highly unlikely, given Tijerina's fugitive status and the fact that Muhammad was under constant FBI surveillance. Clegg notes the FBI files on Elijah Muhammad make no mention of Tijerina, and that Muhammad rarely if ever entertained even his closest associates for this length of time (Personal communication, 17 August 1997).
55. Michel de Certeau, "A Variant: Hagio-Graphical Edification," in *The Writing of History*, Tom Conley, trans. (New York: Columbia University Press, 1988), 277.
56. The strong Catholicism of Fray Angélico Chávez's writing similarly works against his texts in Chicano studies.

57. Tijerina, *Mi lucha por la tierra*, 560.

58. Tzvetan Todorov, "An Introduction to Verisimilitude," in *The Poetics of Prose* (Ithaca, N.Y.: Cornell University Press, 1977), 80–88.

59. For example, a comparison of the last chapter, "La CIA" in the Spanish and English versions reveals the omission of most of the references to scripture and religion in the editing of nineteen pages in the Spanish down to eight in the English edition.

Chapter Six

1. Reies López Tijerina, *Mi lucha por la tierra* (Mexico, D.F.: Fondo de Cultura Económica, 1978), 7.

2. Author's interview with Reies Tijerina, Coyote, New Mexico, April 1990.

3. Author's Tijerina interview, 1990.

4. Peter Nabokov, *Tijerina and the Courthouse Raid* (Albuquerque: University of New Mexico Press, 1969), 279–80.

5. "Tijerina's Thoughts on Justice," *Columnas* (Diocese of Iowa) 1:7 (16 December 1971), 5.

6. See George Marsden, *Fundamentalism and American Culture: The Shaping of Twentieth-Century Evangelicalism, 1870–1925* (New York: Oxford University Press, 1980), 14–21.

7. Tijerina, *Mi lucha por la tierra*, 362.

8. Author's Tijerina interview, 1990.

9. Reies López Tijerina, "From Prison: Reies López Tijerina," in *The Chicanos: Mexican American Voices*, Ed Ludwig and James Santibañez, eds., (Baltimore: Penguin, 1971), 215–22.

10. Letter to author from Renee Barley, FOIA Administrator, Federal Bureau of Prisons, U.S. Department of Justice, 30 June 1997.

11. Letter to Patty Newman from Congressman H. Allen Smith, 25 November 1970, in Patty Newman, *¡Do it up Brown!* (San Diego: Viewpoint Books, 1971), 66; José Armas, "Notas de Aztlán: Reies López Tijerina in Prison," *La Luz* 3:5 (August 1974), 1–2.

12. *El Gallo*, December 1970, quoted in Newman, *¡Do it up Brown!*, 67; Tijerina, "From Prison: Reies López Tijerina," 216; *Mi lucha por la tierra*, 332. Tijerina does not name Castillo in the memoir. I assume he is referring to Castillo in the memoir, as the event occurs in the late summer, early fall of 1969 in both texts. See also, "Tijerina is Given Medical Help at Prison Medical Section," *Albuquerque Journal*, 5 March 1970; "Tijerina Denies Report That He Is Suffering from Throat Cancer," *Albuquerque Journal*, 10 January 1973. In 1971 Tijerina told a crowd after his release from prison that "he had been told that he has a tumor in the esophagus" ("Leader of U.S.-Based Mexicans Freed after 775 Days in Prison," *Los Pensamientos de Aztlán* [Visalia, Calif.] 1:3 [September 1971]). Even in 1996, these rumors were kept alive by raising the issue but leaving it unresolved; Rosales writes in his text: " . . . because of the strange behavior he exhibited after being released, rumors were rife that he had been given mind-altering drugs to control his behavior in jail. In a recent interview, he claimed that being put into prison was a plot to destroy him." (*CHICANO! The History of the Mexican American Civil Rights Movement* [Houston: Arte Público Press, 1996], 169).

13. Letter to author from Renee Barley, FOIA Administrator.

14. Michael J. Churgin, "The Transfer of Inmates to Mental Health Facilities: Developments in the Law," in *Mentally Disordered Offenders: Perspectives from Law and Society*, John Monahan and Henry J. Steadman, eds. (New York: Plenum Press, 1983), 207–9. Issues of justifiable transfer of inmates to medical facilities would not come under scrutiny until the 1980 *Vitek v. Jones* case establishing a set of procedures allowing prisoners to go through an administrative hearing.

15. Author's Tijerina interview, 1990.

16. Churgin, "The Transfer of Inmates," 212.

17. David L. Rosenhan, "On Being Sane in Insane Places," in *Labeling Madness*, Thomas J. Scheff, ed. (Englewood Cliffs, N.J.: Prentice-Hall, 1975), 54–74. See also the critiques of Rosenhan's study in the *Journal of Abnormal Psychology* 84:5 (October 1975). The Rosenhan study not only undermined the foundations of institutional psychiatric care, but also pointed to the error in psychiatric labeling that found medical professionals were "more inclined to call a healthy person sick than a sick person healthy" (58–59).

18. Marcella De La Torre, "Psychological Testing of Incarcerated Hispanics," in *Report: National Hispanic Conference on Law Enforcement and Criminal Justice, Washington, D.C., 28–30 July 1980* (Washington, D.C.: U.S. Department of Justice, Law Enforcement Assistance Administration, 1980), 61–85. See also C. Creary and E. Padilla, "MMPI Differences among Black, Mexican-American, and White Male Offenders," *Journal of Clinical Psychology*, 33 (1977), 171–77; Israel Cuellar, "The Diagnosis and Evaluation of Schizophrenic Disorders among Mexican Americans," in *Mental Health and Hispanic Americans: Clinical Perspectives*, Rosina M. Becerra, Martin Karno, Javier I. Escobar, eds. (New York: Grune & Stratton, 1982), 61–81; Israel Cuellar and Robert E. Roberts, "Psychological Disorders Among Chicanos," *Chicano Psychology*, 2nd ed., Joe L. Martínez, Jr. and Richard H. Mendoza, eds. (San Diego: Academic Press, 1984), 133–61.

19. Tijerina, *Mi lucha por la tierra*, 352; Peter Nabokov, "'Remembering Tierra Amarilla': Chicano Power in the Feudal West," *The Nation*, 8 October 1977, 340.

20. Tijerina, *Mi lucha por la tierra*, 353. In fact, by their own admission, the U.S. Bureau of Prisons admitted that patient psychiatric records were relatively easy to access for anyone inside the institution. See U.S. Bureau of Prisons, *A Handbook of Correctional Psychiatry 1* (Washington, D.C.: Department of Justice, 1968), 26.

21. Tijerina's description of his incarceration activities follows closely the coping and socialization phases of incarceration detailed in *A Handbook of Correctional Psychiatry*, 1–5.

22. Following the original MS, Volume III, 92; *Mi lucha por la tierra*, 354–55. A year prior to his incarceration, the landmark *United States v. ex rel. Schuster v. Herold*, which prohibited the transfer of federal prisoners to medical facilities without diagnosis, had been decided in favor of a prisoner who had languished in a medical facility for more than twenty years. He had been placed there without any clear diagnosis of mental disorder. Had Tijerina been aware of *Schuster*, he no doubt would have attempted to apply it to his situation. See *United States ex.rel. Schuster v. Herold*, 410 F. 2d. 1071 (2d Cir.), 1969. In 1980, the U.S. Supreme Court would rule that the chances that errors are made in diagnosing mental illness warranted legal safeguards such that the "subtleties and nuances of psychiatric diagnosis that justify the requirements of an adversary hearing." Similarly, legal scholars have noted a tendency to "transfer to [Medical/Psychiatric] facilities those inmates who, whether or not mentally ill, were too troublesome for the prisons" (*Vitek v. Jones*, 100 S.Ct. 1254, at 1265).

23. Erving Goffman, *Asylums: Essays on the Social Situation of Mental Patients and Other Inmates* (Garden City, N.Y.: Doubleday & Co., 1961), 210–27.

24. Jocelyn Lieu, "The Courthouse Raid: Twenty Years Later," *Rio Grande Sun*, 28 May 1987; Author's Tijerina interview, 1990.

25. Tijerina, *Mi lucha por la tierra*, 356.

26. Foucault reminds us that before the end of the eighteenth century, the "clinical" sciences were concerned with groups, or, nations, and not the individual ("The Means of Correct Training," in *The Foucault Reader*, Paul Rabinow, ed. (New York: Pantheon, 1984), 200.

27. It is possible that Tijerina's construction of racial cosmogony may have been the fruit of his private conversations years earlier with Nation of Islam leader, Elijah Muhammad, as both of them adopt a theory of white mental and moral deterioration.

28. Tijerina, *Mi lucha por la tierra*, 357.

29. See Luís N. Rivera, *A Violent Evangelism: The Political and Religious Conquest of the Americas* (Louisville, Ky.: Westminster/John Knox Press, 1992), especially Chapter Two, "Alexander's Papal Bulls."

30. Reies Tijerina taped interview with Andrés Guerrero, Coyote, New Mexico, 11 January 1980.

31. My translation of the original MS, Volume III, 97–100; Tijerina, *Mi lucha por la tierra*, 78.

32. Reies Tijerina radio interview with Elsa Knight Thompson, KPFA, Berkeley, California, 5 April 1968. Hayden Library, Arizona State University, Recording #353. His memoir puts this etymology as far back as 1961, but it may be a later insertion (*Mi lucha por la tierra*, 78–79).

33. Tijerina, *Mi lucha por la tierra*, 557.

34. Guerrero interview, 1980.

35. Lieu, "The Courthouse Raid."

36. Guerrero interview, 1980.

37. *Tixerina: Through the Eyes of a Tiger: An Interview with Reies Tijerina* [with Harold Rhodes] [video] (Albuquerque: KNME-TV, University of New Mexico, 1982).

38. Centro de Enseñanza para Extranjeros, *Encuentro Chicano Mexico 1987: Memorias, Testimonios y Ponencias* (Mexico, D.F.: UNAM, 1988), 105.

39. Robert Bunker, "'A Power of Healing': Reies Tijerina at St. John's, September 30, 1967" typewritten photocopy, Nabokov Papers, Box 1, Folder 37, Item 5, 33). Tijerina's speech at St. John's is also mentioned in Richard Gardner, *Grito!: Reies Tijerina and the New Mexico Land Grant War of 1967* (Indianapolis: Bobbs-Merrill Company, 1970), 210–11.

40. Nabokov, *Tijerina and the Courthouse Raid*, 221.

41. See the classic formulation by José Vasconcelos, *La raza cósmica: Misión de la raza Ibero-Americana* (Madrid: Aguilar/Di Ediciones, 1961).

42. The text translates: "Law II. D. Fernando V and doña Juana in Valbuena, on 19 October 1514, and in Valladolid, on 5 February 1515. D. Felipe II and the princess governoress there on 22 October 1556. *That the Indians be allowed to freely marry, and that no royal order impede them.* It is our will, that the Indians have, as they should, complete freedom to marry whom they wish, with Indians, as with those natives from these our kingdoms, or Spaniards born in the Indies, and that in this matter they should not be prohibited. And we command, that no order of ours that might be given, or might have been given, or might impede, not impede the marriage between male and female Indians with male and female Spaniards, and that all have entire freedom to marry whom they desire, and that our courts (*audiencias*) procure that this is protected and accomplished" *Recopilación de Leyes de Los Reinos de las Indias: Mandadas imprimir y publicar por al Magestad católica del rey don Carlos II, nuestro señor*, Vol. 1, 5th ed. (Madrid: Boix, 1841), 217.

43. John Kokish, "Leader Tells Hispano Goals," *The Denver Post*, 6 November 1966, 25. Kokish reports that Tijerina seemed to be playing with the term "Indianas" in 1966.

44. Robert Tice, *The Rhetoric of La Raza* (Kingsville: Texas A & I University/M.A.Y.O., 1971), 8. A recorded version of Tijerina's speech is housed in the Chicano Collection, Hayden Library, Arizona State University, REC 382.

45. Tice, *Rhetoric*, 9.

46. Tice, *Rhetoric*, 10. Text is corrected, following recorded version.

47. Tice, *Rhetoric*, 23. Text is corrected, following recorded version.
48. Jose Armas, "'Entrevista' con Reies López Tijerina," *De Colores: Journal of Emerging Raza Philosophies* 1:1 (Winter 1973), 14.
49. Tijerina's responses to Guerrero's schedule of questions were so startling and troubling that Guerrero was forced to limit his use of this material in his dissertation. I have similarly made judicious use of Guerrero's interview and have tried to locate corroborating statements reported in the press and in public interviews.
50. Ezekiel 37:19–22 reads: "Say unto them, Thus saith the Lord God; Behold, I will take the stick of Joseph, which is in the hand of Ephraim, and the tribes of Israel his fellows, and will put them with him, even with the stick of Judah, and make them one stick, and they shall be one in mine hand. And the sticks whereon thy writest shall be in thine hand before their eyes. And say unto them, Thus saith the Lord God; Behold, I will take the children of Israel from among the heathen, whither they be gone, and will gather them into their own land: And I will make them one nation in the land upon the mountains of Israel; and one king shall be king to them all: and they shall be no more two nations, neither shall they be divided into two kingdoms any more at all" (KJV).
51. Andrés G. Guerrero, *A Chicano Theology* (Maryknoll: Orbis Press, 1987), 129.
52. Author's Tijerina interview, 1990.
53. See the essay by Shalva Weil, "Beyond the Sambatyon: The Myth of the Ten Lost Tribes/Me-Ever La-Sambatyon" in the exhibition catalogue of the same title (Tel Aviv: Beth Hatefutsoth, The Museum of the Jewish Diaspora, 1991), 77–94; "Tribes, Lost Ten," *s.v. The Jewish Encyclopedia*, v. 12 (New York: KTAV Publishing, 1964).
54. Gardner, *Grito!*, 255–56.
55. Guerrero interview, 1980.
56. Weil, "Beyond the Sambatyon," 77–78.
57. James Aho, *The Politics of Righteousness: Idaho Christian Patriotism* (Seattle: University of Washington Press, 1990), 106–8.
58. See Aho, *The Politics of Righteousness*; Michael Barkun, *Religion and the Racist Right: The Origins of the Christian Identity Movement* (Chapel Hill: University of North Carolina Press, 1994); Richard Abanes, *American Militias: Rebellion, Racism and Religion* (Downers Grove, Ill.: InterVarsity Press, 1996); "Anglo-Israelism," *s.v., The Jewish Encyclopedia*.
59. Guerrero interview, 1980.
60. Guerrero interview, 1980.
61. Author's Tijerina interview, 1990; Enrique Flórez, *España Sagrada: Theatro geographico-historico de la iglesia de España*, vols. 1–56 (Madrid: M. F. Rodríguez, 1747).
62. Tijerina owns a complete set of *The Jewish Encyclopedia*, parts of which he has committed to memory, and much of it underlined (Author's field notes, Coyote, New Mexico, April 1990).
63. *Tixerina: Through the Eyes of a Tiger*.
64. Aho, *Politics of Righteousness*, 111.
65. Perhaps the most astonishing Identity theory about race difference is the "two seed" theory that traces Jews to the union of the Serpent and Eve, prior to Eve's union with Adam (Barkun, *Religion and the Racist Right*, 161–62; Aho, *Politics of Righteousness*, 97–98).
66. I recognized Christian Identity materials in his home during my 1990 fieldwork with him.
67. He considers Palestinians to be Christians who were converted to Islam (Author's field notes, 1990).
68. Lieu, "The Courthouse Raid"; Lieu also reports that he admits that the idea of a post-nuclear "rebirth" he got from Elijah Muhammad back in 1961.

69. Rebecca Roybal, "Tijerina Remembers 'Greatest Day,'" *Albuquerque Journal*, 5 June 1997.
70. Michel Foucault, "The Birth of the Asylum" reprinted in *The Foucault Reader*, Paul Rabinow, ed. (New York: Pantheon, 1984), 164.
71. Michel Foucault, "The Means of Correct Training," 197–205.

Epilogue

1. Peter Nabokov, "Reflections on the Alianza," *New Mexico Quarterly* 37:4 (Winter 1968), 343–56; Frances L. Swadesh, "The Alianza Movement: Catalyst for Social Change in New Mexico," in *Spanish-Speaking People in the United States. Proceedings of the 1968 Annual Spring Meeting of the American Ethnological Society*, June Helm, ed. (Seattle and London: American Ethnological Society/University of Washington, 1969), 162–77; Nancie L. González, *The Spanish-Americans of New Mexico: A Heritage of Pride*, 2nd ed. (Albuquerque: University of New Mexico Press, 1969), 93–114, 179–86.
2. Note the excessive religious language in Joseph L. Love's description of Tijerina's work: "Yet there is a sinister element in the Apocalypse which must precede the millennium: Anglos must be driven out. And Hispanos will be judged by whether they aided, stood aside from, or hindered the cause. Those who hindered will be treated harshly" ("La Raza: Mexican Americans in Rebellion," *TRANS-action* [February 1969], reprinted in *Pain and Promise: The Chicanos Today*, Edward Simmens, ed. [New York: Mentor/New American Library, 1972], 279).
3. Nabokov, "Reflections on the Alianza," 352.
4. Carrol Cagle, a reporter with the *Santa Fe New Mexican* at the time of the raid is perhaps the only writer to fully appreciate and acknowledge the essentially religious nature of Tijerina's personality, writing that, "He is a former evangelist tent preacher, and his references are never to Marx or Marcuse, but to Jesus Christ. He is a fundamentalist, a difficult point for most to grasp in this day of semantical debates over minute ideological points" ("The Great Land Grab Game," *The Black Politician: A Journal of Current Political Thought* 1:4 [Spring/April 1970], 19).
5. Carlo Ginzburg, *Clues, Myths and the Historical Method*, John and Anne C. Tedeschi, trans. (Baltimore: Johns Hopkins University Press, 1989), 124–25.
6. Steven Justice, *Writing and Rebellion: England in 1381* (Berkeley: University of California Press, 1994), 255.
7. Leonard Norman Primiano, "Intrinsically Catholic: Vernacular Religion and Philadelphia's 'Dignity'" (PhD diss., University of Pennsylvania, 1993).

BIBLIOGRAPHY

Abanes, Richard. *American Militias: Rebellion, Racism and Religion*. Downers Grove, Ill.: InterVarsity Press, 1996.

Abbott, Carl. *The Metropolitan Frontier: Cities in the Modern American West*. Tucson: University of Arizona Press, 1993.

Acuña, Rodolfo. *Occupied America: The Chicano's Struggle Toward Liberation*, 1st ed. San Francisco: Canfield Press, 1972.

———. *Occupied America: A History of Chicanos*, 2nd ed. New York: Harper & Row, 1981.

———. *Occupied America: A History of Chicanos*, 3rd ed. New York: Harper & Row, 1988.

———. *Occupied America: A History of Chicanos*, 4th ed. New York: Longman, 2000.

Aho, James. *The Politics of Righteousness: Idaho Christian Patriotism*. Seattle: University of Washington Press, 1990.

Alarcón, Norma. "Conjugating Subjects: The Heteroglossia of Essence and Resistance." In *An Other Tongue*, edited by Alfred Arteaga, 125–38. Durham, N.C.: Duke University Press, 1994.

Almaguér, Tomás. "Ideological Distortions in Recent Chicano Historiography: The Internal Colonial Model and Chicano Historical Interpretation." *Aztlán* 18:1 (Spring 1987), 7–28.

Anaya, Rudolfo, and Francisco Lomelí, eds. *Aztlán: Essays on the Chicano Homeland*. Albuquerque: University of New Mexico Press, 1989.

Anderson, Robert Mapes. *Vision of the Disinherited: The Making of American Pentecostalism*. New York: Oxford University Press, 1979.

Anzaldúa, Gloria. *Borderlands/La Frontera: The New Mestiza*. San Francisco: Aunt Lute Press, 1987.

Armas, José. "'Entrevista' con Reies López Tijerina." *De Colores: Journal of Emerging Raza Philosophies* 1:1 (Winter 1973), 13–15.

———. "Notas de Aztlán: Reies López Tijerina in Prison." *La Luz* 3:5 (August 1974), 1–2.

Atkinson, Edwin. "Hispanic Baptists in Texas: A Glorious and Threatened History." *Apuntes* 17:2 (Summer 1997), 41–44.

Barkun, Michael. *Religion and the Racist Right: The Origins of the Christian Identity Movement.* Chapel Hill: University of North Carolina Press, 1994.

Barrera, Mario. *Race and Class in the Southwest: A Theory of Racial Inequality.* Notre Dame, Ind.: University of Notre Dame Press, 1979.

———. *Beyond Aztlán: Ethnic Autonomy in Comparative Perspective.* New York: Praeger Press, 1988.

Billson, Marcus. "The Memoir: New Perspectives on a Forgotten Genre." *Genre* 10:2 (Summer 1977), 259–82.

Blair, Bertha, Anne O. Lively, and Glen W. Trimble. *Spanish Speaking Americans: Mexicans and Puerto Ricans in the United States.* New York: Home Missions Division, National Council of Churches, 1959.

Blauner, Robert. *Racial Oppression in America.* New York: Harper & Row, 1972.

Blawis, Patricia Bell. *Tijerina and the Land Grants: Mexican Americans in Struggle for Their Heritage.* New York: International Publishers, 1971.

Blumhofer, Edith L. *Restoring the Faith: The Assemblies of God, Pentecostalism and American Culture.* Urbana: University of Illinois Press, 1993.

Boyer, Paul. *By Bomb's Early Light: American Thought and Culture at the Dawn of the Atomic Age.* New York: Pantheon Books, 1985.

Brackenridge, R. Douglas, and Francisco O. Garcia-Treto. *Iglesia Presbiteriana: A History of Presbyterians and Mexican Americans in the Southwest.* San Antonio: Trinity University Press, 1974.

Brenneis, C. Brooks, and Samuel Roll. "Ego Modalities in the Manifest Dreams of Male and Female Chicanos." *Psychiatry* 38 (May 1975), 172–85.

———. "Dream Patterns in Anglo and Chicano Young Adults." *Psychiatry* 39 (August 1976), 280–90.

Bruce-Novoa, Juan. "Canonical and Noncanonical Texts." *The Americas Review* 14:3–4 (Fall–Winter 1986), 119–35.

Bryan, C. D. B. *Close Encounters of the Fourth Kind: A Reporter's Notebook on Alien Abduction, UFOs and the Conference at M.I.T.* New York: Penguin, 1995.

Cadena, Gilbert R. "Chicano Clergy and the Emergence of Liberation Theology." *Hispanic Journal of Behavioral Sciences* 11:2 (May 1989), 107–21.

Cagle, Carrol W. "The Great Land Grab Game." *The Black Politician: A Journal of Current Political Thought* 1:4 (Spring/April 1970), 17–21.

Cagle, Carrol W., and Harry P. Stumpf. "The Trial of Reies López Tijerina." In *Political Trials,* edited by Theodore L. Becker, 183–203. Indianapolis: Bobbs-Merrill Company, 1971.

Calderón, Hector. "To Read Chicano Narrative: Commentary and Metacommentary." *Mester: Revista literária de los estudiantes graduados* 11:2 (May 1983), 3–14.

Callanan, Tuss. "Coyote A Town Without Pity." *Chicago Tribune* (12 April 1987), 9–11, 13–20.

Calloway, Larry. "The American Revolution of 1967." *Argosy* (2 February 1968), 121–23.

Carlson, Alvar W. *The Spanish-American Homeland: Four Centuries in New Mexico's Río Arriba.* Baltimore: Johns Hopkins University Press, 1990.

Carrasco, David. "A Perspective for a Study of Religious Dimensions in Chicano Experience: *Bless Me, Ultima* as a Religious Text." *Aztlán* 13 (1982), 195–221.

Centro de Enseñanza para Extranjeros. *Encuentro Chicano Mexico 1987: Memorias, Testimonios y Ponencias.* Mexico, D.F.: UNAM, 1988.

Chávez, Fray Angélico, "The Penitentes of New Mexico." *New Mexico Historical Review* 29 (1954), 635–46.

Chávez, John R. *The Lost Land: The Chicano Image of the Southwest.* Albuquerque: University of New Mexico Press, 1984.

CHICANO! The History of the Mexican American Civil Rights Movement [film]. Hector Galán, Series Producer. Los Angeles: National Latino Communications Group—Galán Productions, 1996.

Chicano Art: Resistance and Affirmation, 1965–1985. Edited by Richard Griswold del Castillo, Teresa McKenna, and Yvonne Yarbo-Bejarano. Los Angeles: Wight Art Gallery, UCLA, 1991.

Choldin, Harvey M., and Grafton D. Trout. "Mexican Americans in Transition: Migration and Employment in Michigan Cities." East Lansing: Department of Sociology, Michigan State University/U.S. Department of Labor, Rural Manpower Center, 1969.

Christiansen, John. "A Real 'Milagro Beanfield War' in New Mexico." *San Francisco Chronicle*, 5 July 1988.

Churgin, Michael J. "The Transfer of Inmates to Mental Health Facilities: Developments in the Law." In *Mentally Disordered Offenders: Perspectives from Law and Society*, edited by John Monahan and Henry J. Steadman, 207–32. New York: Plenum Press, 1983.

Clegg, III, Claude A. *An Original Man: The Life and Times of Elijah Muhammad.* New York: St. Martin's Press, 1997.

Collado, A. B. "Reies Tijerina: ¿Héroe o Malhechor?" *El Hispano* 2:8 (8 August 1967), 1, 3; 2:9 (15 August 1967), 3.

Corona, Bert, and Mario Garcia. *Memories of Chicano History: The Life and Narrative of Bert Corona.* Berkeley: University of California Press, 1994.

Cortés, Carlos E. "New Chicano Historiography." In *Borderlands Sourcebook: A Guide to the Literature on Northern Mexico and the American Southwest*, edited by Ellwyn R. Stoddard, et al., 60–63. Norman: University of Oklahoma Press, 1983.

Couser, Thomas. *American Autobiography: The Prophetic Mode.* Amherst: University of Massachusetts Press, 1979.

Creary, C., and E. Padilla. "MMPI Differences among Black, Mexican-American, and White Male Offenders." *Journal of Clinical Psychology* 33 (1977), 171–77.

Cross, Whitney R. *The Burned-Over District: The Social and Intellectual History of Enthusiastic Religion in Western New York, 1800–1850.* Ithaca, N.Y.: Cornell University Press, 1950.

Cuellar, Israel. "The Diagnosis and Evaluation of Schizophrenic Disorders among Mexican Americans." In *Mental Health and Hispanic Americans: Clinical Perspectives*, edited by Rosina M. Becerra, Martin Karno, and Javier I. Escobar, 61–81. New York: Grune & Stratton, 1982.

Cuellar, Israel, and Robert E. Roberts. "Psychological Disorders among Chicanos." In *Chicano Psychology*, 2nd ed., edited by Joe L. Martínez, Jr., and Richard Mendoza, 133–61. San Diego: Academic Press, 1984.

Darrand, Tom Craig, and Anson Shupe. *Metaphors of Social Control in a Pentecostal Sect.* New York: Edwin Mellen Press, 1983.

Dayton, Donald. *Theological Roots of Pentecostalism.* Grand Rapids, Mich.: Francis Asbury Press/Zondervan, 1987.

DeBuys, William Eno. *Enchantment and Exploitation: The Life and Hard Times of a New Mexican Mountain Range.* Albuquerque: University of New Mexico Press, 1985.

de Certeau, Michel. *The Practice of Everyday Life.* Berkeley: University of California Press, 1984.

———. *The Writing of History.* Translated by Tom Conley. New York: Columbia University Press, 1988.

de la Garza, Rodolfo O. "Chicanos and U.S. Foreign Policy: The Future of Chicano-Mexican Relations." *The Western Political Quarterly* 33:4 (December 1980), 571–82.

De La Torre, Marcella. "Psychological Testing of Incarcerated Hispanics." In *Report: National Hispanic Conference on Law Enforcement and Criminal Justice, Washington, D.C., 28–30 July 1980*. Washington, D.C.: U.S. Department of Justice, Law Enforcement Assistance Administration, 1980.

de Leon, Victor. *The Silent Pentecostals: A Biographical History of the Pentecostal Movement among the Hispanics in the Twentieth Century*. Taylors, S.C.: Faith Printing Co., 1979.

Dibelius, Martin. *From Tradition to Gospel*. New York: Charles Scribner's Sons, 1965.

Dictionary of Pentecostal and Charismatic Movements. Edited by Stanley M. Burgess and Gary B. McGee. Grand Rapids, Mich.: Regency Reference Library, 1988.

Dodson, Ruth. "The Life of Don Pedro Jaramillo: Benefactor of Humanity." *Perspectives in Mexican American Studies* 1 (1988), 69–74.

Duffield, Guy P., and N. M. Van Cleave. *Foundations of Pentecostal Theology*. Los Angeles: L.I.F.E. Bible College, 1983.

Duncan, James, and David Ley. *Place/Culture/Representation*. New York: Routledge, 1993.

Ebright, Malcolm. "New Mexican Land Grants: The Legal Background." In *Land, Water, and Culture: New Perspectives on Hispanic Land Grants*, edited by Charles L. Briggs and John R. Van Ness, 15–64. Albuquerque: University of New Mexico Press, 1987.

Elbaz, Robert. *The Changing Nature of the Self: A Critical Study of the Autobiographical Discourse*. London: Croom Helm, 1988.

Employment Security Commission of Arizona. "Pinal County Agricultural Employment Study, September 1956–August 1957." Phoenix: Arizona State Employment Office, 1957.

Encyclopedia of Southern Baptists. Nashville: Broadman Press, 1958.

Ernst, Eldon G. "The Emergence of California in American Religious Historiography." *Religion and American Culture* 11:1 (Winter 2001), 31–52.

Espín, Orlando. "Popular Catholicism among Latinos." In *Hispanic Catholic Culture in the U.S.: Issues and Concerns*, edited by Jay P. Dolan and Allan Figueroa Deck, 308–59. Notre Dame, Ind.: University of Notre Dame Press, 1994.

Espinosa, Gastón. "'El Azteca': Francisco Olazábal and Latino Pentecostal Charisma, Power and Faith Healing in the Borderlands." *Journal of the American Academy of Religion* 67:3 (1999), 597–616.

Essien-Udom, E. U. *Black Nationalism: A Search for an Identity in America*. Chicago: University of Chicago Press, 1962.

Findlay, John M. *Magic Lands: Western Cityscapes and American Culture after 1940*. Berkeley: University of California Press, 1992.

Flórez, Enrique. *España Sagrada: Theatro geographico-historico de la iglesia de España*, vols. 1–56. Madrid: M.F. Rodríguez, 1747.

Fogarty, Robert S. *Dictionary of American Communal and Utopian History*. Westport, Conn.: Greenwood Press, 1980.

Foucault, Michel. "The Birth of the Asylum." In *The Foucault Reader*, edited by Paul Rabinow, 141–67. New York: Pantheon, 1984.

———. "The Means of Correct Training." In *The Foucault Reader*, edited by Paul Rabinow, 188–205. New York: Pantheon, 1984.

———. "Of Other Spaces." *Diacritics* 16 (1986), 22–27.

Foulkes, David. *A Grammar of Dreams*. New York: Basic Books, 1978.

————. *Dreaming: A Cognitive-Psychological Analysis*. Hillsdale, N.J.: Lawrence Erlbaum Associates, 1985.

Garcia, Ignácio. *United We Win: The Rise and Fall of La Raza Unida Party*. Tucson: University of Arizona Press, 1989.

Gardner, Richard. *Grito!: Reies Tijerina and the New Mexico Land Grant War of 1967*. Indianapolis: Bobbs-Merrill Company, 1970.

Garrett, II, Charles R. "El Tigre Revisited." *Nuestro* 1:5 (August 1977), 16–20.

Gill, Mario. *Nuestros buenos vecinos*, 5th ed. Mexico City: Editorial Azteca, 1959.

Ginzburg, Carlo. *The Cheese and the Worms: The Cosmos of a Sixteenth-Century Miller*. Translated by John and Anne C. Tedeschi. Baltimore: Johns Hopkins University Press, 1980.

————. *Clues, Myths and the Historical Method*. Translated by John and Anne C. Tedeschi. Baltimore: Johns Hopkins University Press, 1989.

Goffman, Erving. *Asylums: Essays on the Social Situation of Mental Patients and Other Inmates*. Garden City, N.Y.: Doubleday & Co., 1961.

Goldschmidt, Walter R. "Class Denominationalism in Rural California Churches." *American Journal of Sociology* 49 (1944), 348–55.

Gómez Quiñones, Juan. *Chicano Politics: Reality and Promise, 1940–1990*. Albuquerque: University of New Mexico Press, 1990.

González, Nancie L. *The Spanish-Americans of New Mexico: A Heritage of Pride*, 2nd ed. Albuquerque: University of New Mexico Press, 1969.

Grayson, Jr., George. "Tijerina: The Evolution of a Primitive Rebel." *Commonweal* 86:17 (28 July 1967), 464–66.

Grijalva, Joshua. *A History of Mexican Baptists in Texas, 1881–1981*. Dallas: Baptist General Convention, 1982.

————. "The History of Hispanic Southern Baptists." *Baptist History and Heritage* 18:3 (July 1983), 40–47.

Griswold del Castillo, Richard. *The Treaty of Guadalupe Hidalgo: A Legacy of Conflict*. Norman: University of Oklahoma Press, 1990.

Guerrero, Andrés G. *A Chicano Theology*. Maryknoll, N.Y.: Orbis Press, 1987.

Guerrero, Dan. "The Milagro Beanfield War." *Vista* 3:7 (6 March 1988), 14–18.

Guillén, Miguel. *La Historia del Concilio Latino Americano de Iglesias Cristianas*. Brownsville, Tex.: Latin American Council of Christian Churches, 1982.

Gutiérrez, David. *Walls and Mirrors: Mexican Americans, Mexican Immigrants, and the Politics of Ethnicity*. Berkeley: University of California Press, 1995.

Hammerback, John C., Richard J. Jensen, and José Angel Gutiérrez. *A War of Words: Chicano Protest in the 1960s and 1970s*. Westport, Conn.: Greenwood Press, 1985.

Harpham, Geoffrey Galt. "Conversion and the Language of Autobiography." In *Autobiography: Essays Theoretical and Critical*, edited by James Olney, 42–50. Princeton, N.J.: Princeton University Press, 1980.

Hawkins, Anne Hunsaker. *Archetypes of Conversion: The Autobiographies of Augustine, Bunyan, and Merton*. London and Toronto: Associated University Presses, 1985.

Hayden, Dolores. *Seven American Utopias: The Architecture of Communitarian Socialism, 1790–1975*. Cambridge: The MIT Press, 1976.

Hillerman, Tony. *The Great Taos Bank Robbery*. Albuquerque: University of New Mexico Press, 1973.

Hobsbawm, Eric. *Primitive Rebels: Studies in Archaic Forms of Social Movement in the 19th and 20th Centuries*. New York: W. W. Norton & Co., 1959.

Hodges. B. A. *A History of the Mexican Mission Work Conducted by the Presbyterian Church in the United States of America, in the Synod of Texas*. Waxahachie: The Woman's Synodical of Texas, 1931.

Holland, Clifton L. *The Religious Dimension in Hispanic Los Angeles: A Protestant Case Study*. Pasadena, Calif.: William Carey Library, 1974.

Hollenweger, Walter J. *The Pentecostals*. London: SCM Press, 1972.

Hough, Richard L. "Religion and Pluralism among the Spanish-Speaking Groups of the Southwest." In *Politics and Society in the Southwest: Ethnicity and Chicano Pluralism*, edited by Z. Anthony Kruszewski, Richard L. Hough, and Jacob Ornstein-Galicia, 169–95. Boulder, Colo.: Westview Press, 1982.

Hunt, Harry T. *The Multiplicity of Dreams: Memory, Imagination, and Consciousness*. New Haven, Conn.: Yale University Press, 1989.

Hynek, J. Allen. *The UFO Experience: A Scientific Inquiry*. New York: Ballentine Books, 1974.

Jackson, Donald Dale. "Around Los Ojos, Sheep and Land are Fighting Words." *Smithsonian* 22:1 (April 1991), 37–44, 46–47.

Jeffrey, David. "Arizona's Suburbs of the Sun." *National Geographic* 152:4 (October 1977), 487–517.

Jenkinson, Michael. *Tijerina: Land Grant Conflict in New Mexico*. Albuquerque: Paisano Press, 1968.

The Jewish Encyclopedia. New York: KTAV Publishing, 1964.

Justice, Steven. *Writing and Rebellion: England in 1381*. Berkeley: University of California Press, 1994.

Kane, Connie M., Ronald R. and Pamela Mellen, and Italo Samano. "Differences in the Manifest Dream Content of Mexican, Mexican American, and Anglo American College Women: A Research Note." *Hispanic Journal of Behavioral Sciences* 15:1 (February 1993), 134–39.

Kelsey, Morton T. *Dreams: The Dark Speech of the Spirit: A Christian Interpretation*. Garden City, N.Y.: Doubleday & Company, 1968.

———. *Tongue Speaking: An Experiment in Spiritual Experience*. New York: Waymark Books, 1968.

Kiev, Ari. *Curanderismo: Mexican-American Folk Psychiatry*. New York: Free Press, 1968.

Knowlton, Clark S. "The New Mexican Land War." *The Nation* 25 (17 June 1968), 792–96.

———. "Tijerina: Hero of the Militants." *The Texas Observer* 61:6 (28 March 1969), 1–4.

———. "Violence in New Mexico: A Sociological Perspective." *California Law Review* 58 (1970), 1053–68.

———. "Reies López Tijerina and the Alianza: Some Considerations." Paper presented at the Rural Sociological Society Annual Meeting, College Station, Texas, 24 August 1984.

———. "Reies López Tijerina and the Alianza Federál de Mercedes: Seekers after Justice." *Wisconsin Sociologist* 22:4 (Fall 1985), 133–44.

Kutsche, Paul, and John R. Van Ness. *Cañones: Values, Crisis, and Survival in a Northern New Mexico Village*. Salem, Wisc.: Sheffield Publishing Co., 1981.

Lalive d'Epinay, Christian. *Haven of the Masses: A Study of the Pentecostal Movement in Chile*, Marjorie Sandle, trans. New York: Friendship Press, 1969.

Lanternari, Vittorio. *The Religions of the Oppressed: A Study of Modern Messianic Cults*. New York: Knopf, 1963.

Larson, Robert W. "The White Caps of New Mexico: A Study of Ethnic Militancy in the Southwest." *Pacific Historical Review* 44:2 (May 1975), 171–85.

Laxalt, Robert. "New Mexico: The Golden Land." *National Geographic* 138:3 (September 1970), 289–345.

Leal, Luis. "El paso y la huella: The Reconstruction of Chicano Cultural History." In *Estudios Chicanos and the Politics of Community*, edited by Mary Romero and Cordelia Candelaria, 19–30. Boulder, Colo.: National Association for Chicano Studies, 1989.

Leddy, Betty. "La Llorona in Southern Arizona." *Perspectives in Mexican American Studies* 1 (1988), 9–16.

Lessa, William A., and Evon Z. Vogt, eds. *Reader in Comparative Religion: An Anthropological Approach*, 2nd ed. New York: Harper & Row, 1965.

Lieu, Jocelyn. "The Courthouse Raid: Twenty Years Later." *Rio Grande Sun*, 28 May 1987.

Lindholm, Charles. *Charisma*. Cambridge, U.K.: Basil Blackwell, 1990.

Lippard, Lucy R., and Chris Takagi. "Land or Death in Tierra Amarilla." *Guardian* (New York) 40:43 (17 August 1988), 7–9.

Lloyd, Rees. "Behind the Mask of Middle-Class Decency: Inside the Albuquerque Journal." *The New Mexico Review and Legislative Journal* 2:2 (February 1970), 1–2, 20–24.

———. "'King Tiger'—Reies López Tijerina—Still Roars for Justice on 'Cinco de Junio' 2003. Is There a Welsh 'Tiger' for Justice?" Online: http://www.welshamerican.com/Rees/tiger.htm.

Love, Joseph L. "La Raza: Mexican Americans in Rebellion." *TRANS-action* (February 1969). Reprinted in *Pain and Promise: The Chicanos Today*, edited by Edward Simmens, 271–85. New York: Mentor/New American Library, 1972.

Luckingham, Bradford. *Minorities in Phoenix: A Profile of Mexican American, Chinese American, and African American Communities, 1860–1992*. Tucson: University of Arizona Press, 1994.

McCarty, Frankie. *Land Grant Problems in New Mexico*. Albuquerque: Albuquerque Journal, 1969.

McClellan, Albert. *The West is Big*. Atlanta: Home Missionary Board, Southern Baptist Convention, 1953.

McCombs, Vernon Monroe. *From Over the Border: A Study of the Mexicans in the United States*. New York: Council of Women for Home Missions and Missionary Education Movement [Methodist Episcopal Church], 1925.

Machado, Daisy L. *Of Borders and Margins: Hispanic Disciples in Texas, 1888–1945*. New York: Oxford University Press, 2003.

Malony, H. Newton, and A. Adams Lovekin. *Glossolalia: Behavioral Science Perspectives on Speaking in Tongues*. New York: Oxford University Press, 1985.

Maril, Robert Lee. *Poorest of Americans: The Mexican Americans of the Lower Rio Grande Valley of Texas*. Notre Dame, Ind.: University of Notre Dame Press, 1989.

Márquez, Antonio. "Richard Rodríguez's *Hunger of Memory* and the Poetics of Experience." *Arizona Quarterly* 40:2 (Summer 1984), 130–41.

Márquez, María Teresa, comp. "A Selected Bibliography of New Mexican Hispanic Literature." In *Paso por Aquí: Critical Essays on the New Mexican Literary Tradition, 1542–1988*, edited by Erlinda Gonzáles-Berry. Albuquerque: University of New Mexico Press, 1989.

Marsden, George. *Fundamentalism and American Culture: The Shaping of Twentieth-Century Evangelicalism, 1870–1925*. New York: Oxford University Press, 1980.

———. "By Primitivism Possessed: How Useful is the Concept 'Primitivism' for Understanding American Pentecostalism?" In *The Primitive Church in the Modern World*, edited by Richard T. Hughes, 34–46. Urbana: University of Illinois Press, 1995.

Matovina, Timothy. *Tejano Religion and Ethnicity: San Antonio, 1821–1860*. Austin: University of Texas Press, 1995.

Meier, Matt S. "'King Tiger': Reies López Tijerina." *Journal of the West* 27:2 (April 1988), 60–68.

———. *Mexican American Biographies: A Historical Dictionary, 1836–1987.* Westport, Conn.: Greenwood Press, 1988.

Meier, Matt S., and Feliciano Rivera. *The Chicanos: A History of Mexican Americans.* New York: Hill and Wang, 1972.

Meinig, D. W. *Southwest: Three Peoples in Geographical Change, 1600–1970.* New York: Oxford University Press, 1971.

Menefree, Selden C. *Mexican Migratory Workers of South Texas.* Washington, D.C.: Federal Works Agency, WPA, 1941.

Miller, Rosanna. "The Peralta Land Grant." *Western Association of Map Libraries* 22:2 (March 1991), 121–26.

Montejano, David. *Anglos and Mexicans in the Making of Texas, 1836–1986.* Austin: University of Texas Press, 1987.

Morales, Alejandro. "Expanding the Meaning of Chicano Cinema: Yo Soy Chicano, Raíces de Sangre, Seguín." *Bilingual Review/Revista Bilingüe* 10:2–3 (May–December 1983), 121–37.

Muhammad, Elijah. *Message to the Blackman in America.* Philadelphia: Hakim's Publications, 1965.

Muñoz, Jr., Carlos. *Youth, Identity, Power: The Chicano Movement.* London: Verso, 1989.

Nabokov, Peter. "Reflections on the Alianza." *New Mexico Quarterly* 37:4 (Winter 1968), 343–56.

———. *Tijerina and the Courthouse Raid.* Albuquerque: University of New Mexico Press, 1969; Berkeley: Ramparts Press, 1970.

———. "'Remembering Tierra Amarilla': Chicano Power in the Feudal West." *The Nation* (8 October 1977), 336–40.

Nericcio, William Anthony. "Autobiographies at 'La Frontera': The Quest for Mexican American Narratives." *The Americas Review* 16:3–4 (Fall-Winter 1988), 145–64.

Newman, Patty. *¡Do it up Brown!* San Diego: Viewpoint Books, 1971.

Nichols, John. "Reies López Tijerina, A Man Like the Northern Weather." *The New Mexico Review and Legislative Journal* 3:11 (November 1971), 12–13.

———. *The Milagro Beanfield War.* New York: Random House, 1974.

Niebuhr, H. Richard. *The Social Sources of Denominationalism.* New York: Henry Holt and Company, 1929.

O'Dea, Thomas, and Renato Poblete. "Anomie and the 'Quest for Community': The Formation of Sects among the Puerto Ricans of New York." *American Catholic Sociological Review* 21 (Spring 1960), 18–36.

Olney, James, ed. *Autobiography: Essays Theoretical and Critical.* Princeton, N.J.: Princeton University Press, 1980.

Orsi, Robert. *The Madonna of 115th Street: Faith and Community in Italian Harlem, 1880–1950.* New Haven, Conn.: Yale University Press, 1985.

Padilla, Genaro M. "The Recovery of Chicano Nineteenth-Century Autobiography." *American Quarterly* 40:3 (September 1988), 286–306.

Paredes, Américo. *"With His Pistol in His Hand": A Border Ballad and Its Hero.* Austin: University of Texas Press, 1958.

Partridge, Christopher. "Understanding UFO Religions and Abduction Spiritualities." In *UFO Religions,* edited by Christopher Partridge, 3–42. New York: Routledge, 2003.

Pascal, Roy. *Design and Truth in Autobiography.* Cambridge: Harvard University Press, 1960.

Phillips, Graciela. "La Gesta de un Pueblo Entre Dos Mundos." *Comercio Exterior* 29:1 (Enero 1979), 113–16.

Pinal County Development Board. "Pinal County Arizona: An Industrial and Commercial Summary." Florence: Pinal County Development Board, 1957.

Pitzer, Donald. *America's Communal Utopias*. Chapel Hill: University of North Carolina Press, 1997.

Polanco, Tomás Alcántara. *Las reales audencias en las provincias de Americanas de España*. Madrid: Editorial MAPFRE, 1992.

Poloma, Margaret M. *The Assemblies of God at the Crossroads: Charisma and Institutional Dilemmas*. Knoxville: University of Tennessee Press, 1989.

Porter, Philip W., and Fred E. Lukermann. "The Geography of Utopia." In *Geographies of the Mind: Essays in Historical Geosophy in Honor of John Kirtland Wright*, edited by David Lowenthal and Martyn J. Bowden, 197–223. New York: Oxford University Press, 1976.

Pred, Allan. *Lost Words, Lost Worlds: Modernity and the Language of Everyday Life in Late Nineteenth-Century Stockholm*. Cambridge: Cambridge University Press, 1990.

Quinn, Anthony. *The Original Sin: A Self Portrait*. Boston: Little, Brown and Company, 1972.

Quoniam, Stephane. "A Painter, Geographer of Arizona." *Environment and Planning D: Society and Space* 6 (1988), 3–14.

Ramírez, Daniel. "Hispanic Pentecostals: History and Mission. Response to Dr. Esdras Betancourt" (Unpublished paper). Paper presented to the Society for Pentecostal Studies Conference, Guadalajara, Mexico, 5 November 1993.

———. "Borderlands Praxis: The Immigrant Experience in Latino Pentecostal Churches." *Journal of the American Academy of Religion* 67:3 (1999), 573–596.

Ramírez, Ricardo. *Fiesta, Worship and Family*. San Antonio: Mexican American Cultural Center, 1980.

Ranaghan, Kevin and Dorothy. *Catholic Pentecostals*. New York: Paulist Press, 1969.

Recopilación de Leyes de Los Reinos de las Indias, 5th ed. Madrid: Boix, 1841.

Rivera, Luís N. *A Violent Evangelism: The Political and Religious Conquest of the Americas*. Louisville: Westminster/John Knox Press, 1992.

Rodríguez, Richard. *Hunger of Memory: The Education of Richard Rodríguez: An Autobiography*. Boston: D. R. Godine, 1982.

Rodríguez, Sylvia. "Land, Water, and Ethnic Identity in Taos." In *Land, Water, and Culture: New Perspectives on Hispanic Land Grants*, edited by Charles L. Briggs and John R. Van Ness, 313–403. Albuquerque: University of New Mexico Press, 1987.

Roll, Samuel. "Chicano Dreams: Investigations in Cross-Cultural Research." Southwest Hispanic Research Institute, Working Paper #107, University of New Mexico (Fall 1984).

Roll, Samuel, and C. Brooks Brenneis, "Chicano and Anglo Dreams of Death: A Replication." *Journal of Cross-Cultural Psychology* 6:3 (September 1975), 377–83.

Roll, Samuel, Richard Hinton, and Michael Glazer. "Dreams of Death: Mexican-Americans vs. Anglo Americans." *Interamerican Journal of Psychology* 8:1–2 (1974), 111–15.

Rosaldo, Renato. *Culture and Truth: The Remaking of Social Analysis*. Boston: Beacon Press, 1989.

Rosales, Francisco A. *CHICANO! The History of the Mexican American Civil Rights Movement*. Houston: Arte Público Press, 1996.

Rosenbaum, Robert J., and Robert W. Larson. "Mexicano Resistance to the Expropriation of Grant Lands in New Mexico." In *Land, Water, and Culture: New Perspectives on Hispanic Land Grants*, edited by Charles L. Briggs and John R. Van Ness, 269–310. Albuquerque: University of New Mexico Press, 1987.

Rosenhan, David L. "On Being Sane in Insane Places." *Science* 179 (January 1973), 250–58. Reprinted in *Labeling Madness*, edited by Thomas J. Scheff, 54–74. Englewood Cliffs, N.J.: Prentice-Hall, 1975.

Roybal, Rebecca. "Tijerina Remembers 'Greatest Day,'" *Albuquerque Journal*, 5 June 1997.

Rutledge, Arthur B. *Mission to America: A Century and a Quarter of Southern Baptist Home Missions*. Nashville: Broadman Press, 1969.

Saldívar, Ramón. "Ideologies of the Self: Chicano Autobiography." *Diacritics* (Fall 1985), 25–34.

———. *Chicano Narrative: The Dialectics of Difference*. Madison: University of Wisconsin Press, 1990.

Saliba, John A. "Religious Dimensions of UFO Phenomena." In *The Gods have Landed: New Religions from Other Worlds*, edited by James R. Lewis, 15–64. Albany, N.Y.: SUNY Press, 1995.

Sánchez, Rosaura. *Telling Identities: The Californio Testimonios*. Minneapolis: University of Minnesota Press, 1994.

Sánchez Walsh, Arlene. *Latino Pentecostal Identity: Evangelical Faith, Self, and Society*. New York: Columbia University Press, 2003.

San Miguel, Jr., Guadalupe. *"Let All of Them Take Heed": Mexican Americans and the Campaign for Educational Equality in Texas, 1910–1981*. Austin: University of Texas Press, 1987.

Saragoza, Alex. "The Significance of Recent Chicano-Related Historical Writings: An Appraisal." *Ethnic Affairs* 1 (Fall 1987), 25–62.

———. "Recent Chicano Historiography: An Interpretive Essay." *Aztlán* 19:1 (1988–1990), 1–77.

Shea, Daniel B. *Spiritual Autobiography in Early America*. Princeton, N.J.: Princeton University Press, 1968.

Smith, Jonathan Z. "Close Encounters of Diverse Kinds." In *Religion and Cultural Studies*, edited by Susan L. Mizruchi, 3–21. Princeton, N.J.: Princeton University Press, 2001.

Soja, Edward. *Postmodern Geographies: The Reassertion of Space in Critical Social Theory*. London: Verso, 1989.

Soleri, Paolo. *The Bridge Between Matter and Spirit Is Matter Becoming Spirit: The Arcology of Paolo Soleri*. Garden City, N.Y.: Anchor/Doubleday & Cosanti Foundation, 1973.

Spengemann, William C. *The Forms of Autobiography: Episodes in the History of a Literary Genre*. New Haven, Conn.: Yale University Press, 1980.

Stang, Alan. "Reies Tijerina: The Communist Plan to Grab the Southwest." *American Opinion* 10:8 (October 1967), 1–22.

———. "Terror Grows: 'War on Poverty' Supports Castroite Terrorists." *American Opinion* 11:3 (March 1968), 1–17.

———. "New Mexico: The Coming Guerilla War." *American Opinion* 12:3 (March 1969), 49–62.

Stevens, Anthony. *Private Myths: Dreams and Dreaming*. Cambridge, Mass.: Harvard University Press, 1995.

Storey, John W. *Texas Baptist Leadership and Social Christianity, 1900–1980*. College Station: Texas A & M University Press, 1986.

Streiber, Whitley. *Transformation: The Breakthrough*. New York: Avon Books, 1989.

Swadesh, Frances L. "The Alianza Movement: Catalyst for Social Change in New Mexico." In *Spanish-Speaking People in the United States, Proceedings of the 1968 Annual Spring Meeting of the American Ethnological Society*, edited by June Helm, 162–77. Seattle and London: American Ethnological Society/University of Washington, 1969.

————. "The Alianza Movement of New Mexico." In *Minorities and Politics*, edited by H. J. Tobias and C. E. Woodhouse, 53–84. Albuquerque: University of New Mexico Press, 1969.

Swanson, G. E. "Trance and Possession: Studies of Charismatic Influence." *Review of Religious Research* 19 (1978), 253–78.

Sylvest, Edwin, "Hispanic American Protestantism in the United States." In *Fronteras: A History of the Latin American Church in the USA since 1519*, edited by Moisés Sándoval, ed., 279–338. San Antonio: MACC, 1983.

Synan, Vinson. *The Holiness-Pentecostal Movement in the United States*. Grand Rapids, Mich.: William B. Eerdmans Press, 1971.

Szasz, Ferenc. *The Protestant Clergy in the Great Plains and Mountain West, 1865–1915*. Albuquerque: University of New Mexico Press, 1985.

Tafolla, Carmen. "The Church in Texas." In *Fronteras: A History of the Latin American Church in the U.S.A since 1519*, edited by Moisés Sándoval, 183–94. San Antonio: Mexican American Cultural Center, 1983.

Taylor, Paul. "Mexicans North of the Rio Grande." *Survey Graphic* 19:2 (May 1931). Reprinted in *On the Ground in the Thirties*, edited by Paul Taylor, 1–16. Salt Lake City: Peregrine Smith Books, 1983.

Tebbel, John. *The Great Change, 1910–1980: A History of Book Publishing in the United States*, Vol. 4. New York: R. R. Bowker, 1981.

Tice, Robert. *The Rhetoric of La Raza*. Kingsville: Texas A & I University / M.A.Y.O., 1971.

Tijerina, Reies López. *¿Hallará Fe en la Tierra . . . ?* N.p., 1954?.

————. "The Spanish Land Grant Question Examined." Albuquerque: Alianza Federál de Mercedes Reales/Pueblos Libres, 1966.

————. "Letter from the Santa Fe Jail, 15–17 August 1969." *El Grito del Norte*, 26 September 1969. Excerpt reprinted in *A Documentary History of the Mexican Americans*, edited by Wayne Moquín and Charles Van Doren, 484–87. New York: Praeger, 1971.

————. "From Prison: Reies López Tijerina." In *The Chicanos: Mexican American Voices*, edited by Ed Ludwig and James Santibañez, 215–22. Baltimore: Penguin, 1971.

————. "Mi lucha por la tierra." Handwritten mss. 4 vols., 1976.

————. *Mi lucha por la tierra*. Mexico, D.F.: Fondo de Cultura Económica, 1978.

————. "Speech at Trinity University, San Antonio, 26 October 1971." *Magazín* 1:32 (December 1971), 2–3, 63–71.

Tijerina, Reies López, with José Angel Gutiérrez, ed. and trans. *They Called Me "King Tiger": My Struggle for the Land and Our Rights*. Houston: Arte Público Press, 2000.

Tixerina: Through the Eyes of a Tiger: An Interview with Reies Tijerina [with Harold Rhodes] [video]. Albuquerque: KNME-TV, University of New Mexico, 1982.

Todorov, Tzvetan. *The Poetics of Prose*. Ithaca, N.Y.: Cornell University Press, 1977.

Turner, Kay F. "'Because of This Photography': The Making of a Mexican Folk Saint." In *Niño Fidencio: A Heart Thrown Open*, edited by Dore Gardner, 120–34. Santa Fe: Museum of New Mexico Press, 1992.

Tyler, S. Lyman, ed, and comp. *Spanish Laws Concerning Discoveries, Pacifications, and Settlements among the Indians*. American West Center, Occasional Papers, 17. Salt Lake City: University of Utah, 1980.

U.S. Bureau of Prisons. *A Handbook of Correctional Psychiatry 1*. Washington, D.C.: Department of Justice, 1968.

U.S. Department of Agriculture. Extension [Service] Farm Labor Program. *Texas-Mexicans in Sugar Beets, Vegetables and Fruits: A Report on Improved Relations between Migratory Farm*

Workers and Agricultural Employers in North Central and Great Plains States, 1943–1947. Washington, D.C.: Department of Agriculture, 1948.

Valdés, Dennis Nodin. *El Pueblo Mexicano en Detroit y Michigan: A Social History.* Detroit: Wayne State University Press, 1982.

Vance, John Thomas. *The Background of Hispanic-American Law: Legal Sources and Juridical Literature of Spain.* New York: Central Book Company, 1943.

Vasconcelos, José. *La raza cósmica: Misión de la raza Ibero-Americana.* Madrid: Aguilar/Di Ediciones, 1961.

Vesey, Laurence. *The Communal Experience: Anarchist and Mystical Counter-Cultures in America.* San Francisco: Harper & Row, 1973.

Villanueva-Collado, Alfredo. "Growing Up Hispanic: Discourse and Ideology in *Hunger of Memory* and *Family Installments.*" *The Americas Review* 16:3–4 (Fall-Winter 1988), 75–90.

Wacker, Grant. "Searching for Eden with a Satellite Dish: Primitivism, Pragmatism, and the Pentecostal Character." In *The Primitive Church in the Modern World*, edited by Richard T. Hughes, 137–66. Urbana: University of Illinois Press, 1995.

———. *Heaven Below: Early Pentecostals and American Culture.* Cambridge: Harvard University Press, 2003.

Weber, Max. *The Protestant Ethic and the Spirit of Capitalism*, Talcott Parsons, ed. London: George Allen and Unwin, 1930 [1904–1905].

———. "The Social Psychology of the World Religions." In *From Max Weber: Essays in Sociology*, Edited by H. H. Gerth and translated by C. Wright Mills, 267–301. New York: Oxford University Press, 1964.

Weigle, Marta. *Brothers of Light, Brothers of Blood: The Penitentes of the Southwest.* Albuquerque: University of New Mexico Press, 1967.

Weil, Shalva. "Beyond the Sambatyon: The Myth of the Ten Lost Tribes/Me-Ever La-Sambatyon." In *Beyond the Sambatyon: The Myth of the Ten Lost Tribes/Me-Ever La-Sambatyon* [exhibition catalogue], edited by Shalva Weil, 77–94. Tel Aviv: Beth Hatefutsoth, The Museum of the Jewish Diaspora, 1991.

Westermann, Claus. *Basic Forms of Prophetic Speech.* London: Lutterworth Press, 1967.

Westphall, Victor. *Mercedes Reales: Hispanic Land Grants of the Upper Rio Grande Region.* Albuquerque: University of New Mexico Press, 1983.

White, Gilbert, Koch, Kelly, and McCarthy, and the New Mexico State Planning Office, *Land Title Study.* Santa Fe: New Mexico State Planning Office, 1971.

Wilson, Bryan R. "An Analysis of Sect Development." *Sociological Review* 24 (February 1959), 3–15.

Woods, Richard D. "The Chicano Novel: Silence after Publication." *Revista Chicano-Riqueña* 4:3 (Summer 1976), 42–47.

———. "An Overview of Mexican Autobiography." *a/b Auto/Biography Studies* 3:4 (Summer 1988), 13–22.

Dissertations and Theses

Busto, Rudy V. "Like a Mighty Rushing Wind: The Religious Impulse in the Life and Writing of Reies López Tijerina." PhD diss., University of California at Berkeley, 1991.

Flores, Raymond Johnson. "The Socio-Economic Status Trends of the Mexican People Residing in Arizona." MA thesis, Arizona State College, 1951.

Haney, Jane B. "Migration, Settlement Pattern, and Social Organization: A Midwest Mexican-American Case Study." PhD diss., Michigan State University, 1978.

Hoover, Mario. "Origin and Structural Development of the Assemblies of God." MA thesis, Southwest Missouri State College, 1968.

Ingraham, Barton Lee. "Reies López Tijerina and the Spanish Americans of New Mexico: A Study in Cultural Conflict." MA thesis, University of California at Berkeley, 1968.

Martínez, Juan Francisco. "Origins and Development of Protestantism among Latinos in the Southwest United States, 1836–1900." PhD diss., Fuller Theological Seminary, 1996.

Mawn, Benedict J. "Testing the Spirits: An Empirical Search for the Socio-Economic Situational Roots of the Catholic Pentecostal Religious Experience." PhD diss., Boston University, 1975.

Officer, James E. "Sodalities and Systemic Linkage: The Joining Habits of Urban Mexican Americans." PhD diss., University of Arizona, 1964.

Primiano, Leonard Norman. "Intrinsically Catholic: Vernacular Religion and Philadelphia's 'Dignity.'" PhD diss., University of Pennsylvania, 1993.

Pulido, Alberto. "Race Relations within the American Catholic Church: An Historical and Sociological Analysis of Mexican American Catholics." PhD diss., University of Notre Dame, 1989.

Remy, Martha. "Protestant Churches and Mexican-Americans in South Texas." PhD diss., University of Texas at Austin, 1970.

Schepers, Emile Markgraaff. "Voices, Visions and Strange Ideas: Hallucinations and Delusions in a Mexican-Origin Population." PhD diss., Northwestern University, 1974.

Stapleton, Jr., Ernest S. "The History of Baptist Missions in New Mexico, 1849–1966." MA thesis, University of New Mexico, 1954.

Vigil, Maurilio. "Ethnic Organizations among the Mexican Americans of New Mexico: A Political Perspective." PhD diss., New Mexico Highlands University, 1974.

Weaver, Thomas. "Social Structure, Change and Conflict in a New Mexican Village." PhD diss., University of California at Berkeley, 1965.

Miscellaneous

Peter Nabokov Papers. Archive #93. Special Collections, Zimmerman Library, University of New Mexico, Albuquerque, New Mexico.

United States ex.rel. Schuster v. Herold, 410 F.2d. 1071, 1091 (2d Cir), *cert. denied*, 396 U.S. 847 (1969)

United States v. Tijerina, 407 F.2d. 349 (1969)

Vitek v. Jones, 100 S.Ct. 1254 (1980)

Wisconsin v. Yoder, 406 U.S. 205 (1972)

INDEX

Meier, Matt, 24, 25, 27
memoirs, 162; and Mexican writers, 160
Menocchio, 14–15, 204
Methodist Episcopal Church, 86
Methodists, 79, 80, 81
Mexican American Catholicism: criticisms
    of, 15; and Virgin of Guadalupe, 125
Mexican Americans: and caste system, 93;
    defined, xi; as healing bridge between
    blacks and whites, 154; and indigenous
    spirituality, 128; and racial oppression,
    28; and racial segregation, 133; and
    religion, 79–80; and supernaturalism,
    124; targeted by Pentecostals, 88
Mexican Baptist Convention, 82
Mexican Catholicism: and dreams and
    visions, 122, 127–28
Mexican Revolution, 85, 87
Mexicans: and bracero labor, 134; as "cos-
    mic" race, 186; defined, xi; and eco-
    nomic caste system, 85; and indige-
    nous spirituality, 128; and racial injus-
    tice, 35; and supernaturalism, 124
The Milagro Beanfield War (film), 74
Mi lucha por la tierra (Tijerina), 4, 7, 9, 22,
    30, 32, 34, 142–46, 156–73; absence
    from Chicano literary canon, 143; fear
    of Anglo-Saxon mentality, 184; hand-
    written text of, 164; heavy-handed
    editing by publisher of, 167; as "out-
    sider" text in Chicano literature, 170;
    prophetic quality of, 162
Montejano, David, 94
Montoya, Joseph, 167
moon landing, 124, 177; and Biblical inter-
    pretation, 175
Moráles, Moisés, 60, 69
Mormons, 86
Muhammad, Elijah, 51–52, 239n27, 240n68
Muñoz, Carlos, Jr., 21, 29
My Life, Judaism, and the Nuclear Age
    (Tijerina), 176

Nabokov, Peter, 7, 8, 15, 16, 18–24, 20, 21,
    32, 41, 44, 45, 55, 64, 97, 154, 174, 180,
    186, 201, 202, 208n14
Naranjo, Benny, 59
National Association for Chicano Studies,
    75
National Association of Evangelicals, 109
National Chicano Moratorium, 70
National Conference for New Politics, 62
National Forest Service, 55

Nation of Islam, 51
The New Chieftain, 54
Newman, Patty, 178
The New Mexico Review and Legislative Journal,
    70, 74
New Mexico State Penitentiary, 69, 152,
    177, 178
New Thought, 86
Nichols, John, 74
Niebuhr, Reinhold, 92
Nixon, Richard, 65, 68, 71
Noverunt Universi (papal bull), 73
nuevomexicano, xi

Occupied America (Acuña), 27–34, 144
O'Dea, Thomas, 93
Olazábal, Francisco, 88
Olney, James, 157

Parham, Charles Fox, 222n35
Penitente Brotherhood, 49–50, 131
Pentecostalism, 5, 77, 83–98, 146, 198; and
    altering of religious landscape, 83; and
    Azusa Street revivals, 84–85; domina-
    tion by males in Latin America,
    222n38; and dreams and visions,
    125–27; as impediment to acceptance,
    33; "Latter Rain" schism in, 108–9;
    "low church" image of, 83; and mis-
    sionaries, 87; rapid growth in Texas
    and Calif., 88; and targeting of
    Mexican Americans, 87
Phillips, Graciela, 144
Poblete, Renato, 93
Poor People's March, 62
Portillo, Ernesto, 71
Poston Relocation Center, 138
Pred, Allen, 138
Presbyterians, 63, 79, 80, 81, 220n16
Primiano, Leonard, 205
Protestant Christianity, 79, 86; few con-
    verts from missionary work, 220n9;
    and Mexican Americans, 81
"The Provokers of Judgment" (sermon),
    99–106; and shaved faces, 108

Quinn, Anthony, 126, 228n24
Quoniam, Stephane, 137

racial injustice, 35; in seminaries, 79–80
racism, 91; and fundamentalist Christianity,
    193
Ramírez, Daniel, 88–89